TRANSLATING IRELAND

TRANSLATING IRELAND

Translation, Languages, Cultures

MICHAEL CRONIN

CORK UNIVERSITY PRESS

For Juliette and Máirtín

First published in 1996 by
Cork University Press
University College
Cork
Ireland

© Michael Cronin 1996

British Library Cataloguing in Publication Data
A CIP catalogue record for this book is available from the British Library.

ISBN 1 85918 018 3 hardcover
1 85918 019 1 paperback
Typeset by Seton Music Graphics Ltd., Bantry, Co. Cork
Printed by ColourBooks, Baldoyle, Co. Dublin

CONTENTS

ACKNOWLEDGEMENTS

The tendency to fetishise individual authorship in the West is well-documented. The truth is that anyone embarking on a book-length study is heavily dependent on a network of friends and acquaintances who encourage, advise, cajole, stimulate and commiserate. I would first like to thank the Governing Body of Dublin City University for leave of absence for the academic year 1993–1994. I am also grateful to Professor Leslie Davis and my colleagues in the School of Applied Languages who supported me in my research work and waylaid panic attacks through their good sense and humour. To Barra Ó Séaghdha I owe a particular debt of gratitude for his attentive reading of chapters and helpful comments. I would like to thank the following for their kind assistance during research on the book: Dorothy Kenny, Liam Mac Cóil, Máirín Ní Dhonnchadha, Éamon Ó Ciosáin, Cormac Ó Cuilleanáin, Eithne O'Connell and Kathleen Shields. It goes without saying that none of them are responsible for opinions expressed in this work which are mine alone. The library staffs of Dublin City University, Trinity College Dublin, University College Dublin and the National Library of Ireland are also to be thanked for their courtesy and resourcefulness.

To Juliette Péchenart who first taught me that translation was possible and who has been a constant source of support over the years *un très grand merci*. To my son Máirtín I can only hope that the mystery of what his father was doing all that time with the 'puter' will finally be elucidated.

Sections of Chapter 5 have appeared in earlier versions in articles in *The Irish University Review*, 21/1, 1991 and *The Irish Review*, 14, 1993.

Outline Chronology of Irish History

7000 BC: Mesolithic food–gatherers and hunters arrive in Ireland after the ice–age.

3000 BC: Arrival of neolithic settlers with a knowledge of agriculture and pottery.

300 BC: Celts bring iron to Ireland. They impose their language and customs on earlier inhabitants. They bring with them their own distinctive culture known as La Tène. Celtic society and laws preserve a number of archaic features of Indo-European culture.

432 AD: Year traditionally attributed to the introduction of Christianity to Ireland. The evangelisation of Ireland is closely linked to the name of St Patrick. Succeeding centuries would see the rapid expansion of Irish monasteries. After the fall of the Roman Empire, Irish missionary monks travelled throughout Europe and played considerable role in the preservation of classical culture within the confines of the former empire.

795: Arrival of Vikings in Ireland. Their settlements along the coast would later grow into the cities of Dublin, Limerick and Waterford.

1172: The Anglo-Norman King Henry II invades Ireland. Anglo-Norman control over Ireland diminished until by the end of the fifteenth century only a small area around Dublin known as the Pale was under effective English control.

1534: Thomas, Lord Offaly popularly known as 'Silken Thomas' and member of the powerful Geraldines of Kildare repudiates allegiance to Henry VIII.

1541: King Henry VIII proclaimed King of Ireland.

1569: First plantations in Ireland. Confiscated lands of native Irish landowners given to English and Scottish settlers in return for defence of the crown. Ulster plantations prove to be the most successful.

1601: Defeat of the traditional Gaelic-Irish leaders Hugh O'Neill and Hugh O'Donnell at the Battle of Kinsale. This followed the consolidation of Tudor power in Ireland throughout the sixteenth century by Henry VIII, Mary and Elizabeth.

1641: Outbreak of Ulster Rebellion directed mainly at new settlers and English forces.

1649: Military intervention by Oliver Cromwell who ruthlessly suppresses rebellion.

1690: Defeat of the Catholic King James II by the Protestant King William III of Orange at the Battle of the Boyne.

1695: Introduction of the Penal Laws.

1791: Establishment by Theobald Wolfe Tone and others of the Society of United Irishmen. The ultimate object of the Society was to unite all Irishmen, Catholic, Protestant and Dissenter under the common aim of breaking the connection with England.

1795: Creation of the Orange Order established to defend the Protestant religion in Ireland and the political link with England.

1798: Rising led by the United Irishmen. Despite assistance from the French the Rising fails.

1800: Act of Union with Britain abolishes the Irish Parliament and makes Ireland part of the United Kingdom.

1829: Catholic Emancipation. Movement led by Daniel O'Connell removes the final disability for Catholics when they are allowed to enter Parliament at Westminster.

1840: Mass demonstrations calling for a repeal of the Act of Union.

1845: Beginning of the Great Famine. As a result of successive failures of the potato crop between 1846 and 1851 almost one million people die of starvation and one million emigrate.

1848: Young Ireland rebellion.

1867: Fenian rebellion.

1875: Charles Stewart Parnell, a Protestant landowner elected to the Westminster Parliament begins to campaign for legislative independence for Ireland.

1912: Home Rule Bill giving Ireland limited independence passed by the British Parliament.

1913: Unionist opposition to Home Rule Bill grows in Ulster with the establishment of the Ulster Volunteers, a group set up to oppose Home Rule by military means.

1914: Outbreak of First World War leads to the suspension of the enactment of the Irish Home Rule Bill.

1916: Easter Rising. Armed rebellion with the object of establishing an independent Irish Republic. After more than a week of fighting the leaders surrender and most of them are executed.

1918: Sinn Féin, the party that championed the ideals of the 1916 leaders wins landslide victory in all-Ireland elections.

1919: Sinn Féin MPs refuse to take up seats in Westminster Parliament and set up their own parliament in Dublin known as *Dáil Éireann*.

1919–1921: War of Independence.

1920: Government of Ireland Act passed by the British Government. This leads to the establishment of a separate parliament for the six north-eastern counties of Ireland: Antrim, Armagh, Derry, Down, Fermanagh and Tyrone.

1921: 6 December. Treaty signed between British and Irish representatives providing for the establishment of the Irish Free State as a Dominion of the British Commonwealth.

1922–23: Civil war between supporters and opponents of the Treaty.

1932: Fianna Fáil come to power, under the leadership of Éamon de Valera, a leader of the 1916 Rising.

1937: New constitution drawn up under the guidance of de Valera. Irish is made the first official language of the country which was henceforth to be called *Éire* in Irish and Ireland in English.

1939–1945: Ireland remains neutral during the Second World War.

1949: Ireland is proclaimed a Republic and withdraws from the Commonwealth.

1967: Northern Ireland Civil Rights Association set up to demand equal rights for Catholics in Northern Ireland.

1968: Violent confrontations between police and civil rights demonstrators.

1969: British troops are sent to Northern Ireland.

1971: Internment without trial introduced.

1972: 31 January, Bloody Sunday. British Army shoot dead thirteen unarmed demonstrators at a civil rights demonstration in Derry.

1973: Ireland becomes a full member of the European Economic Community. Sunningdale Agreement introduces power sharing between unionists and nationalists in Northern Ireland. Strong opposition from loyalists.

1974: Loyalist workers' strike leads to collapse of the Sunningdale Agreement and the power-sharing executive.

1979: Papal visit to Ireland.

1981: Ten Republican prisoners, including Bobby Sands, die on hunger strike for political status.

1983: Amendment to the Irish constitution protecting the life of the unborn child.

1985: Anglo-Irish Agreement gives Irish government limited say in the running of affairs in Northern Ireland.

1986: Referendum to remove the constitutional ban on divorce defeated.

1991: Election of Mary Robinson as first woman President of Ireland.

1992: Two-thirds of Irish electorate support acceptance of Maastricht Agreement in referendum.

1993: Downing Street Declaration. British government recognises the right of the Irish people to national self-determination and Irish government accepts that Irish unity is dependent on the consent of the majority in Northern Ireland.

1994: Declaration of ceasefires by IRA and loyalist paramilitary groups.

INTRODUCTION

TRANSITION ZONES

FOR JOHNNY ROTTEN, Ireland always meant translation difficulties. The Irish grandfather of the Sex Pistols' lead singer, whose real name was John Lydon, found the London speech of his grandson incomprehensible and childhood holidays in Ireland were early exercises in laborious decoding. The desire to decode later became a desire to learn Irish, but his Irish parents refused to teach him, fearing the stigma of difference in their new emigrant home. Translated into new circumstances, language was a faultline that ran through the Lydon household, opening up painful memories of loss and departure. The parents sought a difficult translation into English life and their son would attempt an equally difficult retranslation into Irish life and language.[1] Rotten abandoned the attempt and launched a musical attack on the pieties of conventional rock. The explosive anger of the displaced, of a London-Irish singer lost in translation, was to change the history of popular music.

The history of translation in Ireland is the history of encounters. The encounters have been peaceful, violent, painful and as Rotten found, creative. Translators as inventive mediators have shaped every area of Irish life for centuries, but their role has been largely ignored. If they are remembered at all, it is usually for something else – their sanctity or prowess in the literary or philosophical field. Without translators, however, the emergence and development of different cultures in Ireland would have been literally and metaphorically speaking inconceivable. The dissemination of scientific ideas, the emergence of two national languages, the birth of literatures in English and Irish, the formulation of new ideologies and the spread of religion were crucially dependent on the activities of Irish translators through the ages.[2] Architects of literatures and languages, channels of influence, ambassadors for the Other, they embody at the same time many of the painful dilemmas of Ireland's troubled history. The subjection of Ireland from the sixteenth

1

century onwards demanded, not only military and political but also, cultural, submission. The native Irish had to be *translated*. As Eric Cheyfitz has remarked, 'If Tudor England was not obsessed with racial purity . . . it appears to have been obsessed with linguistic purity; and, indeed, whether implicit or explicit, there appears to have been a close connection between language and racial, or cultural identity.'[3] The process of translation at one level was successful. By the end of the nineteenth century, the majority of Irish people were English-speaking. However, the consequences of translation are rarely predictable and rather than promoting cordial union, many translators in the eighteenth and nineteenth centuries in Ireland found themselves contributing to a movement of cultural and political difference and independence. The Anglo-Irish relationship, as reflected in language and translation, is a fascinating example of the shifting geometry of power, language and resistance, but it should not obscure other equally absorbing episodes of Ireland's long translation history.

Irish cultural and intellectual history, itself the product of multiple translations, has never fully escaped a linguistic schizophrenia which distorts reports of both the past and the present. English-language histories ignore Irish-language material and Irish-language histories focus on exclusively Irish-language material. In this book, I look at the work of translators in both languages in order to give as full a picture as possible of the variety and scale of translation activity in Ireland over the last thousand years. My purpose is to offer a discursive history of translation in Ireland that pays particular attention to the social and political contexts of translation. It is primarily, though not exclusively, concerned with inward translation from other languages into English and Irish and with translation between these two languages. Its aim is to be descriptive rather than prescriptive. My primary concern is not the critical comparison of source texts with target texts to establish the linguistic competence of the translator or bewail the absence of proper equivalence. This prescriptive approach, which has dominated much past commentary on translation in Ireland, has tended to conceal as much as it reveals. Prescriptive commentary practised by scholars who are proficient in both source and target language tends to be retro-spective, i.e. primarily concerned with the faithful translation of the source language. This ignores the fact that most people who read a translation do so because they do not speak the source language and

therefore that questions of reception and target-language acceptability
are central to the translator's practice.

The purposes and effects of translation are also related to dominant
conceptual paradigms in any one period. Translation is not a simple
comparative process between languages but an intellectual discipline in its
own right. Theories of translation can and do radically affect the approach
of translators to their task. This work explores the different theoretical
formulations that have been advanced by Irish translators to present their
work to others. The sources for these formulations vary greatly: prefatory
remarks; explanatory notes; encomia; articles in newspapers and journals;
reviews; interviews; translation commentaries. Despite centuries of translation activity the emergence of translation studies in Ireland has been a
very recent development. Novelty does not excuse amnesia, and it is
important for theoreticians and practitioners that they are aware of the
speculative interest that translation has attracted over the centuries in
Ireland and elsewhere. Robert Welch, Nicholas Williams, David Lloyd,
Máirtín Mac Nioclais and Alan Harrison have pioneered the exploration
of aspects of translation history in Ireland, and the vastness of the subject
will no doubt inspire others to follow suit. The history of translation
activity on the island of Ireland should not be seen, however, as a subject
for purely domestic consumption. Ireland as a European country with a
colonial past, and the experience of a radical language-shift does not fit
easily into the more reductive categories of contemporary theory. One of
the shortcomings of certain contemporary writings on translation and
post-colonialism such as those by Cheyfitz and Tejaswini Niranjana is the
simple opposition of Europe and the New World or Europe and the
Colony.[4] The translation experience of Europe is not homogenous, and
the intense pressures on language resulting from internal colonialism in
Europe itself are ignored in analyses which posit a common European
historical experience and attitude to language. When Vicente Rafael
describes the dissident agenda of the Tagalogs in the Philippines with
respect to the Spanish colonisers and translation, his description would
apply equally well to the different ideological concerns of Irish scribe-
translators working for Anglo-Irish patrons in the early eighteenth century:

> For the Spaniards, translation was always a matter of reducing the native
> language and culture to accessible objects for and subjects of divine and
> imperial intervention. For the Tagalogs, translation was a process less of
> internalizing colonial-Christian conventions than of evading their totalizing

grip by repeatedly marking the differences between their language and interests and those of the Spaniards.[5]

If political relationships in Europe have been characterised over the centuries by asymmetry, languages have been both accomplices and victims. Translation relationships between minority and majority languages are rarely divorced from issues of power and identity that in turn destabilise universalist theoretical prescriptions on the translation process. Contemporary Ireland with a minority language, Irish, and a majority language, English, has experience of both sides of the translation equation. Translation theory must not restrict itself to the perspectives of majority languages and the experience of minority languages greatly complicate facile assumptions that are made concerning the nature of translation. The majority language spoken in Ireland, Hiberno-English, is of course itself in a minority position in the English-speaking world. In addition, writers in Ireland over the last two centuries have been aware of the leakage, the internal translation between the island's two languages, the one ghosting the other. The condition of extraterritoriality that is expressed at a number of levels in the work of Joyce and Beckett is paralleled domestically by the bilingual creativity of Michael Hartnett, Brendan Behan, Pearse Hutchinson, Angela Bourke, Eoghan Ó Tuairisc and Flann O'Brien, among others. Stephen Dedalus, in *Portrait of the Artist as a Young Man*, wonders at how different the words, *home, Christ, ale, master* sound on the lips of the English dean of studies and his own: 'I cannot speak or write these words without unrest of spirit. His language, so familiar and so foreign, will always be for me an acquired speech. I have not made or accepted its words. My voice holds them at bay. My soul frets in the shadow of his language.'[6] The writer Ronan Sheehan, in an 1989 interview, spoke of his own sense of a curious estrangement from English, 'I remember when I'd just finished writing *Tennis Players* and I was reading over it I felt strange it was in English. It's easy to be glib on this subject and make the obvious kind of point but I did genuinely feel an odd kind of alienation from what I'd written myself.'[7] The sense of distance, estrangement and a level of alienation is a common experience of translators who find themselves between languages, suspended in the working space of equivalence. To the extent that all translation involves matching like to unlike, coupling the familiar and the foreign, the translation process has much in common with paradox, metaphor and discovery. Hence, the creative consequences of the state of translation that is modern Ireland. Distance, in addition, suggests a potential for play – objects can be ludically recycled when they are distanced from their real-life uses, e.g., the toy sword or the the old tyre. It is that creative distance, the _Verfremdungseffekt_ of linguistic co-existence, that makes an understanding of translation so necessary for readings of contemporary Irish culture.[8]

Distance, estrangement and alienation are also, however, markers of loss and disorientation. Moving from one language to another is a perilous enterprise, and Julia Kristeva speaks of the 'silence of the polyglots':

> Not to speak your mother tongue. To live in sounds, logics cut off from the nocturnal memory of the body, the bittersweet sleep of childhood. To carry within yourself a secret tomb, or like a handicapped child the language of a another time – treasured and useless – that fades away but never leaves you. You perfect this other instrument as you would algebra or the violin. You can become a virtuoso with this new artifice which also gives you a new body, just as artificial, sublimated – some would say sublime. You feel that the new language is your new resurrection – new skin, new sex. But the illusion is destroyed when you hear a recording and the sound of your voice from nowhere seems strange to you, more like the mumbled stammer of the past than the code of the present . . . So between two languages, your true element is silence.[9]

Seán de Fréine's collection of essays dealing in part with the origins and consequences of language-shift is called _The Great Silence_, while George Petrie spoke in 1855 in connection with traditional song and music of 'this awful, unwonted silence which during the Famine and subsequent years almost everywhere prevailed.'[10] Likewise, the poet Nuala Ní Dhomhnaill sees a reluctance to speak about language-change and links the often violent emotions the subject arouses to a history of repression and pain:

> We all have an emotional block about Irish. Right through the country, even I have it, everyone has it. If you dig away at it -and most of us don't, we run a mile – it's like touching a funny bone but it hurts like all the hurts we have repressed, like being weaned or your Daddy going to England or your first love.[11]

The Great Silence extends to much of Irish historiography which apart from a summary listing of the causes of language-shift in Ireland in the eighteenth and nineteenth centuries pays little attention to the effects of such a shift. There often appears to be an unspoken assumption of ideal equivalence. Translation is a transparent, painless process and full equivalence is possible in the other language. Questions of approximation, mistranslation, conceptual disparities and the consequences of language transfer for self-representation are largely ignored. Translation is not mechanical reproduction. It is transformation.[12] Studying these transformations is a way of understanding how the different peoples on the island of Ireland over the centuries have reacted to the presence of others and the pressures of circumstances. Colin Graham calls for a rethinking of 'the concepts of irony, hybridity, mimicry, the contact zone and transculturation in the Irish context' and the history of translation in Ireland provides countless examples of the strategic uses of these concepts.[13]

If translation transforms, then commentary on translation must effect its own transformation. Readings of the intellectual history of Ireland must take into account the specificity of the translator's task. For example, a proper evaluation of the work of translators in medieval Ireland has been handicapped by a failure to understand the larger context of translation practice in the Middle Ages. Jeannette Beer has pointed out that for medieval translators:

> structural equivalence between source and translation was not of prime importance. By the criterion of appropriateness to target audience a treatise properly could become poetry, epic became romance, and sermons drama – or vice versa! Such dramatic changes in form serve as irritants to those modern theorists, who for the sake of anachronistic criteria, categorise a millenium of translative activity as one thousand years of non-translation.[14]

Therefore, changes, omissions, bold adaptations of source material to the cultural tastes and linguistic habits of the target audience were not automatically signs of linguistic incompetence but a natural response to a translation paradigm of the period. The vitality of translation in medieval Ireland has continued to the present day, and the presence of written translation for over a thousand years challenges homogenous, monolithic, monolingual interpretations of Irish culture. Translation is a meeting ground where all the peoples and languages of Ireland have gathered at one time or another in the island's history. Translation implies in both a geometrical and linguistic sense, movement, a resistance to fixity. Its momentum is dialogical. Joycean fears of hemiplegia and paralysis are gainsayed by a millenium of translation activity that has refused blockage and closure. The contribution of translators to the languages, literatures and cultures of Ireland has been immense. It is a debt which is rarely acknowledged. A full account of all the translation work carried out in Ireland would fill many volumes. A single-volume work is of necessity restricted but I hope to trace the principal patterns of translation activity through the centuries in Ireland and pay due attention to the complexity of that activity.

The title of Roger Doyle's series of musical exepriments *The Babel Project* could be used to describe any translation history. Michael Cunningham, in a text accompanying a CD of Doyle's music, writes of the nature of unpredictability in composition:

> This is another key aspect of *The Babel Project*, the attempt to uncover patterns within sonic turbulence, to find new levels of order in apparent uncertainties, or to map undiscovered transition zones and boundary regions between the totally structured and the completely random.[15]

Ireland's transition zones and boundary regions are not empty. They have been populated for centuries by those most protean and enduring of inhabitants – translators.

Notes

1. Michael Cunningham, 'Rotten Story', *The Irish Times*, 2 April 1994.
2. For a summary description of the different roles of translators see Jean Delisle, 'Projet d'histoire thématique de la traduction', Mladen Jovanović, ed., *Proceedings of XIIth World Congress of FIT*, Belgrade, Prevodilac, 1991, pp. 63–68.
3. Eric Cheyfitz, *The Poetics of Imperialism: Translation and Colonization from 'The Tempest', to 'Tarzan'*, Oxford University Press, 1991, p. 102.
4. Tejaswini Niranjana, *Siting Translation: History, Post-Structuralism and the Colonial Context*, Berkeley, University of California Press, 1992.
5. Vicente Rafael, *Contrasting Colonialism: Translation and Christian Conversion in Tagalog Society under Early Spanish Rule*, Ithaca, Cornell University Press, 1988, p. 213.
6. James Joyce, *A Portrait of the Artist as a Young Man*, Herts., Panther, 1977, p. 172.
7. Michael Cronin, 'Spectacles: Interview with Ronan Sheehan', *Graph*, no. 7, Winter 1989–1990, p. 5.
8. For an examination of these issues in a Canadian context see Sherry Simon, *Le Trafic des langues: traduction et littérature dans la littérature québécoise*, Montreal, Boréal, 1995.
9. Julia Kristeva, *Étrangers à nous-mêmes*, Paris, Fayard, 1988, pp. 26–27 (my translation).
10. Cited in Letter to the Editor from Nicholas Carolan, *The Irish Times*, 16 March 1995.
11. Michael Cronin, 'Making the Millennium: Interview with Nuala Ní Dhomhnaill', *Graph*, no. 1, 1986, p. 7.
12. For a definition of translation as transformation see Paul St-Pierre, 'Translation as a Discourse of History', *TTR*, vol. 6, no. 1, 1993, p. 61.
13. Colin Graham, '"Liminal Spaces": Post-Colonial Theories and Irish Culture', *The Irish Review*, no. 16, 1994, p. 41.
14. Jeanette Beer, ed., *Medieval Translators and their Craft*, Western Michigan University, Medieval Institute Publications, 1989, p. 2.
15. Michael Cunningham, 'Babel Bitmap', *Circa*, no. 69, Autumn 1994, p. 37.

1

Translating the Middle Ages

When Richard II arrived in Ireland in 1394, his problems were not only political and military. They were also linguistic. On the occasion of the visit of the Irish kings to Richard in Dublin that same year, James Butler, the second Earl of Ormond, had to interpret the king's speech into Irish. Loyalty to Richard's kingship did not extend to loyalty to his chosen tongue. The translation skills of another Earl of Ormond would be further called upon in 1541 when the Irish parliament made Henry VIII King of Ireland. The Earl on this occasion interpreted the Speaker's address into Irish for the benefit of the Lords and Commons, although they were predominantly of Anglo-Norman or Old English origin.[1] The act of translation, in this instance, was not without its ironies. James Butler was interpreting into a language that had been outlawed four years previously under the *Act for the English Order, Habit and Language*.

The presence of a translator as historical witness and intermediary in moments of historical shift and transformation was an oblique tribute to the importance of the translation enterprise in Ireland in previous centuries. The medieval translators of Ireland were both lay and ecclesiastical. Irish monasteries from the sixth to the ninth centuries enjoyed a reputation for learning and scholarship. The presence of a large number of Irish monastic scholars in continental Europe added further to this reputation. The reform of the Irish church in the twelfth century and the Norman invasion of Ireland brought many continental religious orders to Ireland who in turn contributed to the cultural and intellectual life of the country. The work of the translators working in monasteries was complemented by the translation work of the different orders of native, professional scholars, the *filid*, brehons and physicians who dominated Irish cultural life for four centuries from 1200 to the Battle of Kinsale in 1601. These scholars translated a wide range of texts; medical, scientific, literary and religious. It is important to understand the role of the *filid* in order to appreciate their involvement in different kinds of translation. They were not so much 'poets' as sages or scholars who were also trained in poetical composition. Fergal McGrath in his account of education in ancient and medieval Ireland describes the different functions of the *filid*:

> The *filid* were guardians of the ancient traditions, history, topography, epics, pedigrees, laws. They were advisers of rulers, witnesses of contracts. By their satires they governed the social conscience. Their knowledge of genealogies was relied on to establish or maintain territorial rights. By their appeal to past glories, they stimulated national pride and military ardour. They held a recognized and honoured place in the social structure. In a sense, they were poets only in the last place, finding poetry an effective tool for their various functions, especially the type of praise-poetry which they took over from lesser poets, known as bards.[2]

The 'brehons' were not so much judges as jurists who were trained experts in the ancient laws of Ireland.[3] The physicians or doctors were the third group of lay scholars in Irish society. As in the case of the *filid* and the brehons, the physicians tended to come from certain families that had become identified with a particular branch of learning. Though their training lasted many years, the lay scholars were rewarded with wealth and prestige in Gaelic society. Translation was an activity that would involve all sections of medieval Irish society. Religious houses, Gaelic-speaking jurists, physicians, and *filid*, Anglo-Norman clerics, English-speaking Crown administrators, all sought out the good offices of translation. The picture that emerges from translation history in this period is one of a multilingual island, creatively alert to the news from elsewhere.

IRISH TRANSLATION ON THE EUROPEAN CONTINENT

The first traces of Irish translation activity lie in the large numbers of glosses that can be found in manuscripts in libraries throughout Europe and which date from the seventh, eighth and ninth centuries. These glosses are translations of single Greek or Latin words or free translations of phrases and sentences into Irish which were used by the Irish monastic teachers or their pupils in deciphering both Christian and non-Christian texts. Examples of these glosses are the *Codex Ambrosianus C.301* which came to Milan from Bobbio, one of Colambanus's monastic foundations, and was in all probability written in Ireland in the first half of the ninth century. Amongst other material, the *Codex* contains a Latin interpretation of the psalms to which the Irish glosses are attached.[4] In the university library in Würzburg, there is the *Codex Paulinus Wirziburgensis* which was begun in the middle of the eighth century. The *Codex* contains a Latin version of thirteen epistles of Saint Paul, as well as part of the epistle to the Hebrews down to xii. 24. It would appear from the scribal styles that three separate Irish monks worked on the glosses at different times.[5] The wide range of material that the Irish monastic scholars glossed is evident in the two-volume *Thesaurus Palaeohibernicus* produced by the noted Celtic scholars Whitley Stokes and John Strachan between 1901 and 1903. The volumes contain glosses on the psalms, the gospels of St Matthew and St Mark, the epistles of St Peter and St Paul, Augustine, Bede, Priscian, Propertius and others.

The range of texts and the handling of both biblical and non-biblical materials is significant. It has often been noted that despite a certain amount of tension, the religious and secular cultures in early Christian Ireland achieved a remarkable degree of harmonious co-existence and interaction. Williams and Ní Mhuiríosa in their history of the Gaelic literary tradition point to the relative absence of hostility to the native, pagan literary culture on the part of the new evangelists:

> it seems that the attitude of the Church towards the pagan culture of Ireland was different from its usual attitude in other pagan countries. Instead of being intensely hostile to that culture, it was friendly towards it; instead of suppressing the old stories which were the back-bone of the native tradition of learning, the Church helped to save them by putting them down on parchment.[6]

The circumstances that allowed for cultural exchange and a more magnanimous attitude to the indigenous culture than that which prevailed elsewhere are crucial in explaining, on the one hand, why Ireland would produce some of Europe's earliest vernacular translations and, on the other, why Irish translators would translate in the way that they did.

TRANSLATION AND EVANGELISATION

Christianity did not come to Ireland on the foot of an invasion. There were no Roman troops to drive home, so to speak, the Christian message. Imperium and faith were not linked entities bent on political domination and cultural submission. Indeed, by the time the evangelisation of Ireland began in the fifth century, the Roman Empire had already gone into irrevocable decline. The native Irish, therefore, would have a response and an attitude to classical culture that was not coloured by the humiliation of political defeat or the apologetic deference of the colonised. For Palladius, Patrick and the other preachers coming to Ireland from abroad, the Christian gospel relied on co-operation rather than coercion and would seek a reasonably harmonious integration into the native culture rather than a violent rupture. D.A. Binchy stressed the already developed state of pre-Christian native learning in 'The Background of Early Irish Literature', where he claimed that 'when Christianity came to this country, it came to a place where there was already a strong native discipline of learning, oral learning, which was organised and administered through learned guilds, if you like to call them such.'[7]

This discipline with its reliance on orality and the ogham alphabet would be bolstered rather than weakened by the arrival of the new Christian learning with its Latin alphabet. By the eighth century, Irish was firmly established in the monastic schools and monks had moved from writing on religious topics to noting down native lore in the form of native learning, sagas and poems.[8] W.B. Stanford argues interestingly that the early Irish Church in competition with the native gods and heroes found it preferable to invoke Homer and Virgil who had the virtue of remoteness: 'the Hiberno-Latin Clergy may well have viewed the pre-Christian classical tradition as an ally rather than an enemy. Better Virgil and Horace rather than the sagas of the druids.'[9] As it turned out, the Irish ended up with both Virgil and the sagas, though it is noteworthy, as Stanford points out, that no medieval Irish cleric felt the necessity to condemn 'the seductive siren-voices of antiquity in the tones of Aldhelm or Pope Gregory'.[10] Thus, the elements for an active translation culture were in place. Attitudes both to foreign classical material and native literary traditions on the part of the new Christian church were largely benign. The vernacular language was not brutally suppressed through imperial conquest. The speakers of the language and the professional literary practitioners were already in possession of a strong literary culture in that vernacular by the time Christianity arrived in Ireland. The Irish were not slow to use the Latin alphabet. James Carney dates a poem by Colmán Mac Lénéni, 'Luin oc elaib', to circa 565 AD. Binchy, following on from Thurneysen, considers, 'Amra Choluim Cille', the poem by Dallán Forguill on the death of Columcille in 597 AD, to be the earliest recorded work of Irish literature.[11] The significance of these dates is that literature was being written down in the vernacular in

Ireland at a time when many other vernaculars in Western Europe remained strictly within the oral sphere. Furthermore, interest in the vernacular was self-reflexive and comparative. The first grammar of Irish, sections of which are contained in a work known as *Auraicept na nÉces* attributed to the scholar-poet Ceann Fhaoladh, dates from the seventh century, a period when most European grammarians remained singularly uninterested in vernacular languages.[12]

Parts of Ceann Fhaoladh's work are based on Isidore of Seville's *Origines*, thus showing the awareness among seventh-century Irish scholars of the classical grammatical tradition. *Sanas Chormaic* or Cormac's Glossary is commonly attributed to Cormac mac Cuilleanáin, a bishop and King of Cashel who died in 908 AD.[13] The glossary consists of the explanations of over a thousand words and phrases that had already become obscure by the ninth century. The derivations of words are traced back and words in Irish are compared with words in the Hebrew, Latin, Greek, British and Norse languages. Douglas Hyde claimed that it was the oldest attempt at a comparative vernacular dictionary in any language in modern Europe.[14] Therefore, at both the grammatical and lexicographical level, there was an attention to the vernacular which would allow it to function as a worthy equal in the marketplace of translation.

BARBARIAN TRANSLATORS AND THE GREEK LANGUAGE

In Forguill's poem on Colmcille he declares that the saint 'at-gaill grammataig greic', which Brian Ó Cuív translates as 'he studied Greek grammar.'[15] Colmcille's interest in Greek would find its most dramatic flowering in the ninth century in the court of Charles the Bald, which brought together three remarkable Irish Hellenists, Johannes Scotus Eriugena, Sedulius Scotus and Martinus Hiberniensis or Martin of Laon. There has been considerable debate over how much these scholars owed their proficiency in Greek to an Irish monastic education, but Stanford concludes that 'the likeliest possibility is that the eminent Irish Hellenists of the ninth century first gained some knowledge of Greek in Ireland and then extended it after they had gone abroad.'[16] Eriugena was an active translator who, at the request of Charles the Bald in 858, had produced a new translation of the writings of Dionysius the Areopagite. Hildiun, the Abbot of the monastery of St Denis to the north of Paris, had produced an earlier translation between 831 and 835 with the assistance of a team of translators. James Kenney stresses the importance of Eriugena's translation for medieval scholarship:

> John seems to have worked resolutely to produce an independent version. His knowledge of Greek was sufficient to enable him not only to make a fairly accurate literal translation of the obscure original, but also to grasp fully its general significance. For this he had been prepared by the neo-Platonic studies of which his *De praedestinatione* had given evidence. It was principally on John's translation, as amended by the papal librarian Anastasius, that the very extensive knowledge and use of Pseudo-Dionysius in the West during the middle ages depended.[17]

Translation demanded vigilance, and Pope Nicholas I in a letter to Charles the Bald requested that the translation be sent to Rome as there were doubts about its orthodoxy. The papal librarian, Anastasius, was given the task of examining and correcting the translation. Returning the edited text to the French monarch in March 860, Anastasius expresses surprise at the linguistic competence of the Irish translator:

> It is a wonderful thing how that barbarian, living at the ends of the earth, who might be supposed to be as far removed from the knowledge of this other language as he is from familiar use of it has been able to comprehend such ideas and translate them into another tongue: I refer to John Scotigena, whom I have learned by report to be in all things a holy man.[18]

Like his fellow countryman Sedulius, to whom a letter is attributed on the problems of translating Greek psalms into Latin,[19] Eriugena reflected on the nature of translation itself. In his preface to his translation of the *De caelistii hierarchia* of the pseudo-Dionysius he states: 'If however the syntactic order of the aforementioned translation will have been judged to be obscure or less open, let me be seen as the translator, not the "expositor" of this work. Indeed I fear that I have committed the fault of the faithful translator.'[20] Rita Copeland argues that, here, Eriugena is echoing Boethius in his prologue to his second version of Porphyry's *Isagoge*. Both Boethius and Eriugena are transferring an approved *modus* for sacred translation, literal fidelity, to the realm of secular translation in their translations from the Greek.[21] In Eriugena's *De divisione naturae*, he rejects allegations that he has been insufficiently literal in his translation[22] and in *Versus de Ambiguis S. Maximi*, another translation produced for Charles the Bald, he warns against the dangers of rhetorical over-indulgence in translation,

Whoever rejoices in the rhetorical cloak of words, let him seek grandiloquence, striving for the Ciceronian camp; but it will be enough for me if I can cull the plain sense, with slow, deliberate speech, following only the matter of the text. The internal value of the text is duly to be grasped; the bombast of words is often deceptive.[23]

Central to the patristic tradition of learned and religious translation of which Eriugena is a leading exponent – alongside Bacon, Boethius and Aquinas – is the notion that meaning is transcendent and that it is the business of translation, through as literal rendition as is possible, to approximate to originary certitude, the language of God.[24] Indeed, the one criticism that Anastasius levelled against the Dionysius translation was an excessive literalism that generated an unnecessary burden of inter-pretation.[25] Eriugena explicitly rejects the Horatian or Ciceronian model of agonistic translation, where the translation in a sense overcomes the original, displaces it and surpasses it in inventive excellence. St Jerome, though sympathetic to the notion of sacred texts as the vessels of trans-cendent meaning, nonetheless espoused a largely agonistic approach to translation. In his *De optimo genere interpretandi*, Jerome states: 'The trans-lator considers thought content a prisoner which he transplants into his own language with the prerogative of a conqueror.'[26] Nietzsche saw in this Roman model the apologia of imperium, when he stated that, for the Romans, 'translation was a form of conquest.'[27]

The fact that Eriugena practised the art of translation outside Ireland is not unusual, as we have already seen with the presence of Irish glosses in Milan, Würzburg, St Gall, Carlsruhe, Turin, Vienna, Berne, Leyden and Nancy. Irish missionary activity on the European continent from the seventh century onwards provided a further stimulus for translation activity in that Irish scholars came into contact with other cultures and other texts.[28] A Latin translation of the Greek text, *Solutiones*, by Lydius Priscus, dating from the ninth century, was attributed to Eriugena, but appears to have been translated by another Irish translator, Fergus, a friend of Sedulius.[29] In manuscripts written in or belonging to the monastery founded by Columbanus at Bobbio, there are extracts from an earlier Greek to Latin translation of Theodore's Commentary on the Psalms. This commentary would appear to be the basis for Columbanus's own commentary on the psalms, and the translation may have been prepared in Ireland as early as the sixth century.[30] The *peregrinatio* then was as much textual as physical. Stanford stresses this wider European dimension to native scholarship:

We must remember . . . that scholars outside Ireland, such as Aldheim and Alcuin, were taught by Irishmen, and that all across Europe from Iona to Vienna the Irish were renowned and revered as teachers. If we add to this the part played by Irish scribes abroad in the preservation of classical texts, it can hardly be denied that the Irish contributed substantially to the maintenance and development of the classical heritage as well as gaining so much from it.[31]

NATURALISATION IN MEDIEVAL TRANSLATIONS

Giolla Caemháin, who is recorded as having died in 1072, is accredited with the Irish translation of Nennius's history of the Britons and the Picts, *Historia Brittonum*.[32] Giolla Caemháin as translator was not an isolated figure, an Irish translation of Dares Phrygius's *De Excidio Troiae Historia* appearing in the tenth century. The *De Excidio* is alleged to be the diary of Dares Phrygius, who took part in the Trojan Wars, and the Latin translator Cornelius Nepos claims that as a direct participant Phrygius is a more reliable witness than Homer. The Irish translation was known as *Togail Troí* and, although the original translation is now lost, versions of it exist in twelve different manuscripts.[33] Outside Ireland, the earliest translation of the *De Excidio* was the *Roman de Troie* produced by Benoît de Sainte Maure around 1160.[34] This makes the Irish translation the oldest extant vernacular translation, which may also be the case with respect to the Irish translations of Statius's *Thebiad*, Virgil's *Aeneid* and Lucan's *Pharsalia*.[35] However, many Irish translators of classical and later material did not share the patristic convictions of their compatriot in the court of Charles the Bald. If they were ready to translate into the vernacular, the activity was not to be one of literal piety but more closely resembled the Roman model of annexation and substitution, with a liberal use of discretion and *inventio* by the translator.

George Calder notes that additions to *Imtheachta Aeniasa*, the Irish translation of the *Aeneid*, were mainly to do with battles, sieges and the different trials through which Aeneas passed. The translator omitted 'genealogies and the speeches of the gods, and all matters peculiarly Roman that would fail to move the interest of an Irish audience'.[36] The battle scenes in the translation of Lucan's *Pharsalia* are greatly elaborated upon as are the descriptions of heroes and weapons.[37] Commenting on the Irish translation of the Gregory Legend (which may have been produced not later than the end of the fifteenth century), Sheila Falconer notes that the play-scene in the legend is naturalised to include a game of hurling and the fish containing the key is a salmon, with its clear echoes in Irish legend.[38] In the fifteenth-century Irish translation of the chronicle falsely attributed to Turpin, Archbishop of Reims, and known in Irish as *Gabhaltas Serluis Mhóir* or the *Conquests of Charlemagne*, the translator leaves out the list of major cities and towns conquered by Charlemagne as well as the one hundred and sixteen lands and islands mentioned in chapter III. Douglas Hyde, editor of the translation also adds that:

> The names of the seven bishops who consecrated the graveyards at Arles and Bordeaux are omitted with the names of their sees, probably as being of small interest to the Irish reader, and also, no doubt for the same reason, the chapter and a half containing the names of those buried at Blaye and Arles does not appear.[39]

In the Irish account of the life of Alexander the Great which is partly a translation of Orosius's *Historia adversus paganos* (iii. 12–23), Robert Meyer claims that 'the Irish love for special figures, for long lists of names, for carefully described articles of clothing or the various kinds of precious stones shows itself . . . even in the prosaic recital of the gests of Alexander'.[40] Translators often indulged an obvious fondness for dogs in lovingly detailed descriptions of the animals whenever they appeared in a text.[41]

This tendency towards target rather than source-oriented translation has been variously interpreted by literary critics and philologists. For Stanford, the tendency towards Drydenesque imitation in free departures from the original text is predicated on self-confidence, on the cultural and linguistic pride of a people that have not been subjected to the rigours of Roman imperial conquest:

> They showed no signs of deferential awe towards classical antiquity. Like Irish raiders in Britain or Gaul, confident in their own military prowess, or like Irish merchants proud of the superiority of their native gold and greyhounds, these anonymous translators and adapters of classical poems and myths took what they found interesting and attractive and used it freely and imaginatively without any sense of inferiority.[42]

Stanford is doubtless correct to refer to the major differences between Irish political experience and that of the Celts in Gaul or Britain and, as we suggested earlier, translation benefited from this in that the development of vernacular language and culture was unimpeded by Roman political hegemony. However, Stanford's thesis (from the point of view of translation history) needs qualification. Assessing the nature of late medieval English translation, J.D. Burnley declares that:

In the literature of secular entertainment, then, as well as in the narratives of saints' lives, there seems to be little concern with accurate rendering of the original text. It is true that there are occasional traces of an author's aspiration to outdo his sources . . . but I do not think that in general the attitude to translation is dependent on a spirit of *aemulatio*, but rather on a widespread obliviousness to the process and problems of translation, which turns the original text into nothing more than a source for literary exploitation by the devices of amplification proper to the literary tradition and idiom of the language.[43]

Speaking more generally of translation in Europe, in *The True Interpreter: A History of Translation Theory and Practice in the West*, Louis Kelly claims that medieval translators did not see 'accuracy apart from the cultural ambience of their readership'.[44] The poetic translators of the Middle Ages were, like pre-Classical dramatists, more given to the use of dynamic than to formal equivalence in their translation practice.[45] Therefore, elements of Irish translation practice were in keeping with translation paradigms in other European vernaculars. As further evidence of this, it is worth considering the activity of another Irish translator, Jofroi of Waterford, a Dominican from an Anglo-Norman background who was educated at the Dominican convent of St Saviour's in Waterford in the thirteenth century. He translated three works from Latin into French, one of the three languages of medieval Ireland, though these translations were produced while Jofroi was living in Paris. The translations were Dares Phrygius' book of the Trojan Wars, which already existed in an Irish translation, Eutropius's history of the Romans and the *Secreta Secretorum*, erroneously attributed to Aristotle and whose translation by Jofroi enjoyed great popularity in the Middle Ages.[46] In his prefatory remarks to his translation of the *Secreta Secretorum* (which he claims to have translated from Greek into Arabic and from Arabic into Latin and finally from Latin into French), Jofroi freely admits to altering his original:

> Being overcome by your entreaties, I have taken care to fulfil this task, and have used more pains in it than I am accustomed to do in my more deep and profound studies. You are further to understand that I have added many other things, which though they are not contained in that book, yet are drawn from other authentic books, and are no less profitable than what is written in that treatise; these things that are added being pertinent to the subject in hand.[47]

In addition to lending the text many ideas incompatible with Greek philosophy, Jofroi omits matter that he considers to be indecent in the section on medical advice, but is careful to devote one chapter to the best vineyards in France and also offers a series of observations on the age, colour, taste and bouquet of wine. Jofroi's translation would later be the basis for a fifteenth-century English translation of the *Secreta* by the Dublin translator and notary public, James Yonge, which was done at the request of James Butler, Earl of Ormond and Viceroy in Ireland (1419–22). The translation contains short tales to illustrate moral points, and Yonge often illustrates these with events from contemporary history. The interpolations allow him to fully express his hatred for the native Irish, quoting instances where men, because they had led good lives, were given grace from God to slay the Irish and ravage their lands.[48] Thus, the translation licence of the indigenous translators was replicated by translators working in other European languages at the same period.

Another feature of Irish translations of the medieval period which has often attracted adverse scholarly criticism is the presence of formulaic passages or 'runs' in descriptions of persons or events. These are aspects of translation licence in that they greatly expand upon what was already present in the original. In a fragment of a translation known as *Imtheachta Generodeis*, Pádraig Ó Fiannachta sees the stock descriptions and runs as clear evidence of an Irish translation. N.J.A. Williams, who dates the text between 1400 and 1550, views alliterative ornamentation, the descriptions of the banquet, sun and city in the tale as evidence of a well-naturalised translation.[49] Cecile O'Rahilly, the editor of the sixteenth-century Irish translation of *William of Palermo* known as *Eachtra Uilliam*, notes that the translator has introduced many stock epithets and similes and a number of alliterative descriptive passages where there is no equivalent in the English original. O'Rahilly adds:

> Sir Frederick Madden deplored the prolixity and repetitions of the English poem. The Irish version is, unfortunately, still more wordy and tedious. This is its most obvious blemish. The alliterative style, together with the use of stereotyped phrases, is partly responsible for this defect.[50]

Commenting on the fifteenth-century translations into Irish from Middle English of the Lives of Guy of Warwick and Bevis of Hampton, F.N. Robinson describes how the English texts are adapted to its Irish audience (including vivid details about four waves of vomit in a dragon-fight in the Bevis translation): 'the manner of the narrative is thoroughly Irish, and they read in general like the native stories in the somewhat ornate prose of the period'.[51] He then, somewhat apologetically, describes this ornate prose, with its accumulation of adjectives and adverbs in alliterating groups of three, and confesses that this presents a problem in his own modern English rendition of the Irish translations:

> In this matter, and in the general structure of sentences, I have adhered in my translation very closely to the original, though the traditions of English prose are so different from those of Irish that the resulting style will sound sometimes monotonous, and sometimes redundant and artificial.[52]

Each period of translation, like each period of literary activity, has implicit or explicit norms that determine what is acceptable literary or translation practice. To judge one period in terms of the norms of the other is to both misunderstand the nature of translation activity in earlier periods and to implicitly present the translation norms of the present as a transcendent, ahistorical standard against which all other productions are measured. Rhetorical elaboration in medieval Ireland in the form of runs or alliterative triads, particularly in the context of what has already been said about the use of licence in medieval translation, corresponds to what Gideon Toury found to be the case in twentieth-century translations into Hebrew i.e., that the operational choices of translators are dictated by teleological considerations and notably the ideological, cultural and stylistic norms of the target culture.[53] The tendency is for translation editors and critics, who in the Irish case have come from a mainly philological or a literary critical background, to ignore the teleological dynamics that inform translation work. Given the powerful presence of the learned schools in the medieval period with their constant practice of the elaborate bardic style, the fact that a number of translators were trained as *filid* in these schools and that runs and stock epithets often facilitated oral delivery (which remained an important avenue of transmission for literature in the medieval period and a central element of the education of the *filid*), it is to be expected rather than regretted that the stylistic norms of Middle Irish should be present in a number of the translations. These norms were a key element of the vernacular of the target culture with respect to non-pragmatic texts.

There is a sense in which the criticism levelled against the translations is part of a more general retrospective idealisation of Irish literary history with its recurrent theme of the Fall.[54] In his *Gaelic Literature Surveyed*, Aodh de Blácam declares that 'we look back . . . to the brilliant sixth and seventh centuries to envisage the Gaelic literary system in its perfect pristine form'.[55] Old Irish is the literary Arcadia from which the bards are subsequently banished. The Early Modern Period (1350–1650) shows clear signs of apostasy, of the abandonment of earlier conciseness and freshness for the bloated rhetoric of prolix poets and scribes who were profligate with parchment:

> In the Early Modern period there arose a turgid style which continued to be practised down to the nineteenth century. Its mark is an overabundance of adjectives chosen for their alliterative value rather than their meaning. Moreover, 'runs' are introduced again and again as if to spare the writer the pains of finding the epithets which are appropriate to his meaning.[56]

De Blácam does not pause to consider whether, in fact, his evaluation of the Gaelic tradition is not driven by the stylistic norms of a more austere form of modernity with its preference for a more pared-down prose, adjectival economy and an avoidance of unnecessary repetition. What is most admirable in the past is that which most closely resembles the present. Robin Flower similarly favours the concrete, epigrammatic concision of speech which he feels characterises the best of Gaelic literature, a literature which is 'confused in the worst periods and examples by the strange pedantries of rhetorical expansion, which appear from a native tendency to display, fostered by the influence of the more degenerate forms of late Latin rhetoric'.[57] Apart from the perplexing vagueness of a 'native tendency to display', there is arguably a view of language and literature which is driven by the unexamined prejudices of modernity and which posits an essentialist aesthetic norm independent of the internal dynamics of language and culture. Flower's thesis was, in part, a reaction to the misty obfuscations of Arnold and Renan in their Romantic depictions of Celtic peoples, and stemmed from his desire to counter this image with evidence of the bright, subtle concreteness of the Gaelic mind. However, the danger is to subsume history to polemic and to treat the translations or literary productions of a particular age as somehow 'degenerate', the vainglorious offspring of noble stock.

The treatment of translation in medieval Ireland is bedevilled by contradiction, in large measure due to a failure to understand what translators did in the period. We have described above the dystopian view of medieval translation practice, the liberties and the stylistic wantonness that convinced Hull that the Irish did not so much translate as paraphrase, and that led de Blácam to declare that Gaelic 'renderings' of classical and mediaeval literature were 'generally very free'.[58] There are examples that substantiate this belief. The Irish translations of Guy of Warwick and Bevis of Hampton,[59] the early Middle Irish translation of the *Thebiad* of Statius known as *Togail na Tebe*,[60] the late fifteenth-century translation of Caxton's translation of Raoul Lefevre's *Recueil des Histoires de Troyes* (known in Irish as *Stair Ercuil agus a bás*),[61] the Irish translation of Francesco Pipino's Latin version of the travels of Marco Polo[62] and the *Pharsalia* translation[63] previously mentioned all demonstrate considerable latitude in translation. In certain instances, the abridgement is such as would appear to justify Hull's charge of paraphrase. The counter-examples are, however, numerous. Commenting on the Middle Irish Alexander, Robert Meyer remarks that 'the Irishman's translation of Orosius is very good, and we may attribute mistakes in translation not so much to his misunderstanding of Orosius's Latin as to the probability of the corruptions in the manuscript he was using'.[64]

Calder underscores the competence of the Irish translator of the *Aeneid*, 'The matter . . . is in the main identical with the the *Aeneid*. The translator was a competent scholar, both in Latin and Gaelic. A few instances of idiomatic phrases, idiomatically rendered, place his scholarship beyond the reach of cavil.'[65] O'Rahilly defends the translation abilities of the translator of *Eachtra Uilliam*, abilities which he defines in terms of fidelity: 'The Irish tale is not a mere adaptation or free rendering.' He goes on to claim: 'In the dialogues and soliloquies especially, we can see how closely the Irish translator adheres to the original.'[66] Standish O'Grady concedes that 'the mediaeval Irish were, when they gave their minds to it, excellent translators and could solve the problem of how to render closely from a strange tongue without distorting the idiom of their own.'[67] There is, therefore, a tradition of faithful, exact translation that exists alongside the more extravagantly liberal translations that caught the attention of de Blácam, Hull and others. The tradition of relative fidelity is, of course, even more obvious in the area of pragmatic translation, the Irish translations of medical, philosophical, religious and scientific texts of the Middle Ages. These will be considered separately (in another section), given the different pragmatics of reception governing the production and use of these translations.

If we consider the different translation strategies of fidelity, expansion, contraction, naturalisation and paraphrase, what is most striking in medieval Irish translation is the prevalence of rewriting. In the examples quoted above of closeness and fidelity, the claims that the latter-day editors make must be qualified. The Alexander translation in the Book of Ballymote, the *Imtheachta Aeniasa* and *Eachtra Uilliam* bear multiple traces of modification, omission and elaboration. On the other hand, the freer non-pragmatic translations of the period contain many passages that are recognisably close to the original source text. If this was not the case, it would be difficult to identify them as translations in the first place. What we have in effect is translation as a form of what André Lefevere calls 'rewriting'.[68] These target-oriented, prospective translations were source texts rewritten for an Irish audience, initially for the Gaelic chieftains and Anglo-Norman lords, monasteries and native schools of learning, and violated free/literal distinctions. It was less a case of either/or than of both/and. The retrospective Romantic concern with the sanctity of the original not only belittles the role of the translator generally, but it also leads to misrepresentation of the context of translation activity and sets up false dichotomies with respect to translation norms. The central concern of literary translators in the period was to provide translations that would be wholly acceptable to the native reader and which would function within the native literature. As Quin points out in the case of the *Ercuil* and *Togail Troí* translations:

> While the main theme is on the whole faithfully adhered to, the adapter is by no means a slavish follower of his original. In addition to adopting a peculiarly Irish phraseology and making free use of the commonplaces of the native literature he draws wherever it suits him on other sources and alters proper names at will. The result is a tale which except for its central theme is thoroughly Irish.[69]

The translator's aim was to make the translation conform to the linguistic and stylistic norms of the target-language literature. That this aim was achieved through a mixture of dynamic and formal strategies does not seem to have greatly troubled the translators since the important considerations were teleological rather than originary. This is not to say that the source was obscured. Translation was an important source of new heroic models, images and motifs for medieval Irish literature whether the source was the *matière de Rome, matière de France* or *matière de Bretagne*.[70] The original did not, however, exercise the power of veto that it would in the patristic or romantic periods.

The Irish practice, in a sense, predates by centuries Lawrence Venuti's 'fluent strategies' in translation which he sees as the consequence of contemporary Anglo-American cultural hegemony:

> A fluent strategy aims to efface the translator's crucial intervention in the foreign text: he or she actively rewrites in a different language to circulate in a different culture, but this very process results in a self-annihalation, ulti-

mately contributing to the cultural marginality and economic exploitation which translators suffer today. At the same time, a fluent strategy effaces the linguistic and cultural difference of the foreign text: this gets rewritten in the transparent discourse dominating the target-language culture and is inevitably coded with other target-language values, beliefs, and social representations, implicating the translation in ideologies that figure social differences and may well arrange them in hierarchical relations (according to class, gender, sexual orientation, race, nation).[71]

The Irish practice of fluent strategies, seen in this light, is predicated on cultural confidence. The interest in and attention to the vernacular that we noted earlier was not diminished by the Viking raids of the eighth to tenth centuries or by the Norman invasion in the twelfth. This is not to say that the vernacular was unaffected by contact with Norse, Latin, French or English. The Danish and Norwegian settlements would provoke the shift from Old to Middle Irish and the Norman presence precipitated the transition from Middle Irish to Early Modern Irish.[72] Englishmen adopting Irish names, dress, customs or speech ran the risk of forfeiture of all lands and tenements under the 1366 Statutes of Kilkenny (the Statutes, seen by historians as a measure favouring English, were in fact written down in French). However, the English language between 1200 and 1500 did not flourish in Ireland, with the notable exception of a small number of towns and cities. By 1495, Poyning's Parliament had repealed the language decree of the 1366 Statutes, and by 1500, Curtis notes, 'English had lost most of the ground to Irish'.[73] The gradual hibernicisation of the Norman lords, the migration of the small tenantry back to England, the ravages of the Black Death in the Pale (the area stretching from Dundalk and Ardree to Kilcullen and the Wicklow mountains that remained under English control at the start of Henry VIII's reign), and English military involvement in France meant that the fourteenth and fifteenth centuries could be described by one commentator from the point of view of the Irish language as centuries of national revival and restoration respectively.[74]

These are also the centuries of the most prolific translation activity and, in the light of Venuti's observation, it is hardly suprising that the translation strategies adopted by the indigenous translators were fluent and not otherwise. This conversely means that the scale of translation activity in Ireland in the Middle Ages was evidence of political and cultural assurance, translation a sign of cultural health rather than linguistic decrepitude. The Irish experience, however, calls into question Venuti's claim that fluent strategies efface the translator's crucial intervention in the translation of the foreign text. On the contrary, the translator's signature is everywhere in these medieval translations which are manipulated, expanded, adopted to the expectations, desires and cultural referents of the target culture. The manner in which the prerogatives of the target culture are interpreted by the translator are in many ways as intensely subjective as the foregrounding of those features of the foreign source text which the translator deems to be irreducibly other. The translators are not passive instruments of aesthetic orders from the target culture but active makers and shapers of the translated texts. Writing on Fingin O'Mahony's 1475 translation of the *Buke of John Mandeville* into Irish, M.C. Seymour declares that:

> On comparison with the English text, for example that extant in MS. Queen's 383, the Irish version is seen to be a deliberate and successful redaction. Much of the somewhat dull detail of itinerary, historical fact, and prosaic information, together with the names and characters of the Hebrew and Saracen alphabets, is suppressed. What remains is a collection of the best stories in *Mandeville's Travels*.[75]

Describing the Virgil translation, Calder stresses the narrative preoccupations of the translator which made his work akin to that of a modern novelist. The translator in the *Aeniasa* 'has the requisite literary talent. A thorough knowledge of his orginal enables him to begin effectively; to select, curtail, amplify, or transpose his materials in order to meet the taste of his readers.'[76] Again, it is worth remembering that this narrative interventionism, as we have already noted, does not preclude close translation. Venuti, in his eagerness to denounce Anglocentric cultural arrogance and the imbalance in the direction of translated literature (North-South rather than South-North or South-South), may, in fact, contribute even further to the marginalisation of translators by failing to recognise that a fluent strategy is an active, not a passive, process and that in certain respects the translator is even *more* present than in a retrospective translation because of the multiple modifications to the source text. Effacement in translation rules out self-effacement. The translator's background is also worth considering in this light. Many translators were trained as poet-scholars in the native schools of learning and these schools, together with the learned families, constituted a powerful intellectual caste in medieval Ireland. In addition to their study of Irish language and literature, they also studied poetic composition. It was therefore quite natural for them to adopt, as they did, an interventionist approach to non-pragmatic texts. They rarely took refuge in transparency.

PRAGMATIC TRANSLATION IN MEDIEVAL IRELAND

The intellectual needs of medieval Ireland were supplied in part by
literary translation. There was in addition, however, the need for
translations of medical, scientific and philosophical texts. As Williams
and Ní Mhuiríosa point out:

> Dá shuimiúla iad na scéalta rómánsacha go léir ní bhfaighfear pictiúr cruinn
> de litríocht Ghaeilge na meánaoise mura gcuimhnítear nach raibh iontu ach
> cuid amháin den ábhar a rugadh isteach ó theangacha eile. Ba líonmhar iad
> na téacsanna oideachasacha a aistríodh i gcaitheamh na n-aoiseanna sin, idir
> théacsanna diaga, théacsanna leighis agus eile.[77]

The reform of the Irish Church in the twelfth century, with the creation
of territorial dioceses and the arrival of religious orders such as the
Cistercians, Augustinians, Franciscans and Dominicans, further strengthened Irish links with the continent. As Michael Richter has observed: 'In
the twelfth century the Irish Church was more closely linked to the
Continental Church than ever before.'[78] From a translation point of view,
this meant that there was a ready source of texts for the vernacular translator, particularly but not only devotional texts. The arrival of the Anglo-
Norman aristocracy, with their links to England and the continent, was
another important source of material that, in those cases where the aristocracy became hibernicised, would become available to native scholars.[79]
Thurneysen gives us some idea of the scale of scholarly activity in the
Middle Ages when he notes that from the earliest times to the eighteenth
century there were over a thousand known native scholars.[80] This figure
does not take into account, of course, the many lesser-known scholars,
who because of Ireland's troubled history have disappeared without a
trace. The religious, philosophical, medical and scientific texts that were
translated were primarily for use as text-books or for private study.[81]

The translation of philosophical and medical texts was done primarily
by scholars from the native Irish medical schools. In this, the Irish translators were following the general medieval tradition where medicine was
inextricably bound up with philosophy. Both Hippocrates and Galen
linked medicine to philosophical speculation, a link that was further
emphasised by Arab scholars from the eighth century onwards. Thus,
when Aristotelian theory in philosophy and Hippocratic teaching in medicine became widely known in medieval Europe as a result of translations
from the Arabic, it was not surprising that medicine and philosophy

should be closely associated with one another. Aristotelian philosophy would, in a sense, provide the theoretical basis for the new medicine. Aspiring doctors, therefore, would be expected to familiarise themselves with philosophical precepts as part of their medical education.[82] From the number of extant manuscript copies of medical translations, it appears that they enjoyed wide circulation and were extensively used.[83] The standard medieval texts that were translated were more remarkable for their erudition than for their clinical observations, and the Irish translators were content to follow in this tradition by interpolation of quotations from well-known Arab authorities in their Irish translations. Two works that were particularly popular were the *Rosa Anglica* of John of Gadesden or Johannes Anglicus, and the *Lilium Medicinae* of Bernard of Gordon, both English physicians. In an interesting example of intertextual strategies in translation, John of Gadesden used Bernard's *Lilium Medicinae* extensively in compiling the *Rosa Anglica* while the Irish translator of the *Rosa* borrowed heavily from the *Lilium* but not always in the same places or in the same manner as John.[84] The contents of the *Rosa Anglica* were varied:

> From the medical point of view the *Rosa Anglica* is a hotch-potch of medieval teaching, genuine or fabulous results of the application of remedies, oriental leechcraft and superstition, native English cures and charms, prayers and religious practices, interwoven with the native beliefs of the people at different periods and in different parts of the country.[85]

Though the translator was free in his use of matter from Bernard's work, he did not introduce materials from the pre-medieval native tradition in Ireland or indigenous cures and charms that would have differed from those found in England.[86] This would appear to be largely due to the respect in which the new medicine was held and a reluctance on the part of the translators to be associated with older, discredited native traditions. The identity of the translator of the Royal Irish Academy manuscript of the *Rosa* edited by Winifred Wulff is unknown, but a translation of the text was attributed to Nicól Ó hÍceadha in 1400, and another translation is attributed to him and Aonghus Ó Callanáin in a British Museum manuscript dated to 1482. The Ó hIceadha and Ó Callanáin translation of Hippocrates' aphorisms was made in 1403.[87] Both the *Rosa* and the *Lilium* were translated from Latin.

The O'Hickeys, a Munster family and hereditary doctors to the O'Briens, were one of the best known native medical families of the medieval period, along with the O'Cassidys and the O'Shiels. Another

26

famous medical family from the period were the Ulster family of Mac Duinntshléibhe, hereditary physicians to the O'Donnells. In the fifteenth century, a member of that family, Cormac mac Duinntshléibhe, made a translation of the *Lilium Medicinae* as well as a number of other translations including Thomas Aquinas's *Operationibus Occultis Naturae*,[88] and the *Gualterus de dosibus* or *Gualterus on the doses of decoctions* to which is attached the following note by the translator: 'Here ends Gualterus his book of the doses of medicines. Cormac mac Duinntsleibhe has put this summary into Irish for Dermot mac Donall O'Lyne; and to him and his sons may so profitable a comentary render good service. On the 4th day of the Kalends of April this lecture was finished at Cloyne in the year 1459.'[89] Whereas the standard of the *Rosa Anglica* translation is high, it is not always easy to make definitive statements about the translation abilities of medieval translators of non-literary texts. Commenting on a collection of medieval medico–philosophical translations in 1940, Francis Shaw singles out one particular translation, that of Gualterus Burley's *De Potentiis Animae*, and states that the 'translation, which is excellent, renders very faithfully and with scrupulous care the whole thought of the original'.[90] On the other hand, translations such as those of Thomas Aquinas's *De Mixtione Elementorum* and his *De Motu Cordis* are deficient with omissions and a failure to capture part of the sense of the original. Shaw observes of the twenty texts in the collection he is studying that:

> The quality of translations varies very considerably: a few reach a high standard of excellence; some are very unsatisfactory. However, in the case of these latter, it is not always easy to apportion blame. The defects may be due to a faulty original, to the incompetence or carelessness of a copyist, or to the translator. It is possible, too, that in some cases we have before us what is only the first draft of the Irish translation.[91]

In a Thomas Davis lecture given over twenty years later, Shaw claims that with respect to the Irish medico–philosophical translations, 'At times, the translation is very imperfect.'[92] No new evidence is adduced for this statement, but one assumes he is referring to the texts in his 1940 article. If this is the case, then he is misrepresenting his own conclusions, as in only three of the twenty texts does he identify serious problems of mistranslation or unintelligibility. Further, he ignores the methodological problems posed by a manuscript tradition that he himself mentioned in the above extract. Unfortunately, opinions quoted out of context become dangerous certitudes. Nessa Ní Shéaghdha, in her 1983 Statutory Public Lecture to the Dublin Institute of Advanced Studies on translation, says of the philosophical translations: 'Most are very unsatisfactory, often the translation "fails to render the sense of the original even where all the Latin words are put into Irish".'[93] The quotation in Ní Shéaghdha's remarks is from Shaw's 1940 article, but Shaw's comments refer specifically to the translation of Aquinas's *De Mixtione Elementorum*, whereas Ní Shéaghdha gives the reader the mistaken impression that they somehow apply to virtually all medieval Irish philosophical translations.

Though there is clear evidence of lacunae on the part of certain native scholars as to their knowledge of Latin, the overwhelming bulk of translation in the Middle Ages, when one considers literary, devotional, medical, philosophical and scientific translations as a whole, point to a more than adequate knowledge of a language which was an important source of translation material. It would be unfortunate, therefore, if the efforts made by these medieval translators were to be misrepresented through injudicious quotation. It is interesting to note that both Shaw in his 1961 lecture, and Ní Shéaghdha in her 1983 lecture, both quote Edmund Campion's 1571 *Historie of Ireland*:

> Without either precepts or congruity they speake Latin like a vulgar tongue, learned in their common schools of leach-craft and law, whereat they begin children, and hold on sixteen or twentie years, conning by roate the Aphorisms of Hippocrates.[94]

The quotation in each instance is offered uncritically as if Campion was an utterly reliable source. However, as is clear from the accusation of unbridled fornication among the native Irish (a standard element in the rhetorical arsenal of colonial propagandists), Campion's comments can hardly be deemed impartial. In addition, Stanford points out that Campion was writing from the point of view of a scholar trained in the strict Ciceronianism of the Renaissance period. Another equally legitimate tradition existed where Latin was adapted to the requirements and idioms of the vernacular language, so that it remained in a sense a living language.[95] Thus, the general standard of translation of Latin throughout the medieval period does not bear out the truth of Campion's criticism as a general comment on the linguistic abilities of the native scholars whatever about its relevance to standards in specific schools. Again, ill-judged quotation misleads rather than enlightens.

Aodh de Blácam making a special case for the Irish contribution to Latin literature ignores the important Latin influence on Irish translation practice in the Middle Ages. He sees the Vikings as the harbingers of doom for the Latin tradition: 'The interruption of the fruitful intercourse between the Gaelic genius and the Latin culture was the chief injury that the Norwegian and Danish invasions inflicted on Irish culture.'[96] If de Blácam is referring to Hiberno-Latin and the works produced by Irish scholars in the Latin language, his argument makes some if not total sense. However, in considering the medieval period, account should be taken of the extensive contact that Irish scholars, both lay and clerical, had with the Latin language. 'Latin culture' is, of course, a vague term and the political entity that sustained it had long gone into a decline before the Danes and Norwegians arrived in Ireland. The language did, however, survive and was in many respects more important than English from the point of view of the translator working in medieval Ireland. For this reason, it is difficult to accept that 'the fruitful intercourse between the Gaelic genius and the Latin culture' was interrupted or terminally affected by the political events of the ninth and tenth centuries. The intercourse was, indeed, to continue for another six centuries. One of Latin's functions, as we noted earlier, was to act as an intermediary for the transmission of Arabic thought and culture in medieval Europe. An example of this was Gerard of Sabionetta's Latin translation of an Arabic treatise attributed to Mascha Allah or Messahalah, a Jewish astronomer of Alexandria who was active in or around 800 AD. Gerard's translation was edited by J. Stabius and was printed in Nuremberg in 1504 under the title *De Scientia Motus Orbis*.

The Irish translation which possibly dates from the sixteenth century, is partly similar to Stabius's text but adds material from other unidentified Latin texts. There is a reference to spectacles in chapter vii which could not have been in Messahalah's work as spectacles did not come into use until the early fourteenth century.[97] The mixed translation strategy that was employed in translation of literary texts is similarly used in this instance though there is an important difference in style and register. The editor of the Irish translation, Maura Power declares that:

> The Irish text cannot be said to be a literal translation of Stabius. It is rather an adaptation. In parts the rendering is indeed literal, but there is scarcely a chapter where there is neither more or less matter than in the corresponding Latin version.[98]

If a certain conscious striving after archaism characterises poetic and historical writing in the sixteenth century, resulting, Power claims, in 'a pedantic mass of bombast, wholly unnatural, and quite valueless artistically or philologically', the astronomical translation is refreshingly different. Here she argues:

> The subject-matter of our text precludes all that rhetoric and expansion so popular in translation of narrative matter. Lucidity being the chief object, the style is simple and straightforward, sometimes even bald in description; it bears no trace of affectation, becoming almost colloquial in places, so that one is tempted to put it down as a sample of the spoken Irish of the fourteenth or fifteenth centuries.[99]

Power, in making her case for the stylistic directness of the Irish translation of Stabius has resort to caricature, e.g., 'a pedantic mass of bombast', and ignores the substantial contribution made by translators of literary and devotional literature in extending the range of styles available to Irish scholars. Cainneach Ó Maonaigh, in his edition of Tomás Gruadha Ó Bruacháin's fifteenth-century Irish translation of the *Meditationes vitae Christi*, speaks of the fifteenth century as a period of intense activity in devotional translation in Ireland. He argues that what characterised this literature was a concern with content rather than form and that, due to the intrinsic difficulties of translating from one language to another, the translators were less concerned with the pursuit of an exaggerated formalism and the deliberate cultivation of archaism in language.[100] Ó Maonaigh, in fact, claims that these translators rather than the Franciscans in Louvain must be credited with the birth of a more simplified and direct Modern Irish:

> De dheasca na faillí a tugadh ins an litríocht seo na 15ú aoise, bhí a lán ar intinn gur do Fhroinsiascánaigh Lobháin a bhí an chreidiúint ag dul mar gheall ar tús a chur leis an nua-Ghaelige simplí seo. Ach ní headh. Lean drong amháin, go mór-mhór lucht na filíochta agus fiannaíochta, ag saothrú na seanGhaeilge casta i gcomhnuí, ach bhí dream eile, agus go háirithe lucht leabhar cráibhtheachta a scríobhadh ag soláthar leabhar i gcanúint na ndaoine. Níorbh é a gcuspóir, mar adubhairt Aodh Mac Aingil féin an Ghaeilge a mhúineadh ach an aithrí.[101]

Ó Maonaigh does not confine his comments to devotional translations, however, and declares that translators of medical literature were equally intent on providing knowledge about diseases of the body rather than lessons in grammatical excellence.[102] Ó Maonaigh may have been overly optimistic concerning the observational powers of medieval doctors schooled in the new Aristotelian medicine, but he is correct to emphasise the centrality of translated literature to the evolution of Irish language and culture in the Middle Ages.

CIRCULATION, VISIONS AND THE TRANSLATOR'S SIGNATURE

We shall see in further chapters the role played by translation in post-medieval Ireland but it is worth remembering that, where they survived the ravages of the Cromwellian and Williamite wars, translations enjoyed, in Walter Benjamin's words, a considerable afterlife. Ó Bruacháin's translation of the fourteenth-century work of Friar John of Caulibus appears to have been made sometime between 1430, and the date of the earliest manuscript copy, 1461. Between 1461 and 1847, thirty-eight manuscript copies of the translation were made in different parts of Ireland. The circulation of translations was, of course, facilitated by the peripatetic nature of scholarship. The medieval scholars travelled from castle to castle and monastery to monastery and, owing to the existence of a standard literary dialect in Irish, there were no problems of inter-dialectical incomprehension. Fingin O'Mahony's 1475 translation of Mandeville's travels made in Cork, in the south, was by 1484 being copied in the north of the country, in Cavan.[103] Domhnaill Ó Conaill, a Munster scholar, assisted Ó Bruacháin in writing down his translation known in Irish as *Smaointe Beatha Chríost*. In 1443 Ó Conaill, according to Ó Maonaigh, took down from oral dictation Uiliam Mac Duibhne's translation of Pope Innocent III's work, *De contemptu mundi*. Mac Duibhne was recovering from a sword wound at the time and no doubt his choice of source text was dictated, in part, by his own personal circumstances.[104]

The work, indeed, seems to have been popular with Irish translators, as Walter Stanihurst, brother of the more famous Richard, produced an English translation of the *De contemptu* in the sixteenth century.[105] Ó Bruacháin was choir canon in Killala in County Mayo so it is quite possible that, after working with Ó Bruacháin, Ó Conaill travelled to Leitrim to take down Mac Duibhne's translation. Thus, the political economy of translation in medieval Ireland involves, externally, the ready importation of source material from Britain and the continent and, internally, the circulation of translations through a network of travelling scribes. John MacKechnie indicates the extent of mobility in a period when travel was difficult. In his edition of the Irish translation of the *Instructio Pie Vivendi et Superna Meditandi*, he points out that the Irish text would appear to be connected with a religious house on the continent that had a Latin text of the work. This Latin text may have come to Ireland via Cashel in Tipperary. MacKechnie notes the stylistic similarities between Mac

Duibhne's translation of the *De Contemptu*, and the translation of the *Instructio*, and suggests that the Leitrim translator may have also been responsible for the latter translation.[106] If MacKechnie's hypotheses are correct we have a text that travels from the continent to Ireland and then travels from the south northwards to be translated.

Irish translations of the Latin lives of saints, the Visions and apocryphal literature are prominent in the devotional translations of the Middle Ages in Ireland. Augustine Mac Raighin, a canon on Saint's Island, Lough Ree, is mentioned in the manuscript known as *Liber Flavus Fergusiorum* as the translator of a life of St John the Divine. Seán Ua Conchubhair, who died in 1405, is also mentioned as the translator of the *Dialogus de passione Christi* in *Liber Flavus*, which contains the translated lives of a number of saints as well as the translation of a popular medieval work.[107] The *Visio Sancti Pauli* or the Vision of Saint Paul, one of the sources used for the Vision of St Patrick's Purgatory, exists in a translated version in both the *Liber Flavus* and in a Royal Irish Academy manuscript (MS 24 P2) dated 1513–14.[108] These Visions of the otherworld were popular with medieval readers, and they offered great imaginative scope within the confines of devotional or hagiographical literature. The popularity of these Visions endured for the Irish, and as late as the seventeenth century an Irish translation, known as *Fís Mherlíno*, was made in a Franciscan monastery either in Rome or in Prague.[109]

One of the most popular *visio* was the *Visio Tnugdali* which was composed in Latin in the monastery of Regensburg in present-day Germany by Marcus, an Irish monk from Cashel. The *visio* was composed around 1149 AD. Tnugdalus, an Irishman, has a dream where his soul is separated from his body. During that dream, he visits the otherworld, where he meets saints like Patrick and Ruadhán and many of his contemporaries. The *Visio Tnugdali* was translated into many European vernaculars, though an Irish translation was not available until one was made sometime between 1510 and 1520 by Muirgheas mac Páidín Uí Mhaolchonaire.[110] As we shall see in the next chapter, Muirgheas mac Páidín's grandson, Flaithrí Ó Maolchonaire, would continue the family's distinguished translation tradition in Belgium, a century later. The language of Uí Maolchonaire's *Aisling Tundail* is the archaic literary language of the filid, which differs significantly from the language in the Ó Bruacháin translation.[111] This is undoubtedly a result of both the subject matter and the personality of the translator. With their imaginative freedom and poetic potential, the Visions would have excited the literary interests of those scholars translating this type of devotional literature. In addition, Uí Maolchonaire had a reputation as a scholar and a poet, a reputation that he would no doubt be eager to confirm through a knowledgeable handling of literary language in Irish.

The case of *Aisling Tundail* illustrates the danger in translation history of generalisations that ignore questions of the translator's signature or generic constraints, for example, the nature of the *visio* material made more prosaic translations less likely. Even in the case of saints' lives, the background of the translator was relevant. For example, the translation of the Life of Saint Margaret is written in the formal, adjectival style of the bardic romances. Pilib Ó Dálaigh, the translator, was a canon in the monastery on Trinity Island in Lough Key, County Roscommon. However, he had been trained as a *file* before entering religious life so that the aesthetic norms in his translation practice would be strongly influenced by bardic conventions.[112] One of the more famous scribes of the fifteenth century was Uilliam Mac an Leagha who came from a famous medical family. Trained as a scholar in the native schools, he worked for the Anglo-Norman Butlers among other patrons. Gordon Quin believes that the Lives of Guy and Bevis, *Stair Ercuil agus a bás* and *Betha Mhuire Eigiptachdha* were all translated by Mac an Leagha. In all cases, the translator appears to have used an English intermediary text. Quin adds:

> Even when allowance is made for the fact that he was only one of the many writing a fairly uniform Early Modern Irish, the method of relation, the style, and many idiosyncrasies in diction point to him as translator. Especially significant is the fact that no one of the tales is found in a second MS, and the wealth of archaism points in the same direction. This is more striking in SE [Stair Ercuil] and Betha Mhuire than in Guy, but as we can see from SE itself Mac an Lega was by no means consistent in this respect.[113]

The influence of the individual translator on the translated text is once more apparent but, more interestingly in the light of our present discussion, there would seem to be a certain tension with respect to the operational choices of the translator when he is dealing with religious literature (though the *Betha* is clearly at the romantic end of the devotional spectrum). Freeman in his edition of the *Betha* notes that:

> The language is quite modern and in places colloquial; witness *a'dul* and *in mac's a' t-atbair*, which looks odd beside alliterative passages and archaic expressions which are such prominent features of the style.[114]

If Quin is correct in his attribution of the *Betha* translation to Mac an Leagha, then there is a sense in which the inconsistency that he describes is the result of uncertainty as to what translation strategy is appropriate to the religious subject matter. The romantic treatment of the events in the source text appears to call for a style and register appropriate to the more formally elaborate literary translations (though, as we have seen, many literary translations cannot be seen uniquely as products of conservative bardic style), yet the religious theme would invite comparison with other devotional translations of the same period that opted for a more direct, less ornate style. The result is, one could argue, the uncertainty noted by Freeman with respect to the use of register in the Irish translation.

The translator's signature could take more radical forms than inconsistent use of register, and the work of another Irish translator, Richard Stanihurst, is either a cautionary tale or a hymn to the creative autonomy of the translator. Stanihurst, who was born in Dublin in 1547 and is better known for his writings on Irish culture and history, moved later in life to Leyden and there published his English language translations of Books I–IV of Virgil's *Aeneid*, along with such other poetical pieces as translations of Sir Thomas More's Latin epigrams.[115] In his 'Introduction to the Reader', he supports Gabriel Harvey's theory of English prosody that quantity rather than accent ought to be the guiding principle of both English and Latin metre. To prove this proposition, he translated Virgil into hexameters. Goethe would praise Johann Heinrich Voss in 1819 for a similar initiative in translating Homer into hexameters, seeing Voss's work as that of the third epoch of translation where the translation achieves perfect identity with the orginal. Goethe does note that this kind of translation meets with the 'most resistance in its early stages.'[116] The critic D. St John Seymour appears to feel that, in the case of Stanihurst, the resistance was justified. He is withering on Stanihurst's translation project:

> The result was a literary monstrosity. The Latin was recklessly paraphrased in a grotesquely prosaic vocabulary, which abounded in barely intelligible words invented by the translator to meet metrical exigencies. Frequent inversions of phrase heightened the ludicrous effect.[117]

Seymour may be overstating the case, but the result of Stanihurst's new metrical scheme for the reader was singularly unhappy. His scant regard for the reception of his translation, and the difficulties even highly literate readers would encounter in reading it, did not lead to any further demand for his translation work and no further translations appear under his name.

However, Stanihurst was a genuine classical scholar, and Stanford claims that his 'analyses of Virgil's prosody and metre . . . were sensible and acute.'[118] Stanihurst as translator had perhaps the ultimate consolation of visibility, if not that of readability.

Religious belief and practice in the Middle Ages involved, for those who had the desire or the means, a pilgrimage to the Holy Land. For those who had the former and not the latter, there was translation. A certain number of medieval translations in Ireland fulfilled the function of providing the readers (or listeners) with accounts of the marvels of the East. This orientalism *ante verbum* was, in essence, a secular *visio*, a presentation of an otherworld which existed not in the dreams of the divine but in Kingdoms on Earth. The Irish translation of the tale of the Seven Wise Masters,[119] or the translations of the Letter of Prester John, are examples of translated texts that allowed Irish readers the pleasures of largely fictitious travel.[120] In the early fifteenth-century translation of the Letter from the Latin, the translator interpolates a description of the marvels of India from Bartholemus Anglicus's *Proprietates Rerum* to further heighten the exoticism of the text for the target audience. The wonders of India are similarly a focus of the translator's attention in the medieval Irish Alexander translation where the *Epistola ad Aristotelem*, Alexander's epistle to his teacher Aristotle, known in Europe since the ninth century, is translated in its entirety by the Irish translator. The *Epistola* details the wonderful sights that are to be beheld in India.[121] Robert Meyer claims that 'medieval man found his thirst for the miraculous, the strange, and the awesome somewhat satisfied in hearing retold the deeds of Alexander and the portrayal of the Wonders of the East'.[122] The translators did not always see their activity in this light, however, and Fingin O'Mahony in his preface to his translation of Maundeville's Travels would appear to advance admirably prosaic reasons for the translation enterprise:

> And whosoever would fain know the best way to wend from every country to Jerusalem and the holy places that are thereabout, Fingin, son of Diarmait Mór Húa Mathgamna, will tell it.
>
>   For 'tis he that put this book out of English and Latin and Greek and Hebrew into Gaelic to shew the ways, on sea and on land to Jerusalem unto everyone who may desire to go in pilgrimage thither.'[123]

Flower takes O'Mahony's motives seriously and argues that Maundeville's Travels, the Travels of Marco Polo and the Letter of Prester John were translated into Irish 'to satisfy the interest in oriental things aroused by the practice of pilgrimage to Palestine'.[124] The translations, therefore, responded to both imaginative and practical needs, even if, in the case of the latter, excessive belief in the fidelity of the accounts was likely to lead to certain disappointment for the intrepid pilgrim. The demand for these translations illustrates a more general point about translation and Irish culture in general.

TRANSLATION, INSULARITY AND PERIPHERALITY

Insularity was certainly a geographical fact for the medieval Irish, but as the extent of translation activity indicates, it was not a cultural one. In the case of the other two languages of medieval Ireland, French and English, St John D. Seymour reaches the same conculsion, 'Ireland did not adopt an insular attitude . . . there was a considerable amount of literary intercourse between it, England, and the Continent.'[125] A danger of Irish cultural history is to project later experiences onto earlier ones and to assume the existence of ahistorical constants in the history of the island and its peoples. The political circumstances that from the seventeenth century onwards reduced intercourse with the continent (though even this is often exaggerated) can often colour analyses of earlier periods and sustain the romantic, if inaccurate, image of a beleagured peripherality. There is, in addition, a tendency to adopt excessively terrestrial as opposed to maritime readings of the sources of cultural influence and exchange. This readily leads to the view of Ireland at the 'edge' of the terrestrial world rather than being at the 'crossroads' of seaways from Scandinavia to North Africa.[126] The dominant image of the period, and this is borne out by the language, sources and circulation of translated materials, is one of movement. Irish monks going to the continent, the Anglo-Normans, Norwegians, Danes coming to Ireland, the continental orders and monks establishing themselves on the island, the regular travel between Britain and Ireland, the trade with England, France and Spain, the native scholars regularly moving from one patron, one castle to another – translation was only to be expected in a culture where that degree of openness and cultural contact was a feature of religious and secular life.

The wider dimension of translation activity has been largely obscured by a regrettable tendency to see translations almost exclusively as lexicographical quarries. The distinguished Celtic scholar, Max Nettlau, at the end of nineteenth century called for scholarly work to be done on what he correctly saw as the much neglected medieval translations into Irish. He stated that the language of these translations:

> forms a counterpart to that of the romantic tales of the same or later ages . . . and so it is not without interest as affording means to control in several instances the meaning and the genuine or traditionary use of words or expressions in the later native productions.[127]

Commenting on the translation of the *Rosa Anglica*, Winifred Wulff states rather baldly: 'The value of the treatise from an Irish point of view is chiefly lexicographical.'[128] In his edition of the Irish Marco Polo translation, Whitley Stokes mentions cultural contact as a feature of medieval translations. He also mentions 'Celtic' translations of French texts, but most extant evidence would seem to indicate that much material of French origin came into Irish through intermediary texts in English or Latin. Indeed, Thomas O'Rahilly in an article in the journal *Studies* declared that: 'So far as I know, no medieval Irish translation from the French has come down to us.'[129] Stokes, however, quickly moves on to issues of lexicography:

> It is needless here to enlarge upon the desirability of printing the Celtic translations of Latin and French texts. They are the best evidence that the mediaeval Irish and Welsh were in touch with the literary life of the continent: they add considerably to our vocabularies; and in the case of many words and idioms they enable Celtists to ascertain meanings which would otherwise remain unintelligible or ambiguous.[130]

The lexicographical concerns of the Celtic scholars were perfectly legitimate, and to this day, medieval translations represent important source material for terminologists working in the Irish language. However, the lexical interest can also be reductive in that it fails to take account of questions that are supra-lexical and specific to both translation *per se* and its role in a culture. The tendency is to see translation as a form of transcoding, the substitution of one lexical unit for another, and to ignore any questions that would arise from a linguistics of utterance or a politics of translation.[131] Thus, the very advocates of the study of medieval translation may, paradoxically, have marginalised its contribution to Irish life and thought through an excessively narrow focus.

Creative interaction with literature in Irish was one of the signal contributions of translation to Irish culture. This was inevitable, given the scale of translation and the popularity of the translations themselves. The number of surviving manuscript copies of *In Cath Catharda*, the translation of Lucan's *Pharsalia*, meant that there must have been a strong demand for it.[132] The demand had consequences. The most obvious example is Seán Mac Craith's account of the battles between the O'Briens of Munster and the Anglo-Norman de Clares known as *Caithréim Thoirdhealbhaigh* (The Wars of Turlough), which is clearly based on the translation of Lucan's text.[133] The influence of Arthurian literature on writing in Irish has been well documented,[134] though what is notable is that few complete translations from the *matière de Bretagne*, such as *Eachtra Uilliam* and *Lorgaireacht an tSoidhigh Naomtha*, have come down to us.[135]

Williams and Ní Mhuiríosa emphasise the influence of devotional translation on the development of particular themes such as Christ's descent into Hell in the vernacular literature, while Stanford views Irish translations of classical texts as evidence of a constant concern in Irish contributions to world literature. He defends the translations against modern scholars who cherish fidelity as a consequence of their reverential attitude to the classical texts, and declares that what should be recognised is that 'in these Irish versions . . . we have a new literary fusion which is both scholarly and creative, derivative and inventive, classical and Celtic, which cannot be fitted into any of the orthodox genres'. Stanford generalises his observation to take in twentieth-century literature:

> As in other manifestations of the Irish genius – one thinks of Joyce's or Beckett's later work – the conventional categories are broken down and new modes, sometimes monstrous or barbaric by conventional standards, come to birth.[136]

Stanford does indeed identify the salient contribution of translation to the development of national literatures, the breaking down of barriers, the creative interaction between different languages, styles, mentalities. However, this fact is not peculiarly Irish and is true for most languages where contact with other literatures or cultures has featured in their development. What he characterises as peculiar to the Irish mind is in fact intrinsic to the translation process in most historical periods, namely that target-culture expectations and values are crucially important but that this does not prevent the source text and source culture from having a decisive impact on the cultures into which they are translated. The impact can range from the presentation of historical narrative as in *Caithréim Thoirdhealbhaigh*, and its debt to the Lucan translation, to the birth of a new medical tradition by way of the *Rosa Anglica*, *Lilium Medicinae* and other translations.

Translation is always unsettling for essentialism. One of the recurrent fictions of certain kinds of history-making is the Fall from Linguistic Grace. In other words, once upon a time there was a Gaelic Ireland untainted by predatory ambitions of barabarian tongues, a 'pristine' state that would eventually give way to the corruption of the longboats and late Latin rhetoric. The opposite is the case. Literature and culture in Irish would never be stronger than when engaged in constant exchange with Latin and English in medieval Ireland. The very fact and nature of translation in the medieval period testified to the confidence of the vernacular and its supporting culture. The subsequent misfortunes of Irish are not to do with language contact *per se*, but with the *context* of language contact. The translation enterprise which played a constructive role in the development of indigenous language and culture would become increasingly problematic in that its purposes became suspect, and its achievements questionable. The later history of translation in Ireland has the unfortunate consequence of obscuring its earlier history and, by association, translation is habitually perceived as a source of danger rather than as a sign of creative renewal. A feature of medieval Ireland is the coexistence of the impulses to conserve and assimilate. On the one hand, there is a profoundly conservative bardic culture which polices language and poetry and seeks scrupulous fidelity to tradition. On the other, there are the translators bringing new words, motifs, materials into the language and continually extending its range. The danger for cultural historians is to present either the conservative or the assimilationist features of medieval Irish culture as constituting the essential Ireland of the period, whereas both flourished in their respective contexts. A further aspect of the capacity to assimilate which is endemic in the translation act is that language is rooted in plurality. Babel puts an end to the transparency of the human community and translation is born.

Ireland for centuries has been the site of not one but several languages. Multingualism and translation did not arrive on Irish shores with the European Economic Community in 1973. As we have seen, Latin, English, French and Irish all featured as target languages for Irish translators. The cultural reality for many medieval Irish scholars was not monolingual but plurilingual. The dominance of one world language in late twentieth-century Ireland, or nostalgia for the Lost Kingdom of the monoglot Gael, can too often produce readings of history which simplify linguistic realities and ignore translation practice. In this respect, peripherality can become a misleading if fashionable fetish. In the wake of deconstructionist/post-colonial criticism and its emphasis on the margins, de-centring, the peripheral, it is relatively easy to portray Ireland for historical reasons as the much-maligned periphery that has a decisive impact on imperialist culture at key moments in its development. The peripheral argument is important, and as we shall see in later chapters, there is an important relationship between translation in Ireland and the process of de-centring culture and language. However, the rationale for increased European Union funding should not become the guiding principle of cultural history. The history of translation shows constant contact with a world beyond the surrounding seas. There is little sense in the medieval period of a beleagured outpost of Western culture struggling on the edge of darkness. The geographical periphery was in translation terms a cultural centre and the examination of translation activity in Ireland in the Middle Ages 're-centres' the notion of peripherality by highlighting the scale of inter-cultural and interlingual contact. Richard's second visit to Ireland in 1399 had a less happy conclusion than the first, language notwithstanding, a conclusion that Shakespeare would turn into tragedy. In *Richard II*, the King addressing the Duke of York and the Earl of Northumberland in Act II Scene 1, declares:

> So much for that. Now for our Irish wars.
> We must supplant those rough rug-headed kerns,
> Which live like venom where no venom else
> But only they have privilege to live.

In the next chapter, we shall examine the dramatic implications of the 'Irish wars' of the seventeenth century for translators and translation in Ireland.

Notes

1. Edmund Curtis, 'The Spoken Languages of Medieval Ireland', *Studies*, vol. 8, 1919, p. 251.
2. Fergal McGrath, *Education in Ancient and Medieval Ireland*, Dublin, 'Studies' Special Publications, 1979, p. 37.
3. McGrath, pp. 39–40.
4. Whitley Stokes and John Strachan, *Thesaurus Palaeohibernicus*, Dublin, Dublin Institute for Advanced Studies, 1975, 2 vols., pp. xiv–xxi and pp. 7–483.
5. Stokes and Strachan, pp. xiii–xxv, 499–714.
6. 'is cosúil narbh ionann ar fad dearcadh na hEaglaise i leith chultúr págánach na hÉireann agus a gnáthdhearcadh i dtíortha eile. In ionad a bheith ina deargnamhaid don chultúr sin, is amhlaidh a bhí sí báúil leis; in ionad na seanscéalta a

bhí mar chnámh droma don léann traidisiúnta a chur faoi chois, is amhlaidh a chuidigh sí lena dtaisciú agus lena gcur ar phár.' J.E. Caerwyn Williams and Máirín Ní Mhuiríosa, *Traidisiún Liteartha na nGael*, Baile Átha Cliath, An Clóchomhar, 1978, p. xviii. This is not to argue that the influence of Christian culture on native culture was wholly benign. The ravages of its patriarchal biases are detailed in Mary Condren, *The Serpent and the Goddess: Women, Religion and Power in Celtic Ireland*, San Francisco, Harper and Row, 1989.

7. D.A. Binchy, 'The Background of Early Irish Literature,' *Studia Hibernica*, 1, 1961, p. 10. For a more detailed account of native learning prior to the arrival of Christianity see Fergal McGrath, *Education in Ancient and Medieval Ireland*.

8. Binchy, p. 8.

9. William Bedell Stanford, *Ireland and the Classical Tradition*, Dublin, Allen Figgis, 1976, p. 11.

10. Stanford, p. 10.

11. James Carney, 'Three Old-Irish Accentual Poems', *Ériu*, no. 22, 1971, p. 63 and Binchy, p. 18.

12. George Calder, *Auraicept na n-Éces*, Edinburgh, John Grant, 1917, p. xxxi.

13. Kuno Meyer, ed., *Sanas Chormaic*, Lampeter, Llanerch Publishers, reprinted 1994.

14. See McGrath, p. 84.

15. Brian Ó Cuív, *The Linguistic Training of the Mediaeval Irish Poet*, Dublin Institute for Advanced Studies, 1973, p. 1.

16. Stanford, p. 9.

17. James Kenney, *The Sources for the Early History of Ireland*, vol. 1, New York, Columbia University Press, 1929, pp. 581–2.

18. Kenney, p. 582.

19. Kenney, p. 569.

20. J.–P. Migne ed., *Versus de Ambiguis S. Maximi*, *Patrologia latina*, Paris, 1864–64, 122, col. 1032.

21. Rita Copeland, 'The Fortunes of "Non Verbum pro Verbo": or Why Jerome is not a Ciceronian', Roger Ellis, ed., *The Medieval Translator*, Cambridge, Brewer, 1989, pp. 30–31.

22. Migne, *Patrologia latina*, 122, col. 567. 'Ideoque solus eorum intellectus separatis verbis per periphrasin tranferetur, ut eorum solummodo virtus intelligatur, quorum interpretation de verbo ad verbum non exprimitur.'

23. Copeland's translation:
    Quisquis rhetorico verborum syrmate gaudet,
    Quaerat grandiloquos, Tullia castra pretens:
    Ast mihi sat fuerit, si planos carpere sensus
    Possem tardilocus pragmata sola sequens.
    Interior virtus sermonum rite tenenda:
    Verborum bombi fallere saepe solent.
Original in Versus de Ambiguis S. Maximi *Patrologia latina*, 122, cols. 1235–6.

24. Copeland, p. 22.

25. Kenney, p. 582.

26. Cited in Hugo Friedrich, 'On the Art of Translation', Rainer Schulte and John Biguenet, eds., *Theories of Translation*, Chicago University Press, 1992, pp. 12–13.

27. Friedrich Nietzsche, *The Gay Science*, trans., Walter Kaufmann, New York, Random House, 1974, p. 90.
28. For an account of the geographical spread of this missionary activity see Tomás Ó Fiach, *Gaelscrínte san Eoraip*, Baile Átha Cliath, Foilseacháin Ábhair Spioradálta, 1986.
29. Kenney, p. 575.
30. Kenney, p. 665.
31. Stanford, p. 12.
32. J.H. Todd, ed., *Irish Nennius*, Dublin, Irish Archaeological Society, 1848.
33. R.I. Best and M.A. O'Brien, *Togail Troí*, Dublin Institute for Advanced Studies, 1966; also Gearóid Mac Eoin, 'Dán ar Chogadh na Traoi', *Studia Hibernica*, vol. 1, 1961, pp. 19–20.
34. Stanford, p. 74.
35. Stanford, p. 81; William Beddell Stanford, 'Towards a History of Classical Influences in Ireland', *Proceedings of the Royal Irish Academy*, vol. 70 section C, 1970, p. 37; also Neasa Ní Shéaghdha, 'Translations and Adaptations into Irish', *Celtica*, vol. 16, 1984, pp. 107–9.
36. George Calder, ed. and trans., *Imtheachta Aeniasa: The Irish Aeneid*, London, Irish Texts Society, 1907.
37. Whitley Stokes, ed., *In Cath Catharda*, Leipzig, Verlag von S. Hirzel, 1909, Irische Texte iv/2.
38. Sheila Falconer, 'An Irish Translation of the Gregory Legend', *Celtica*, vol. 4, 1958, p. 57.
39. Douglas Hyde, *The Conquests of Charlemagne*, London, Irish Texts Society, 1917, p. viii.
40. Robert Meyer, 'The Sources of the Middle Irish Alexander', *Modern Philology*, vol. 47, no. 1, 1949, p. 6.
41. Stanford, p. 84.
42. Stanford, p. 73.
43. J.D. Burnley, 'Late Medieval Translation: Types and Reflections', in Roger Ellis (1989), op. cit., p. 46.
44. Louis G. Kelly, *The True Interpreter: A History of Translation Theory and Practice in the West*, Oxford, Basil Blackwell, 1979.
45. Kelly, p. 156.
46. St John D. Seymour, *Anglo-Irish Literature 1200–1582*, Cambridge University Press, 1929, p. 31.
47. Author's translation cited in Seymour, p. 32.
48. Seymour, p. 139.
49. Pádraig Ó Fiannachta, 'A Fragment of an Irish Romantic Tale', *Irish Ecclesiastical Record*, vol. 109, 1968, 166–81. N.J.A. Williams, 'The Source of Imthechta Ghenerodeis', *Éigse*, vol. 17, 1977–79, pp. 297–300.
50. Cecile O'Rahilly, ed., *Eachtra Uilliam*, Dublin Institute for Advanced Studies, 1949.
51. F.N. Robinson, 'The Irish Lives of Guy of Warwick and Bevis of Hampton', *Zeitschrift für Celtische Philologie*, vol. 6, 1908, pp. 9–180 and pp. 273–338.
52. Robinson, pp. 19–20.

53. For an account of influence of Toury's Hebrew fieldwork on his theoretical pronouncements see Edwin Gentzler, *Contemporary Translation Theories*, London, Routledge, 1993, pp. 125–134.

54. For an exploration of this notion in its effects on the reception of eighteenth-century poetry in Irish, see Breandán Ó Buachalla, 'In a Hovel by the Sea', *The Irish Review*, vol. 14, 1993, pp. 48–55.

55. Aodh de Blácam, *Gaelic Literature Surveyed*, Dublin, Talbot Press, 1973, p. 28.

56. de Blácam, p. 178.

57. Robin Flower, *The Irish Tradition*, Oxford, Clarendon Press, 1947, p. 110.

58. de Blácam, p. 9; Vernam Hull, 'The Middle Irish Version of Bede's *De Locis Sanctis*', *Zeitschrift für Celtische Philologie*, vol. 17, p. 225.

59. Robinson, pp. 14–15.

60. George Calder, ed., *Togail na Tebe*, Cambridge, Cambridge University Press, 1922, p. xix.

61. Gordon Quin, ed., *Stair Ercuil agus a bás*, Dublin, Irish Texts Society, 1939, p. xvii.

62. Whitley Stokes, 'The Gaelic Abridgement of Ser Marco Polo', *Zeitschrift für Celtische Philologie*, vol. 1, 1897, p. 245.

63. Stokes, *In Cath Catharda*, p. v.

64. Meyer, p. 4.

65. Calder, *Imtheachta Aeniasa*, p. xv.

66. O'Rahilly, p. xvii and p. xviii.

67. Standish O'Grady cited in Winifred Wulff, *Rosa Anglica*, London, Irish Texts Society, 1929, p. xxxiv.

68. André Lefevere, *Translation, Rewriting and the Manipulation of Literary Fame*, Routledge, London, 1992.

69. Quin, p. xxvi.

70. See Stanford, p. 73; and Flower, p. 137.

71. Lawrence Venuti, ed., *Rethinking Translation*, London, Routledge, 1992, pp. 4–5.

72. de Blácam, p. 12.

73. Curtis, p. 245.

74. de Blácam, pp. 180–181.

75. M.C. Seymour, 'The Irish Version of "Mandeville's Travels"', *Notes and Queries*, vol. 208, 1963, p. 366.

76. Calder, *Imtheachta Aeniasa*, p. xv.

77. 'As interesting as these romance stories are, in order to get a clear picture of medieval Irish literature it is important to remember that they represent only a part of the material that was translated from other languages. The translations of educational texts, religious, philosophical, medical and so on, were more numerous [my translation].' Williams and Ní Mhuiríosa, p. 132.

78. Michael Richter, *Medieval Ireland – The Enduring Tradition*, Dublin, Gill and Macmillan, 1988, p. 129.

79. Flower, p. 132.

80. McGrath, p. 44.

81. Maura Power, ed., *An Irish Astronomical Text*, London, Irish Texts Society, 1914, p. i.

82. Francis Shaw, 'Medieval Medico–Philosophical Treatises in the Irish Language', John Ryan, ed., *Essays and Studies presented to Professor Eoin Mac Neill*, Dublin, Three Candles, 1940, pp. 144–45.
83. Winifred Wulff, ed., *Rosa Anglica*, London, Irish Texts Society, 1929, p. L.
84. Wulff, p. xv.
85. Wulff, p. xviii.
86. For comments on our scanty knowledge of this early native medical tradition see Francis Shaw, 'Irish Medical Men and Philosophers' in Brian Ó Cuív, ed., *Seven Centuries of Irish Learning 1000–1700*, Dublin, Stationery Office, 1961, pp. 87–90.
87. Williams and Ní Mhuiríosa, p. 144.
88. Shaw, 'Medieval Treatises', p. 150.
89. Wulff, p. xlvi.
90. Shaw, 'Medieval Treatises', p. 153.
91. Shaw, 'Medieval Treatises', p. 145.
92. Shaw, 'Irish Medical Men', p. 94.
93. Ní Shéaghdha, p. 116.
94. Cited in Ní Shéaghdha, pp. 116–17.
95. Stanford, p. 26.
96. De Blácam, pp. 42–3.
97. Power, pp. ii–iv.
98. Power, p. iii.
99. Power, p. x.
100. Cainneach Ó Maonaigh, *Smaointe Beatha Chríost*, Baile Átha Cliath, Institiúid Ard-Léighinn, 1944, p. xxxix–xl.
101. Ó Maonaigh, p. xl. 'Because of the neglect of this fifteenth-century literature, many believed that the credit for this simple Modern Irish was due to the Franciscans in Louvain. This is not so. One group, particularly those working with poetry or the tales of the Fianna, continued to use the complicated Old Irish. But there was another group, particularly writers of devotional literature, who provided books in the spoken language of the people. Their aim, as Aodh Mac Aingil himself said, was not to teach Irish but repentance [my translation].'
102. Ó Maonaigh, p. xl.
103. Flower, p. 124.
104. Ó Maonaigh, pp. xvii–xviii.
105. Seymour, p. 146.
106. John MacKechnie, ed., *Instructio Pie Vivendi et Spuperna Meditandi*, vol. 2, Dublin, Irish Texts Society, 1946, pp. ix–xii.
107. Edward Gwynn, 'The Manuscript known as the Liber Flavus Fergusiorum', *Proceedings of the Royal Irish Academy*, vol. 26, 1906–7, pp. 15–41; also R.A.Q. Skerrett, 'Two Irish Translations of the *Liber de Passione Christi*', *Celtica*, vol. 6, 1963, pp. 82–117.
108. J.E. Caerwyn Williams, 'Irish Translations of *Visio Sancti Pauli*', *Éigse*, vol. 6, pp. 127–34.
109. Robin Flower, *British Museum Catalogue of Irish Manuscripts*, vol. 2, p. 338.

110. Williams and Ní Mhuiríosa, p. 142.
111. A copy of the Uí Maolchonaire translation is to be found in TCD H.3.18.
112. Williams and Ní Mhuiríosa, pp. 134–5.
113. Quin, p. xi.
114. A. Martin Freeman, 'Betha Mhuire Eigiptacdha', *Etudes Celtiques*, Vol. 1, p. 104.
115. Richard Stanihurst, *Aeneid*, ed., E. Arber, Constable, London, 1880; see also Colm Lennon, *Richard Stanihurst: The Dubliner 1547–1618*, Dublin, Irish Academic Press, pp. 57–67.
116. Johann Wolfgang Von Goethe, 'Translations', Schulte and Biguenet, p. 61.
117. Seymour, p. 159.
118. Stanford, p. 163.
119. David Greene, 'A Gaelic Version of the Seven Wise Masters', *Béaloideas*, vol. 14, 1945, pp. 219–236.
120. David Greene, 'The Irish Versions of the Letter of Prester John', *Celtica*, vol. 2, 1954, pp. 117–45.
121. Meyer, 'Middle Irish Alexander', p. 4.
122. Meyer, 'Middle Irish Alexander', p. 2.
123. Author's translation in Stokes, *The Gaelic Maundeville*, p. 3.
124. Flower, p. 132.
125. Seymour, *Anglo-Irish Literature*, p. 10
126. This is the argument advanced by Bob Quinn in *Atlantean: Ireland's North African and Maritime Heritage*, Quartet, London, 1986, pp. 23–25. Though Quinn's work has generated much controversy on specific claims made in his book and the accompanying television series, his basic thesis that interpretations of Irish culture have suffered from Graeco-Roman based terrestrial histories (with the notion of 'culture spread' and cultural developments 'eventually' reaching Ireland) to the neglect of the maritime dimension seems perfectly plausible. For further evidence of the importance of the sea as a channel of influence see John de Courcy Ireland, 'Ireland and the Sea'; John de Courcy Ireland and Eoghan Ó hAnluain, eds., *Ireland and the Sea*, Dublin, Cumann Merriman, 1983, pp. 12–24. See also John de Courcy Ireland, *Ireland's European Tradition*, Drogheda, Vanguard, 1970 and the same author's *Ireland's Maritime Heritage*, Dublin, An Post, 1992.
127. Max Nettlau, 'On Some Irish Translations from Medieval European Literature', *Revue Celtique*, vol. 10, 1889, p. 179.
128. Wulff, p. xiii.
129. Thomas F. O'Rahilly, review of *The Conquests of Charlemagne*, ed., Douglas Hyde, *Studies*, vol. 8, 1919, p. 670.
130. Stokes, *Marco Polo*, p. 245.
131. For a discussion of the problems inherent in a transcoding approach to translation see Robert Larose, *Théories contemporaines de la traduction*, Québec, Presses de l'université du Québec, 1989, pp. 15–16.
132. Williams and Ní Mhuiríosa, p. 123.
133. Standish Hayes O'Grady, *Caithréim Thoirdhealbhaigh*, London, Irish Texts Society, 1929.

134. See Gerard Murphy, *The Ossianic Lore and Romantic Tales of Medieval Ireland*, Cork, Mercier Press, 1971; Williams and Ní Mhuiríosa, pp. 125–132.
135. Sheila Falconer, ed., *Lorgaireacht an tSoidhigh Naofa*, Dublin Institute of Advanced Studies, 1953.
136. Stanford, p. 87.

2

TRANSLATION, CONQUEST AND CONTROVERSY

AN ESSAY ON TRANSLATED VERSE, published in 1685 and written by
the Anglo-Irish nobleman Wentworth Dillon, the Earl of Roscommon,
became a highly influential work in late seventeenth and eighteenth
century English translation theory. The essay was an important English
source for Alexander Pope's own *Essay on Criticism*. John Dryden, in his
prefatory poem to the *Essay* is fulsome in his praise for his Irish friend's
achievements and firmly locates Dillon's work in the larger context of
the conflictual relationship between the two neighbouring islands:

> How much in him may rising *Ireland* boast,
> How much in gaining him has *Britain* lost!
> Their Island in revenge has ours reclaim'd,
> The more instructed we, the more we still are sham'd.
> 'Tis well for us his generous bloud did flow
> Deriv'd from *British* Channels long ago,
> That here his conquering Ancestors were nurst;
> And *Ireland* but translated *England* first:[1]

Dryden's metaphorical play on origin and practice, the translator who is
himself translated, affirms the conqueror's antecedence. The alarming
prospect of Irish pre-eminence is dismissed through the agency of
translation. Dillon's competence is rooted in the source text of racial
origin, his Irishness a mask disguising his essential Englishness. Dryden's
reading of translation history is explicitly agonistic and imperial:

> For conquering *Rome*
> With *Grecian* Spoils, brought *Grecian* Numbers home;
> Enrich'd by those *Athenian* Muses more
> Than all the vanquish'd world could yield before.[2]

Knightly Chetwood, in his prefatory poem to the *Essay* entitled 'To the
Earl of Roscommon on his Excellent Poem', brings Dryden's reading
forward to more recent translation into English from the classical
languages:

And some who *merit* as they *wear*, the Bays.
Search'd all the *Treasures* of *Greece* and *Rome*,
And brought the *precious spoils* in Triumph *home*.[3]

For Chetwood, English translators are simply carrying on a tradition of enrichment through conquest and expropriation nobly illustrated in earlier times by the Romans. Dillon himself makes the identification between Britain and Imperial Rome explicit in the closing lines of his *Essay*:

O may I live to hail the Glorious day,
And sing loud Paeans through the crowded way,
When in Triumphant State the British Muse,
True to her self, shall barb'rous aid Refuse,
And in the Roman Majesty appear.[4]

CULTURAL SUBMISSION AND TERRITORIAL TRANSLATION

The vision of translation articulated by Dryden, Chetwood and Dillon in a century of protracted struggle between Ireland and England was not a disinterested one. The wars, rebellions, massacres and plantations of the sixteenth and seventeenth centuries led to an increasing politicisation of the translation process that crucially affected the relationship between the two languages on the island of Ireland and the subsequent fortunes of translation itself. The Tudor and Cromwellian conquests of Ireland sought not only military but cultural submission. Already in 1536, Henry VIII was writing to the Burghers of Galway saying that:

every inhabitant within the saide towne indevor theym selfe to spek Englyshe, and to use theym selffe after the Englyshe Facion; and specially that you, and every of you, do put forth your childe to scole, to lerne to speke Englyshe.[5]

In 1537 the Parliament in Dublin passed the Act for the English Order, Habit and Language which demanded that the Irish 'to the utmost of their power, cunning and knowledge' shall 'use and speake commonly the English Tongue and Language'.[6] Irish speakers were in effect being asked to translate themselves into another language and culture. Failure to do so was tantamount to disloyalty. Edmund Spenser, in *A View of the Present State of Ireland* (1596), argued that 'the speech being Irish, the heart must needs be Irish for out of the abundance of the heart the tongue speaketh'.[7] Spenser was unwittingly invoking notions of linguistic relativism, identifying a specific language with a specific world-view, to suppress Irish. The same notions would, in fact, be invoked in later centuries to maintain and revive the language. Spenser, in language that is remarkably similar to the pronouncements of translators a century later, outlines the prerogative of the conqueror: 'for it have ever been the use of the conqueror to destroy the language of the conquered and to force him by all means to learn his'.[8] Translation both complicates and simplifies Spenser's responses to Ireland. He confesses that the poems of the Gaelic bards savour of 'sweet wit and good invention' because 'I have caused diverse of them to be translated unto me'.[9] It is not possible, therefore, to dismiss the culture of the native Irish as the barbarous product of literary ineptness. Translation checks condemnation.

His other uses of the word 'translate' suggest another logic, one of conquest and control. In outlining his proposals for the pacification of Ireland, Spenser recommends that people living in the north of the country should be sent to settle on lands in the south, and that the 'Byrnes, Tooles and Cavanaghs' should be sent up north. He declares, 'I will translate all that remain of them into the places of the other, in Ulster, with all their creet and what else they have left them.'[10] To avoid ghettoisation, Spenser wants to see the Irish scattered among the English, and to achieve this, he again proposes the 'translating' of the Irish. Thus, translation at a cultural level – the embrace of English acculturation – is paralleled by translation at a territorial level, the forcible displacement and movement of populations.

For Spenser, the threat to English begins at birth. Women are a particularly potent source of linguistic corruption as the role of the wet-nurse and the power of the 'mother' tongue can be dangerously conflated:

> The child that sucketh the milk of the nurse must of necessity learne his first speech of her, the which being the first that is enured to his tongue is ever after the most pleasing unto him. In so much as though he afterwards be taught English yet the smack of the first will always abide with him and not only of the speech but also of the manners and conditions. For besides the young Children be like Apes which will affect and imitate what they see done before them specially by their nurses whom they love so well. They moreover draw into themselves together with their suck, even the nature and disposition of their nurses.[11]

Language was a contagion that would lead inevitably to that degeneracy believed by Tudor and Cromwellian propagandists to characterise Irish life. In an epistle to his friend Henry Wotton who has to go to Ireland, John Donne warns him against the dangers of 'Irish negligence' and 'Lethargies'. As Andrew Hadfield and Willy Maley note: 'Like Spenser, Donne percieves in the colonial experience the risk of a loss of identity, an abandonment of self.'[12] The Old English, those descendants of the Anglo-Norman settlers who had invaded Ireland in the twelfth century, were vivid reminders of the pernicious effects of Irish acculturation, many of them adopting Irish customs and, in particular, the Irish language. They had, in a sense, subverted the reassuring closure of Dryden's translation process. In the case of these 'conquering Ancestors', Ireland had indeed 'translated England first' and their embrace of the Irish language was, for the Tudor English, evidence of translation as a fallen state. Certain intellectuals among the Old English such as the translator Richard Stanihurst were keen to distance themselves from the inculturation process and stress their linguistic separateness from the Gaelic Irish. Writing in *Holinshed's Chronicles*, Stanihurst makes the following observation:

> The inhabitants of the English pale have beene in old time so much addicted to their civilitie, and so farre sequestered from barabarous savageness, as their onlie mother toong was English. And trulie, so long as these impaled dwellers did sunder themselves as well in land as in language from the Irish: rudeness was daie by daie in the countrie supplanted, civilitie ingraffed, good lawes established, loyaltie observed, rebellion suppressed, and in fine the coine of a yoong England was like to shoot in Ireland.[13]

The Old English, in fact, suffered doubly from the dilemmas of translation. In the first place, as we have seen in Chapter One, there were those who had abandoned English for Irish. In the second, the twelfth-century colonists spoke the English of Bristol and the south-western counties whereas by Tudor times, north-midland speech had become the standard English spoken by Tudor officials. In addition, centuries of co-existence meant that many Irish loan-words had entered their language. For the New English, the problems of translating the language of these older colonists were as intractable as those presented by Irish. Stanihurst tells a story in his chronicle of an English lord who goes to Ireland and boasts that he can understand Irish. He had, in fact, been listening to a dialect spoken by the Old English and assumed it was Irish because he could not fully understand it.[14]

In his *Description of Pembrokeshire* (1603), George Owen, Lord of Kernes, describes the linguistic plight of the Old English, who like colonists in later periods in many other situations, had become foreigners in their own country: 'these for the most part speak the English tongue . . . as many as come out of the country say that they understand no Irishe . . . neither doth anye well understand his [their] English'.[15] For some Old English intellectuals such as Geoffrey Keating the proper role of the Old English was to celebrate the achievements of Gaelic culture and language, to effect a full translation into the culture of the conquered, while others like Stanihurst, in Holinshed's *Chronicles*, argued that to speak the language of the Gaelic Irish was to savour the evil customs of those who spoke it.[16] Stanihurst acknowledged, however, the complexity and antiquity of the Irish language and defended himself against charges of denigrating the language in his *De Rebus in Hibernia Gestis* (1584). He continued to believe in the cultural superiority of English language and culture, and remained hostile to the Gaelic acculturation of the Anglophone community in Ireland.[17]

THE REFORMED CHURCH, PRINTING AND VERNACULAR TRANSLATION

The most common trope throughout the sixteenth and seventeenth centuries was simply that the Irish were barbarians. This notion had already been advanced by Bernard of Clairvaux and Gerald of Wales in the twelfth century, but the charge would take on a new virulence in the writings of Tudor and Cromwellian commentators on Irish affairs.[18] John Milton, in his *Observations upon the articles of peace with the Irish Rebels* (1649), a tract largely designed to justify the Cromwellian campaign in Ireland claims that the Irish Catholics

> rejecting the ingenuity of all other Nations to improve and waxe more civill by a civilising Conquest, though all these many yeares better known and taught, preferre their own most absurd and savage Customes before the most convincing evidence of reason and demonstration: a testimony of their true Barbarisme and obdurate wilfulnesse to be expected no less in other matters of greatest moment.[19]

The insistence on the civilising mission of the Cromwellian army was partly to circumvent the inherent contradictions of their actions. In April 1649, a pamphlet appeared entitled *Certain Queries propounded to the consideration of those who are intended for the service of Ireland*. The

51

pamphlet called on the soldiers of the New Model Army to stop Cromwell's expedition to Ireland by applying the ideas of natural rights, government by consent and rejection of rule by conquest to the Irish.[20] Propagandists, including Milton, were quick to respond that civilised criteria could not be applied to the Irish who were barbarous and therefore less than human. Thus, there was no contradiction between espousing a philosophy of individual rights and liberties and indulging in the large-scale dispossession of a people. These contradictions were not so easily resolved, however, at the level of religious practice, as is evidenced by the attempts of the Reformed Church to use the vernacular language in religious services. The translation history of the sixteenth and seventeenth centuries does, in fact, point to the complexity of the process of colonisation and how the realities of language difference ran counter to the dictates and analyses of the propagandists.

Elizabeth I and Henry VIII differed on what was to be done with the Irish language. Henry's 1537 Act had among other provisions ordered that each member of the Protestant clergy shall:

> endevour himself to learne, instruct and teach the English tongue, to all and everie being under his rule, cure, order or governance, and in likewise shall bid the beades in the English tongue, and preach the word of God in English if he can preach.[21]

Although the Irish Parliament in Dublin added a special provision to the Act of Uniformity in 1560 expressly prohibiting the use of Irish in Church of Ireland services, Elizabeth, who had acceded to the the throne in 1558, did not share the English-dominated Dublin Parliament's antipathy to Irish. In 1565 Críostóir Nuinseann provided her with a grammar of the Irish language, and her policy in the late sixteenth century was to appoint clergymen such as Hugh Brady, Robert Dale and Christopher Browne to dioceses in Ireland because of their knowledge of Irish. Even more importantly, Elizabeth's government would provide the money in the 1560s to have a set of characters made in order for the New Testament to be printed in Irish.[22]

The connection between technology and translation is clear throughout the Renaissance and Reformation period as is their political importance. The acquisition of a printing press for Irish by the Franciscans in Louvain in 1611 and their prompt production of translated material was largely prompted by the fear that the combined power of the translated and printed word would prove fatal to Catholicism in Ireland. The first printed work in Irish was in fact a translation. *Foirm na nUrrnuidheadh* was published in Edinburgh in April 1567 and was a translation of the 1562 *Book of Common Order* of the Reformed Church. The translator, a Presbyterian, Seon Carsuel, is suitably self-deprecatory in his prefatory epistle to the reader:

> dá bfadhadh saoi ré h-ealadhain locht sgríobhtha nó deachtaidh sa leabhar
> bheag-sa, gabhadh sé mo leithsgél-sa, óir ní dhearrna mé saothar ná foghluim
> sa nGaoidheilg acht amháin mar gach duine don phobal choitcheand.[23]

Nicholas Williams argues on the basis of the translation that Carsuel's claim is difficult to accept at face value and that he clearly had a proper linguistic training in an Irish or Scottish bardic school. As we shall see below, when we come to consider translators' prefaces more closely, proclamations of unworthiness were commonplace in sixteenth, seventeenth and eighteenth-century translations. However, it is worth noting here that Carsuel has high expectations of the linguistic competence of his readership, whereas later translators into Irish will blame any deficiencies in their Irish less on their own inability to write in the language than on the diminished capacity of their readers to understand it.

The Presbyterian head-start in the area of translation may have helped to concentrate minds in the Church of Ireland, for by 1571 Seán Ó Cearnaigh's *Aibidil Gaoidheilge 7 Caiticiosma* had been published in Dublin and by 1603 Uilliam Ó Domhnaill's (William Daniel) New Testament had appeared in Irish. The *Aibidil* contained a translation of the catechism of the 1559 *Book of Common Prayer* in addition to a translation of *A Brief Declaration of Certain Principal Articles of Religion*.[24] Ó Cearnaigh, a graduate of Cambridge who was born in Sligo, produced competent translations and was the first translator in Irish to have his work published in Ireland. The translation of the New Testament was largely based on Erasmus's Greek *Textus Receptus* which first appeared in 1516. The use of the *Textus Receptus* is somewhat ironic in the light of Erasmus's prefatory comments to his Greek translation, where he notes that 'I would have these words translated into all languages, so that not only the Scots and the Irish, but also the Turks and the Saracens might read them.'[25] Presumably, the Irish and the Turks were both equally situated at the antipodes of the civilised world as viewed by the Renaissance thinker.

In addition to the *Textus Receptus*, the translators of the New Testament would also appear to have used the Geneva Bible and the Latin Vulgate.[26] Although Ó Domhnaill did much of the translation work, particularly in the 1590s, he was assisted by others such as Seán Ó Cearnaigh, Nioclás Bhailís and Fearganainm Ó Domhnalláin. Ó Domhnaill was born in Kilkenny and was one of the first three students in Ireland's first university, Trinity College, Dublin, which opened in 1592. He was also the first recipient of a doctorate for work done in the area of translation studies in Ireland as he was awarded a Doctorate in Divinity in 1602, largely it would appear for the work he did in translating the New Testament and having it printed.[27] The function of his translation was clear for Ó Domhnaill. It would rescue the Gaelic Irish from the intolerable darkness of their ignorance and superstition so that they would no longer be in the shadow of spiritual death, the image that is used by Ó Domhnaill in his prayer or 'Urrnuighthe' at the end of the New Testament translation.[28] In view of the centrality of the Bible to the Protestant faith, translation was indeed seen as a form of salvation, particularly for a Puritan like Ó Domhnaill. The light of the translated word would reveal the superior truth of the reformed faith. Therefore, to see the work of Ó Domhnaill and other Irish Protestant translators of the sixteenth and sevententh centuries as merely forms of prosleytism is reductive, and fails to situate vernacular translation at the heart of a genuine Reformation commitment to making the Bible directly available to people in their own language.

The intemperate, anti-Catholic language of the prefaces can sometimes obscure the deeply-held religious convictions that motivated translation practice in Reformation and post-Reformation Europe. The translators were not operating in a vacuum, however, as became apparent in the relative lack of success of Ó Domhnaill's translations. In addition to the New Testament, he published in 1609 a translation of the *Book of Common Prayer* under the title *Leabhar na nUrnaightheadh gcomhchoidchiond*. (The book was in fact printed a year earlier.) The work has been hailed in this century as 'one of the monuments of Irish translation', but its impact in the seventeenth century seems to have been rather limited.[29] Ó Domhnaill is sensitive to the political context and his translation prefaces dwell not on technical points of translation theory but on the political and religious climate in which he is working. In 'The Epistle Dedicatorie' to the New Testament translation that appears in 1602, just a year after the Battle of Kinsale, Ó Domhnaill laments the 'manifold stumbling blocks that Sathan in his wonted malice had cast in the way, and the small encouragement that I received (such hath been the iniquitie of the times.)'[30] Only the erection of a new college near Dublin (Trinity College), and the encouragement and financial assistance of Sir William Usher, allowed him to persist in his task:

> And that in a time of blackness, & darkness & tempest, wherein al hope of proceeding was in a maner cut off, by reason of the general garboiles, and universal floud of rebellion that overflowed the face of the Kingdome.[31]

Prefixed to the translation of *The Book of Common Prayer* is an 'Epistle Dedicatorie' to Sir Arthur Chicester, the Lord Deputy General of Ireland. It shows that rebellion is still on Ó Domhnaill's mind and he defends the English policy of the plantation of Ireland:

> The Land having partly swallowed up in displeasure the disturbers of our peace, and partly spued them out into Straunge Countryes, craving better Inhabitants to enjoy her blessings, and discovering her riche bosome for their kinder entertainment.[32]

In 1623 James I ordered that the Irish translations of the New Testament and the *Book of Common Prayer* be used more often in parishes with large numbers of Irish speakers. Although only five hundred copies of the New Testament were printed, they were slow to move and copies were still available in 1628, twenty-six years later.[33] The apparent reluctance to use the translations was not based on objections to their adequacy but on the perceived threat of translation to the successful completion of the colonisation process. Recurrent emphasis on the barbarous, uncivilised nature of the Irish, whose very language was seen as synonymous with sedition, did not sit happily with efforts to supply the Gaelic Irish with printed translations in their own language. Ó Domhnaill is conscious of these tensions and offers a justification of his translation project which defends both Gaelic culture, through an appeal to antiquity, and English policy in Ireland as the necessary political basis for bringing the light of Reformation to the native Irish. He reminds Chicester that 'if learning & religion were hereditarie to any Nation . . . this noble land . . . might compare with any other whatsoever'.[34] Ó Domhnaill then cites Ireland's reputation in earlier centuries for scholarship and sanctity, invoking the authority of foreign commentators. In an argument that anticipates Dryden and cultural inversion in translation, the Irish translator sees other nations, including England, coming to Ireland in this earlier period for enlightenment:

> God that caused light to shine out of darkness in the beginning, caused also the beames of piety, learning, and religion, to shine from thence into other

Nations, that sate in darkness and in the shadow of death; for as there came many swarmes hither from forainne Countryes to be trayned up in learning and religion (..The neighbour Saxons learning then their very characters from us, the same in a manner with the characters of this Booke:)[35]

However, this golden age was superseded by the liberation of 'Satan' and the primary aim of the Reformation in Ireland in Ó Domhnaill's eyes is to restore Irish Christianity to its former glory. Ó Domhnaill's use of the monastic period in his argument bears eloquent witness to the malleability of historical interpretation, as it is precisely the same period that will be used by cultural nationalists in the late nineteenth century to decry the malign influence of English intervention in Irish affairs. Notwithstanding the rationale offered by Ó Domhnaill, and the personal interest of Elizabeth I and James I in the Irish language, many Tudor and Cromwellian administrators viewed with profound misgiving any initiative that might be seen to encourage the Irish to keep their language, a language which bore all the traces of unacceptable difference.

At the 1634 Convocation of the Church of Ireland, Canons VIII, LXXXVI and XCIII contained provisions relating to the use of Irish. They were accepted after much debate. One of the most ardent advocates at the Convocation for the use of Irish in religious services and the continued translation of religious material into Irish was an Englishman, William Bedell.[36] Bedell had been educated in Essex and Cambridge and in 1607 became Chaplain to the English Ambassador to the Republic of Venice, Sir Henry Wotton, who apparently had successfully warded off the dangers of Irish lethargy. While in Venice, Bedell translated *The Book of Common Prayer* into Italian. On the recommendation of James Ussher, Bedell was appointed Provost of Trinity College, Dublin, in 1627 and later became Bishop of Kilmore. Bedell embarked on his project of translating the Old Testament into Irish in 1632. Muircheartach Ó Cionga (Murtagh King) was the chief translator and his assistant Séamas de Nógla (James Nangle) worked as a translation editor, correcting Ó Cionga's text. Bedell was almost sixty when he began learning Irish and had been learning it for only four years when the translation work began. He was therefore clearly unable to undertake such an ambitious translation task in a language that was not his own. This did not stop him, however, from making corrections to Ó Cionga's translation, not all of which were felicitous.[37] Ó Cionga himself was nearly seventy when he began his translation of the Old Testament and did not live to see its completion. He was thrown into prison in 1638 on foot of a number of allegations made by William Baily concerning his fitness for religious office and died soon afterwards. The translation was completed in 1640 but plans to print it were interrupted by the 1641 rebellion. Bedell, who was then Bishop of Kilmore, was imprisoned along with his two sons by the rebels. After he was released he was able to take refuge in Donncha Ó Sioradáin's house. He had, however, developed a fever while in captivity and died in Ó Sioradáin's house in 1642. Ó Sioradáin was friendly with the Catholic bishop, Eoghan Mac Suibhne who had taken over Bedell's house, and Ó Sioradáin was able to rescue the manuscript translation.

The translation would in fact remain in manuscript form for over forty years and it was only thanks to the intervention of Andrew Sall, a Jesuit who later became an Anglican minister, and Robert Boyle, the famous chemist, that the translation with corrections would eventually appear in 1685. An irony of translation history is that what has come to be known as Bedell's translation almost fell foul of the political insurgents whose language it celebrated. It also, however, fell foul of the politics of the period, when despite support from the Church of Ireland in 1704 and 1709 for preaching in Irish and the use of material translated into Irish, little was done to further these aims in practice. When the House of Commons of the Irish Parliament was presented with a scheme for the conversion of Irish Catholics through the medium of the Irish language, it recommended that there be a legal obligation on 'Papists' to send their children to charitable schools whose aim would be to ensure that 'in Time the Irish Language may be utterly abolished'.[38] A translation policy that was guided by the object of conversion could only be sustained as long as there was a belief that conversion was worthwhile.

In the light of the legislative changes occurring at the end of the seventeenth century the prospect of large-scale conversion was more alarming than reassuring for members of the largely Protestant landed aristocracy. The result of war, confiscation and plantation in the seventeenth century had led to two-thirds of Irish land changing hands. From 1692 a number of Acts, directed mainly though by no means exclusively against Catholics, were passed by the Dublin Parliament and were known collectively as the Penal Code. Catholics were not allowed to vote, could not enter Parliament, could not take commissions in the Army, Navy and Civil Service. They could not open or teach in a school and were barred from the manufacture and sale of newspapers and books. Catholic archbishops and bishops were banned from the country, while only one priest was allowed per parish and he was obliged to register with the local authorities. Priests were not allowed to enter the country, and the land rights of Catholics were severely restricted. These laws which were to be roundly denounced by Edmund Burke at the end of eighteenth century and by the historian William Lecky in the nineteenth were, above all else, a confession of failure. The Ascendancy class that controlled the Dublin Parliament had clearly abandoned any serious commitment to converting the majority Catholic population and decided that a policy of containment and economic and cultural subjection would, at the very least, ensure the continuation of their privileges. The very enactment of the laws was predicated on the assumed non-adherence of most Irish Catholics to the Established Church. As Bradshaw argues:

> By the end of the seventeenth century the catholic challenge had been defeated, and Ireland emerged with an apartheid constitution in law and in practice, religion providing the criterion for discrimination. The protestant ascendancy had acquired a strong incentive to leave Ireland for the greater part catholic.[39]

In such circumstances, the outlook for translation activity by Protestant translators was bleak. Gofraidh Mac Domhnaill's 1652 translation of William Perkins's *The Christian Doctrine or the Foundation of Christ's religion, Gathered into six principles, necessary for every ignorant Man to learn* has been described by Williams as a gem of translation in Irish – 'is seoid bheag d'aistriúcháin Gaeilge é' – but it never received a second printing. John Richardson, in his 1712 translation of John Lewis's church catechism, echoes sentiments similar to those expressed by Ó Domhnaill a hundred years earlier when he states in the Dedication to Robert Nelson, 'I was apprehensive nevertheless, when this Work was begun, that it would meet with some Discouragement and Opposition'.[40] Published the previous year, his collection of translated sermons *Seanmora ar na Priom Phoncibh na Chreideamh* unwittingly highlighted the dilemma in which Richardson and other translators like him found themselves. In his Dedication to James, Duke of Ormond and Lord Lieutenant General of Ireland, Richardson reviews Ireland's recent past and justifies the introduction of the Penal Code:

> It is too manifest to be denied, that the many dreadful Calamities with which that unfortunate Island hath been miserably Afflicted since the

Reformation, are in a great measure owing to the unhappy differences of Religion in it. To prevent them for the time to come, several Laws have been made to weaken and, at last to extinguish Popery in that Kingdom.[41]

In the context of discriminatory legislation, it was unlikely that those who drafted such legislation were going to be very sympathetic to the efforts to promote a language that was identified almost exclusively with the principal victims of the penal laws. Secondly, the use of religion as the basis for social and economic segregation meant that the 'Natives' were less likely to come to an 'Acknowledgement of the Truth', as Richardson hoped, than to greatly resent it.[42] Richardson as a translator fell foul of these contradictions and none of his translations, including his 1712 translation of the *Book of Common Prayer*, met with any notable success. The particular skill or accomplishment of individual translators could not in itself validate or consolidate the translation process. The translation theoretician, André Lefevere talks about 'patronage' as part of the literary system, understanding it to mean 'the powers (persons, institutions) that can further hinder the reading, writing and rewriting of literature'.[43] If translation is taken to mean a form of rewriting, it is clear that its survival depends on patronage which is determined *inter alia* by ideological considerations. The increasing paucity of translations into Irish by Protestant translators as the eighteenth century progresses demonstrates the tangible effects of official indifference or hostility to the continued use of the Irish language. The political imperatives of control would gradually silence the religious imperatives of conversion.

PATRONAGE AND CONTINENTAL TRANSLATION ACTIVITY

As we saw in Chapter One, the primary sources of patronage for the medieval translators were either religious orders or the Gaelic and Anglo-Norman/Old English aristocracy. These patrons would be the principal victims of the Tudor and Cromwellian campaigns in Ireland. The dissolution of the monasteries by Henry VIII, the defeat of the confederate army at Kinsale in 1601, the Flight of the Earls in 1607, the Cromwellian campaign beginning in 1649, the defeat of James II at the Battle of the Boyne in 1690, and the plantations of Munster and Ulster were all events that severely weakened both the economic basis for translation activity and the sections of the Irish community that would be expected on a cultural and ideological level to legitimise the process of translation into Irish. Political events would force a change in the geography of translation activity, with an increasing number of translations being produced by translators in exile on continental Europe. Thus, writing on the seventeenth century, Cainneach Ó Maonaigh notes, 'Aistríodh téacsanna go Gaeilge sa Bhoithéim, sa Bheilg, sa Fhrainc, sa Spáinn agus san Iodáil.'[44] In Prague, for example, an Irish Franciscan College was opened in July 1631.[45] In 1650, Bonaveantúr Ó Conchúr, a Franciscan translator based in the college produced a translation of Jerome Savonarola's *Triumphus Crucis* under the title of *Buaidh na Naomhchroiche.*[46] The translation was from the Latin and the translator remained scrupulously faithful to the original. However, although a request for permission to print the translation had been presented to the Vatican's Propaganda Fide in December 1652, the translation did not appear in printed form for another three hundred years.

In 1670, Filip Ua Raghallaigh, another Irish translator based in Prague, produced *An Bheatha Chrábhaidh*, a translation of the Latin work written by Saint Francis de Sales but better known as the *Introduction à la vie dévote*. Again, this translation did not appear in printed form but a copy was made by Eoghan Ó Raghallaigh, a member of a religious order in Flanders, in 1710 and another copy was made in 1824.[47] Although the name of the translator does not appear on the Irish translation of the *Vita Divina seu Via Regina ad Perfectionem*, it may have been produced by Anraí Mac Ardghail, another Franciscan who was associated with the Prague college.[48] The *Vita Divina* was originally written in Spanish by a Jesuit, Juan Eusebio Niremberg, and the Latin translation by Martino Sibenio was published in Westphalia in 1642. This translation served as a basis for the Irish version known as *An Bheatha Dhiadha nó an tSlighe Ríoghdha*. The translation circulated in manuscript form but was not printed. Thus, although the Franciscans in Prague had found patronage in the form of political and economic support for the establishment of their college, the dissemination of translated material was still reliant on a medieval system of circulation.

The acquisition in 1611 by the Franciscans based in St Anthony's College, Louvain of a printing press with Irish characters represented a decisive shift in the production and distribution of translated literature in Irish.[49] The decision to acquire the press was directly related to the propaganda war that was being fought in Ireland in the seventeenth century for the religious allegiance of the Irish. The decision by Elizabeth to provide funds for a printing press in Ireland and Uilliam Ó Domhnaill's use of the press in publishing his two translations greatly concerned the Franciscans on the continent, who felt that the Protestant churches would enjoy an incomparable advantage through the production of religious literature in Irish. In the preface to his 1618 devotional work, *Scáthán Shacramuinte na hAithridhe*, Aodh Mac Aingil explicitly mentions Ó Domhnaill's translations as part of the efforts to spread what he deemed to be heresy in Ireland:

> Mar atá leabhar Aifrinn ag an Eaglais Chatoilc, do-conncas d'eiricibh na hÉirionn gné leabhair Aifrinn do bheith aca féin dá ngoirid Leabhar an Chumainn agus nírbh olc an t-ainm sin dhó, dá gcuiridís "fallsa" leis. Ó Nar chuireadar, ní leasainm dhó Leabhar Iffrinn Eireaceachda do thabhairt air. Do chuirsead an leabhar so agus mórán don Bhíobla a nGaoidhilg agus as lór a neimhchirti sgríobhthar iad.[50]

The polemical tone of Mac Aingil's remarks, which mirror the belligerent denunciations of Uilliam Ó Domhnaill and Gofraidh Mac Domhnaill, are ample evidence that the stakes were high in seventeenth-century Irish translation activity. If the translations decried by Mac Aingil had circulated in manuscript form, it is doubtful whether he and the other Franciscans in Louvain would have reacted with such alarm and alacrity. The difference in impact of printed translations is ironically borne out by what appears to be the use of the 'heretical' translation in biblical references in the *Scáthán* and in writings by other scholars associated with Louvain such as Flaithrí Ó Maolchonaire, Seathrún Céitinn and Froinsias Ó Maolmhuaidh.[51] The Franciscan scholars had no option but to refer to Ó Domhnaill's translation as there was no Irish translation available to them at the time of the Douai Bible.

The availability of the printing press and the concentration of a group of scholars skilled in Irish and other languages provided an important impetus for translation work in Louvain. One of the founding members of the college in Louvain, Flaithrí Ó Maolchonaire, was a distinguished scholar with a European reputation for his theological work.[52] He came from a family in Roscommon with a long tradition of involvement with Gaelic scholarship, and was closely associated with political events of the period. He sailed with Don Juan d'Aquila and the Spanish fleet to Kinsale in 1601, and when the Irish were defeated he returned to Spain with Red Hugh O'Donnell to seek further assistance from the Spanish King Philip III. He was with O'Donnell when he died. In 1607 when the Gaelic leaders who had left Ireland arrived in Douai, he was waiting for them with another scholar, Roibeárd Mac Artúir. The Gaelic chiefs spent the winter with Ó Maolchonaire in Louvain and he accompanied them the following year to Rome, a city where he was appointed Archbishop of Tuam in 1609. Ó Maolchonaire had been educated in Salamanca, where he was received into the Franciscan Order in 1584. He was thus intimately acquainted with the Spanish language and his first translation was from Spanish into Irish. The translation was of a catechetical work from an unknown Spanish original (the author was not mentioned) and was completed in 1593. Ó Maolchonaire sent the translation in manuscript form to Ireland five years later, in 1598.[53] His first printed translation in Irish was *Sgáthán an Chrábhaidh*, also known as *Desiderius*, which came out in Louvain in 1616.[54]

The original work on which the translation is based, *Spill de la vida religiosa*, was written in Catalan and was published in Barcelona in 1529. However, it appears that Ó Maolchonaire worked mainly from *El Desseoso*, a six-part Spanish translation of the work, possibly the 1588 edition published in Lisbon. The Irish scholar Seán Ua Súilleabháin mentions other sources: *El Desideroso. Nelquale si contiene il modo di cercare & ritrovare la perfettione della vita Religioso*, an Italian translation that is based directly on the Catalan original, and a French version based on the Latin translation contained in the *Thesaurus Devotionis*. The Latin translation was published in 1554.[55] In his preface to the reader, Ó Maolchonaire signals an important change in the use of the target language in his translation: he is writing for ordinary people who are not skilled in the arcane niceties of literary language, 'chum leasa na daoine simplidhe, nach foil géarchúiseach i nduibheagán na Gaoidhilge'.[56] Ó Maolchonaire's declared intention to write an Irish that is more readily understandable to readers who are not steeped in the linguistic knowledge and lore of the bardic schools is making explicit a process that was already at work in the translation of non-literary works in the late medieval period. The primary objective of the translation for Ó Maolchonaire is to communicate knowledge and not to display virtuosity. However, it is not just the specific text-type which allows a more instrumental approach to language. There is also the wider context of the target culture and the ideological concerns of the translators. In the combative atmosphere of the Reformation and the Counter-Reformation, the protagonists were primarily concerned with communicating directly with their audience, whose salvation they believed to be imperilled by heresies, whether of Roman or Lutheran origin. The passing on of religious beliefs assumed an urgency that must bypass syntactic niceties, or as Mac Aingil puts it in his preface to *Scáthán Shacramuinte na hAithridhe*, 'nách do mhúnadh Gaoidhilgi sgríobhmaoid, achd do mhúnadh na h-aithrídhe, agus as lór linn go ttuigfidhear sinn gé nach bíadh ceart na Gaoidhilgi aguinn'.[57] The other factor dictating changes in target-language reception was the serious erosion of the institutional structures under-pinning Gaelic culture to which Ó Maolchonaire refers in his prefatory remarks, an erosion greatly accelerated after the defeat at Kinsale in 1601.

As a member of a family that was closely tied to the bardic system of learning, Ó Maolchonaire would be particularly conscious of the changes that were wrought by political upheaval and the consequent withdrawal of patronage. The trauma of the seventeenth century had, in one sense, a curiously liberatory effect. The translations, the contact with other languages on continental Europe and the weakening hold of a bardic orthodoxy on the Irish language would in fact ultimately lead to the birth of modern Irish. As Cáinneach Ó Maonaigh puts it:

> Teangacha na hEorpa ag soláthair tuairimí nua don Ghaeilge, agus téarmaí nó cora cainte úra lena gcur i gcéill. Borradh nua ag teacht faoi scríbneoireacht na Gaeilge dá bharr. Roinnt de na seanrialacha a bhí ag fáscadh agus ag tachtadh na teanga idir phrós is fhilíocht, a gcaitheamh uaithi.[58]

The emphasis on greater simplicity and communicative effectiveness that guided the translation work in Louvain and elsewhere would embolden others in their rejection of strict adherence to bardic conventions. In his *Cathecismus sen Adhon, an Teagasc Críostuí iar na fhoillsuí a Laidin & a Ngaoilaig*, published in Brussels in 1639, Theobold Stapleton points to the wilful obscurantism of bardic hierophants as one of the reasons for the decline of Irish. Part of the blame, he feels, rests with the 'Aois Ealaghain noch as udair dhon Teangain do chuir i fá fórdhorcatheacht 7 cruas focal, dha scribha a nodaibh 7 fhocalaibh deamhaire, doracha, do thuicseanta'.[59] Louvain's importance in the Gaelic translation network is indicated by the fact that dozens of reports and letters were sent by Franciscans from the Scottish Gaeltacht to be translated into Latin or Italian. These translations would then be forwarded to the Congregatio de propaganda fide in Rome.[60] One of the two original copies of *Annals of the Four Masters* was intended for translation into Latin in St Anthony's College, Louvain, where it was to be printed.[61] Thus, translation was one of the central activities of the college alongside teaching, historical and linguistic scholarship and the production of original devotional works.

63

The rules relating to the Third Order of the Franciscans were translated into Irish from Latin by Brian Mac Giolla Coinnigh and published in Louvain in 1641 under the title *Riaghuil Threas Uird S. Froinsias, dá ngoirthear Ord na hAithrighe*. The decision to translate the Rule would appear to have been prompted by the adoption of the Rule by the Franciscans at their General Chapter in Toledo in 1633 and the resolution at the meeting that the Rule should be translated into Latin and French.[62] Mac Giolla Coinnigh, who was from Connacht, studied at St Anthony's College and was a chaplain to Captain Somhairle Mac Domhnaill's troops in the Netherlands in 1623. Three years later he was at St Isidore's College in Rome and the following year he went to Ireland. After his period as President of St Anthony's College, he returned again to Ireland where he was put in charge of the convent in Ros Oirbhealaigh. In 1650, he gave shelter in his convent to Protestant refugees who were fleeing from attack, but this did not prevent him from being arrested by English troops in 1653. He died in captivity in 1662. His translation style, in keeping with other translations from Louvain, favoured directness and simplicity and avoided excessive adjectival ornamentation. Mac Giolla Coinnigh's chaplaincy to Irish troops on the continent is significant in pointing to another section of the target audience for material translated from Irish. The seventeenth century saw thousands of Irish soldiers enlisting in foreign regiments, particularly the armies of France and Spain. They were an important constituent of the Irish diaspora and for many, though not all, their mother tongue was Irish. Thus, translations would meet both a domestic and foreign demand.

A project that occupied the energies of the Franciscans in Louvain for a number of years was their hagiographical work. The aim was to compile the lives of Irish saints by collecting information on the saints that was scattered throughout Ireland and Europe. The second stage, once the information was collected, was to produce lives of the saints in Latin; this often involved translating material where the source material was not in Latin (or rewriting it, if necessary, to conform to the Latin style of the seventeenth century). The chief motivator behind this project was a Donegal Franciscan, Aodh Mac a' Bhaird and he was greatly assisted by, among others, Mícheál Ó Cléirigh, the main compiler of the *Annals of the Four Masters*, and Pádraig Pléimeann, who became head of the Irish College in Prague. The murder of Pléimeann in Bohemia in 1631 and Mac a' Bhaird's untimely death in Louvain in 1635 seemed to cast doubt over the project, but another Franciscan from Donegal, Seán Mac Colgán, took over the editorial and translation work on the death of Mac a' Bhaird. The *Acta Sanctorum Hiberniae*, the *Triadis Thuamaturgae* and the *Collectanea Sacra* (Tomás Ó Sírín was principally involved in the publication of this last work) were the published fruits of the Franciscan labours. The lives of Irish saints would not only provide source material for the important Latin translation project in Louvain but they would also influence the translation process in the other direction. In the Irish version of the life of St Francis based on translated material from two Latin works, St Bonaventure's *Legenda maior* and the *Liber Confirmitatum* by Bartholomeus of Pisa, the language contains a mixture of the classical and the modern. Pádraig Ó Súilleabháin, a later editor of the seventeenth-century text known as *Beatha San Froinsias*, speculates that the archaisms derived in part from a conscious attempt to imitate the language of the lives of the Irish saints composed in earlier centuries: 'Séard is bun le cuid den arsaíocht, b'fhéidir gur dócha go ndearna an t-aistritheoir iarracht ar an mbeatha seo San Froinsias a mhunlú ar bheathaí na naomh Éireannach le go mbeadh crot agus cuma dhúcasach uirthi.'[63]

The Irish translators working outside Ireland did not concentrate, however, on exclusively religious material. Maghnus Ó Domhnaill, a priest who was educated in Salamanca in the latter half of the seventeenth century, translated a work entitled the *Lunario* of Geronymo Cortès into Irish. The *Lunario* was largely didactic in its concerns, providing the reader with the main facts or theories that were considered to be of importance in the physical, astronomical and agricultural sciences. The translation was from Spanish and there are a number of hispanicisms such as a redundant use of the article and an incorrect use of the plural adjective in Irish. He also leaves out sentences containing the names of foreign fruits for which there are no equivalents in Irish, in much the same way as medieval translators omitted material that would not be familiar to their readers.[64] Ó Domhnaill was not restricted in his choice of text-types and also translated three stories by the Spanish writer Juan Perez de Montalván into Irish as *Eachtra an phálais dhraíochtúil*, *Eachtra an cheatharnaigh choille chompáisigh*, and *Eachtra Risdeaird agus Lisardha*. Montalván's stories were published in his *Para Todos: Exemplos Morales, Humanos y Divinos*. The year given for these manuscript translations is 1706.[65]

TRANSLATED AUDIENCES

Translation activity in Irish was not confined to expatriate Irish scholars on the European continent. We have seen the formidable translation tasks undertaken by Protestant translators in the seventeenth century, and translators based in Ireland continued to work to respond to the demand for translations. The Poor Clares, who had a convent on Merchant Quay in Dublin in 1629, had an Irish translation of the First Rule of St Clare made for them by Aodh Ó Raghallaigh and Séamas Ó Siaghail, and transcribed by Mícheál Ó Cléirigh in 1636. That same year, after their expulsion from Dublin, they settled on a piece of a land near Athlone which they christened Bethlehem.[66] In 1642 they left Bethlehem and moved to Galway, where they looked for more translations – duly provided by An Dúbhaltach Mac Fhir Bhisigh in 1647.[67] Mac Fhir Bhisigh who came from a distinguished bardic family apologises for the standard of Irish in the translation and blames not the translator but his audience. The 'bacuighe', lameness or the simpleness of his Irish does not come 'tré ghainne na Gaeilge', from the poverty of his Irish, but 'tre esbaidh a heoluis ar chách, ionnus gurob usa leó focail choimhightheca do thuisgin ináid focail fhíre na Gaoidhelge'.[68] Mac Fhir Bhisigh's dilemma is that of translation itself.

Translation had a distinct energising effect on the Irish language in the seventeenth century and the presence of other languages, world-views and literatures was in many senses enabling and enriching as it had been in previous centuries. This sense of linguistic possibilty and intellectual opportunity has always been translation's most important gift to world culture. However, when a language and its speakers come under intense pressure from another language or languages and culture, then translation becomes instantly problematic. Do translators become the grave-diggers of their own language by accepting borrowings on a large-scale and so damage the language's specificity, its very *raison d'être*, or do they fight a rearguard action, maintaining standards of linguistic purity at the risk of being misunderstood or not understood at all? Though it could be argued that Mac Fhir Bhisigh's remarks are dictated by a nostalgia for the linguistic privileges of a bardic élite, he does point up the predicament of a translator who finds not only that he is translating but that his very audience is being *translated*. This, in one sense, is a constant feature of language. Societies, cultures and peoples change over time, whence the constant demand for new translations of old works. History is perpetual translation and readers are translated by their centuries. In periods of crisis, this normal process is greatly accelerated and translators occupy a central if invidious position. They are either agents of decay or harbingers of renewal, but it is often circumstances rather than intentions that determine the consequences of their activities. The political and military forces deciding the future linguistic allegiances of the Irish could not be altered by the translations of An Dúbhaltach Mac Fhir Bhisigh and others, but translation itself was powerfully affected by them.

The Emergence of English-language translation

The seventeenth century marks the emergence of Ireland as a locus for English-language translation. The emergence was related to a new system of patronage. The elements that combined to consitute an infrastructure for translation activity in English came into being in the sixteenth and seventeenth century. Firstly, there was the establishment in 1592 of Ireland's first university, in the modern sense of the word. Although it provided for the teaching of Irish and through the agency of Uilliam Ó Domhnaill and William Bedell was centrally involved in translation projects into Irish, Trinity College in Dublin was predominantly English-speaking. This was hardly surprising as it had been founded on the initiative of the new English authorities in Ireland. Secondly, the massive land transfers of the seventeenth century had led to the emergence of a new landed aristocracy, the Ascendancy, who were almost exclusively English-speaking. This new class provided both the prestige and the support that was considered both desirable and necessary in order to have translations published. Thirdly, many of the settlers in the new plantations in Ireland spoke English and there was little economic or political incentive for them to change their linguistic habits. Fourthly, the language of the established church was mainly English, despite valiant efforts by individual churchmen to adopt a more generous policy towards Irish. When Bishop Dopping of Meath appeared to lose interest in his efforts to have a number of the psalms translated into Irish for Bedell's Bible, Archbishop Marsh in a letter to Robert Boyle on the 22 March 1685 noted: 'The unwelcomeness of this undertaking to many in this country I believe, was the reason, why the bishop of Meath flew off from prosecuting what he designed and promised, and has ever since been wholly unconcerned and sat neuter.'[69]

The area of theatrical translation provides a small, if telling, example of the interplay between translation, language and the fraught emergence of the new infrastructure. John Ogilby, an English translator of Virgil, was taken into the Earl of Stafford's household to teach his children in 1633. When Stafford was appointed Lord-Deputy of Ireland, Ogilby became one of his troop of guard and in Ireland he was appointed deputy-master of the revels. He built a small theatre in Werburgh Street, but when war broke out in 1641 Ogilby lost everything. He narrowly escaped being blown up in Rathfarnham Castle and was shipwrecked on his passage back to England.[70] Ogilby's theatre, the Smock Alley Theatre, hosted the first performance of Katherine Philips's English translation of Pierre Corneille's *Pompéi* in 1663. Philips who had come to Ireland to prosecute her husband's claim to lands, became friendly with another translator, Roger Boyle, and he encouraged her to complete the Corneille translation. The play was a great success in Dublin and she had begun working on a translation of Corneille's *Horace* when she was struck down by smallpox and died at the age of thirty-three.[71] In his history of early Irish theatre, William Smith Clark attaches particular significance to the Irish *première* of Philips's translation:

> Few in the large and brilliant audience presided over by the Lord-Lieutenant realized that once again . . . Dublin had taken the lead over London in an historic stage presentation. *Pompey* marked the first in a long succession of Restoration performances of French plays in English.[72]

Philips was not the only translator of Corneille in Ireland in the late seventeenth century. John Dancer, an Irish horsetrooper and *littérateur*, translated *Nicomède* and the play was performed in the Smock Alley Theatre in 1670.[73]

Philips's choice of classical themes for her French translations is significant, in that many of the English translations produced by Irish translators in the late seventeenth and eighteenth centuries reflected the strong interest in translations from classical authors that had given translation much of its impetus in the Renaissance period. Edward Wetenhall, the Protestant Bishop of Kilmore, was one of the clergymen at the beginning of the eighteenth century who supported the scheme for the translation of religious works into Irish.[74] He was himself a translator and a former Fellow of Trinity College Dublin. In 1675, his Pindaric translation

of the Tenth Satire of Juvenal was published in Dublin and dedicated to
Lord Viscount Blessington. Wetenhall's 'Dedication' to the translation
decribes its genesis. On his journey to Clonmel for legal business he
decides to pass the time by indulging in comparative translation criticism:

> Some perplex't business drew him to the terms at Clonmel, in which Jour-
> ney, for diversion of law thoughts, and entertainment of time, which was
> not very capable of more serious studies, he took with him Juvenal and his
> learned Translators, Sir Robert Stapleton, and Dr. B. Holiday, only with the
> design of pleasing himself by comparing the Original and Translations: a
> pleasure truly worthy of an ingenious mind, at once to view the product of
> Three so great Wits employed on the same conceits.'[75]

During a stopover in Kilkenny, a friend suggests that Wetenhall produce a Pindaric version of Juvenal because Juvenal would lend himself
to this poetic treatment and the translator would thereby avoid competing with those 'great Names' who had already translated the Roman
writer. Writing on the Renaissance discourse on translation, Theo
Hermans has described the protestations of humility that were prefatory
commonplaces in European translations of the Renaissance period and
later: 'the translator will . . . understate his own abilities and achievement in order to highlight the difficulty of the task, the excellence of
the model and/or the erudition of his patron'.[76] Wetenhall does indeed
defer to the knowledgeable judgment of his patron, who is to decide
whether he has succeeded or not in his translation, but the Dedication
is not mere sycophantic formula. It indicates that his approach to
translation is not haphazard. Wetenhall is aware of translating within a
tradition (the 'great Names'), and his comparative studies on the
Dublin–Clonmel journey are testimony to that anxiety of influence
which is a recurring feature of literary translation. Mere replication
would make the translation redundant so a new Juvenal translation
must employ a strategy of renewal, in this case, a Pindaric version.

In his 1692 translation of Epictetus's *Enchiridion*, the Derry translator,
Ellis Walker, is similarly concerned with translation as revitalisation.
Walker's 'Epistle Dedicatory' directly alludes to Ireland's troubled state
and the refuge that he sought in the house of his uncle and patron,
Samuel Walker of York: 'When I fled to you for shelter at the breaking
out of the present Troubles in Ireland, I took Epictetus for my com-
panion; and found that both I, and my friend were welcome.'[77] In
Walker's case, it is not the friend but he himself who suggests a
'Poetical dress' for Epictetus. In the laudatory poems that accompany

the translation, it is significant that Will Peirse from Emmanuel College Cambridge situates Walker in a poetic tradition that would appear specifically Irish to many of his contemporaries:

> Such were these Rules; but 'tis to You we owe,
> That they in Numbers and in Measure flow;
> So Bards and Druids under awful shade
> Of Reverend Aged Oak of old conveyed
> Their sacred verse to the admiring throng,
> And taught 'em Vertue as they heard their Song
> These were our native Prophets; such are you
> Prophet, Philosopher and Poet too.[78]

This is precisely the tradition that is rejected by another Irish translator, Wentworth Dillon, whose *Essay on Translated Verse* appeared seven years before Walker's translation:

> I grant that from Mosie, Idol Oak,
> In Double Rhymes our Thor and Woden spoke;
> And by Succesion of unlearned Times,
> As Bards began, so Monks Ring on the Chimes.[79]

Dillon's desire to distance himself from the 'Bards' and the 'Monks' can be seen as a specific repudiation of the cultural tradition of the country in which he lived, but it can be seen more generally as part of a post-Renaissance insistence on the pre-eminence of Greece and Rome. Monks and bards are the high priests of a medievalism that is to be banished by the superior graces of classical learning. It is, for Dillon and others, translation itself that will produce the miracle of access and allow the celebration of classical excellence. This sentiment is clearly articulated in Ezekiel Bristed's 'Acrostick, on the ingenious Translator Mr E.W.', where poetic translation is synonymous with fusion and revelation:

> E ngland and Athens now are joyn'd in one;
> L earned Epictetus sings in th'English Tone.
> L ay by his rusty Book of crabbed Greek;
> I n English Poetry you hear him speak.
> S o all the dark-tongu'd Oracles of Greece,
>   (peace,
> W hen Truth Shot forth full Beams did hold their
> A ll you, that would Philosophers appear,
> L earn Natures Laws, in charming Numbers here:
> K eep home, you need no more to Athens run:
> E 're long, they'l all from thence to England come:
> R ead here and you will find them all out done.[80]

The fusion ('joyn'd in one') is suspiciously like submission. The readers can spare themselves the philological journey to 'crabbed Greek' and Athens as they can now enjoy the delights of Greek learning in the comfort of their own 'home'. The praise of foreign genius becomes the exaltation of native domesticity. Translation thus occupies a somewhat paradoxical position. It is the way into the wit and beauty of other and earlier cultures, yet it can also act as the guarantor of cultural complacency. Even allowing for the ritual hyperbole of Bristed's acrostic, the implications are clear. Translation is a form of homage to England's cultural superiority, and readers in English will soon find themselves granting the favour of poetic improvement to classical authors rather than remaining in mimetic thrall to their accomplishments. Dillon in his translation essay is explicit in his identification of poetry and empire:

> By secret influence of Indulgent Skyes,
> Empire and Poetry Together rise.
> True Poets are the Guardians of a State,
> And when They Fail, portend approaching Fate.[81]

Translation is the continuation of war by other means, and Dillon is at pains in his essay to show that England's main political rival in the seventeenth century, France, has a language that is intrinsically deficient for translation purposes: 'Vain are our Neighbours Hopes, and Vain their Cares, / The Fault is more their Languages, than theirs.'

Dillon's identification with the English imperial project, and his ready acceptance into English literary circles, highlight an important aspect of the operation of patronage in the widest sense. Horace's *Art of Poetry* first appeared in an English translation by Dillon in 1680, and a second edition came out in 1685. Both of these editions were published in London. In 1733, his translation of Horace was published in Dublin and dedicated to the Provost, Fellows and Scholars of the University of Dublin (Trinity College).[82] Dillon therefore had an audience and a market in both Ireland and England. Irish translators in English not only had ready access to printers but, more importantly, had access to a wider audience than translators working in Irish. The economies of scale of publishing greatly favoured those who were translating for a growing English-language market in Ireland and an already substantial British market.

PLAIN DRESS AND PICTURES

Theo Hermans has remarked on the prevalence of the '"garment" meta-phor' in Renaissance translation discourse, where the poor dress of translation lies in stark contrast to the rich apparel of the source text.[83] The plainness can of course be seen as a virtue, particularly in post-Reformation thinking, in which plain speaking and unadorned churches are seen as the outward manifestations of a direct and honest relationship with God and the Word. In the 1696 translation of the Psalms of David by two Irishmen, Natum Tate and Nicholas Brady, the methods employed in the translation are explained at the end in an 'Advertisement'. They claim that they have kept 'strictly to the text' but their intention has been 'to make the whole version easie and intelligible'.[84] Source-language exoticism and target-language confusion are avoided, as Brady and Tate affirm that they have rendered the 'Hebraisms in their plain Sense and Meaning as agreed on by the best Commentators'. Plainness is truthfulness. Insofar as the translation that Tate and Brady produced was widely used in church services for many years, they had indeed succeeded in making their 'version easie and intelligible'. However, many critics questioned the accuracy of the metrical version, suggesting that sense had been sacrificed to intelligibility.[85]

In his translation of the *Satires* of Persius, Thomas Sheridan draws an analogy between certain translators and those 'modern Orators' who 'rather dazzle and perplex the Understandings of the Hearers, than inform their Judgements; whereas Reason and Truth show always to the best Advantage, in the plainest Dress'.[86] In this, Sheridan is at one with Dillon.[87] Hence, the very image that was earlier used to show up the inadequacy of translation is now employed to point to translators' commitment to honesty and truth in their textual practices. In advocating the special virtues of unadorned translations, the premises are not solely theological. They are also political. Dillon pities the French, for their language is 'Courtly, florid and abounds in words'. He celebrates the invigorating energy of English, which by implication scorns the mellifluous wordiness of French.[88] Thus, plainness becomes a linguistic marker of national specificity and indeed superiority. In vaunting plainness of dress, translators such as Dillon, Brady, Tate and Sheridan are not simply embracing a credo of reader-oriented intelligibility but are echoing religious and poli-tical concerns that inform the political and cultural environment of their translation practice.

Thomas Sheridan was an active translator in Ireland in the first half of the eighteenth century who also devoted a certain amount of attention to the process of translation itself. He was a grandson of Donncha Ó Sioradáin, known in English as Dennis or Dionysius Sheridan, who (as we saw earlier) saved Bedell's manuscript translation from destruction and had in fact assisted Bedell in his task.[89] Thomas Sheridan graduated from Trinity College, Dublin, with a Bachelor of Arts in 1711 and a Doctorate in Divinity in 1726. For a while he ran a school in Capel Street where he was described by Swift as a 'master of the Greek and Roman languages'.[90] Swift often stayed with Sheridan in the latter's country house in County Cavan and they were close friends. (The relationship later became somewhat embittered as the result of a long recuperation by Sheridan in Swift's house.) Sheridan died in Rathfarnham, County Dublin in 1738. His extravagance and inconstancy did not always prove attractive to his contemporaries. The Earl of Orrery wrote of him as:

> ill-starred, good-natured, improvident . . . a punster, a quibler, a fiddler and a wit. Not a day passed without a rebus, an anagram, a madrigal. His pen and his fiddle-stick were in continual motion, and yet to little or no purpose.[91]

This judgement ignores Sheridan's achievements in translation and his decidedly purposeful approach to speculation on the nature of the activity.

In his preface to his 1727 translation of the *Battle of the Frogs and Mice*, a text that was falsely attributed to Homer, Sheridan describes a fictional encounter with a translator of Homer's *Iliad*. The translator would appear to have taken seriously Dillon's friendship theory of translation ('No longer his Interpreter, but He'), because he has taken to physically resembling a statue of Homer described by Cedrenus. Sheridan proceeds to describe to the Homeric translator various 'arts of success' which are, in effect, an ironic comment on aspects of contemporary translation practice that Sheridan obviously deplores.[92] These include prefixing a copy of Greek verses to the translation, calling the Titles of each Book not First and Second but *Iliad* Alpha and Beta. One should retain names that the world is least acquainted with in choosing proper names and put many Greek verses in the notes. Chapman is seen as particularly guilty in his pedantic use of esoteric names such as Ephaistus for Vulcan and Baratrum for Hell.[93] Dillon in 1685 had already called for the purging of the soil of translation of rank pedantic weeds, and Sheridan's Homeric translator is equally trenchant in his condemnation of wanton displays of scholarship:

A success, says he, founded on the Ignorance of others, may bring a temporary Advantage, but neither a conscious Satisfaction nor future Fame to the Author. Men of Sense despise the affectation which they easily see through, and even they who were dazzled by it at first, are no sooner inform'd of its being an Affectation, but they imagine it also a Veil to cover Imperfection.[94]

Sheridan is here anticipating the Matthew Arnold and F.H. Newman debate in the nineteenth century as to the true role of scholarship and learning in the translation of texts. For Sheridan, translating for an English audience, the element of national rivalry that is present in seventeenth-century translations is still alive. His interlocutor urges Sheridan to use poetry rather than prose in his translation declaring somewhat grandly:

Let the French whose Language is not copious, translate in Prose; but ours which exceeds it in Copiousness of Words; may have a more frequent Likeness of Sounds, to make the Unison or Rhime easier; a Grace of Musick, that attones for the Hardness our Consonants and Monosyllables occasion.[95]

In addition to translation in verse as further proof of intrinsic national excellence, there is the equation of translation with a form of aesthetic morality. When Sheridan wonders whether the 'air' accompanying his translation should be antiquated (Chapman) or modern (La Motte), his adviser uses an extended visual metaphor. If one observes a painter whose paintings are always in fashion:

He neither chooses to draw a Beauty in a Ruff, or a French-Head; but with its Neck uncover'd, and in its natural Ornament of Hair curl'd up, or spread becomingly: So may a writer choose a natural Manner of expressing himself which will always be in Fashion, without affecting to borrow an odd Solemnity and unintelligible Pomp from the Past Times, or humouring the present by falling into its Affectations, and those Phrases which are born to die with it.[96]

The emphasis on 'a natural Manner' will assume increasing importance throughout the eighteenth century as it becomes a core concept of Romanticism. It implies a commitment to truth that is evident in the celebration of 'plainness', but without the distinct theological overtones of the latter concept. The translator in the embrace of naturalness eschews modishness (antiquity in this sense is an affectation, a variant of fashion), and seeks for an essential meaning that is immanent in the text itself. The metaphor that Sheridan uses is not innocent in its directly addressing questions of representation and gender in translation, but it also relates to a tradition in translation theory that dates from Quintillian's *Institutio Oratoria*. Quintillian, in Book X, clearly marks the limits to imitation and declares that whatever 'is like another object must necessarily be inferior to the object of its imitation, just as the shadow is inferior to the substance (and) the portrait to the features which it portrays'.[97] The pictorial metaphor is used to explain the unpredictability of target-language reception of translations. A man need only go to a painter to find what 'he hears said of a picture' also applying to a translation:

> There is one Spectator tells you, a Piece is extreamly fine, but he sets no Value on what is not like the Face it was drawn for, while a second informs you, such another is extreamly like, but he cares not for a Piece of Deformity, tho' its Likeness be never so exact.[98]

Quintillian's image, which had become a commonplace in Renaissance translation prefaces,[99] is employed by Sheridan less to suggest the intrinsic inadequacy of translation as imitation than to underline the status of translation as an open system.[100] In this sense, reception in literary translation is in the realm of aesthetics. The reader's response to a literary translation and the viewer's response to a painting are affected by a complex of public and private histories that make accurate forecasts of reaction problematic.

Sheridan is suggesting that endless debates about freedom versus fidelity (to which he contributes) may be misguided. The success of translation rests not on the degree of licence or faithfulness used by the translator but on what readers expect translation to do for them. If the reader believes that translation is a doomed art, a hostage to derivative mediocrity, s/he will remain unconvinced no matter what strategy is adopted by the translator. Translation criticism as it has been practised for centuries in language classrooms is generally informed by this spirit. The teacher shows how inadequately the target language renders the untranslatable beauties of the source text, and the emphasis is almost invariably on what translation cannot do rather than what it can. Furthermore, even if the reader accepts translation as possible, the translation may still be rejected because readers do not like what they see. The text offends strongly-held beliefs about source-language language and culture, with 'deformities' scarring imagined purity. Translators from Irish in the late nineteenth century, as we shall see in the next chapter, periodically abandoned their policy of meticulous fidelity when they baulked at translating sexually frank imagery, preferring to sacrifice their scholarship to convention. Despite the anticipation of dissatisfaction, there is in Sheridan's writing a note of self-confidence that would embolden translators from the mid-seventeenth century onwards, as they

came to regard themselves less as dutiful serfs and more as inventive crea-
tors in their own right. Ó Domhnaill in 1602 offers us an image of
translation as hard labour, a linguistic penance:

> Under which burden how carefully and conscionably I have groaned, they
> onely can judge, that can confer this translation with the original Greeke,
> unto which I tyed my selfe, as of dutie I ought: having laboured therein in
> all sinceritie, as in the presence of God, the Judge of all, to express the text
> truly and fully, as neare as I could, without either detraction or addition,
> saving only in such places, where the necessitie of the phrase or sentence
> required it, (as it is usual in all translations, that cannot attaine unto the grace
> and proprietie of the originall) to give the full sense.[101]

Even allowing for the difference between religious and secular translation
– in the former the latitude for the translator's intervention, free from
Augustinian strictures, has always been greater – there is nonetheless a
strong affirmative note in the translator's credo as expressed by Sheridan in
his 1727 Preface:

> When I am literal, I regard my Author's Words; when I am not, I translate
> in his spirit. If I am low, I choose the narrative Style; if high, the Subject
> requir'd it. When I am enervate, I give an Instance of ancient Simplicity;
> when affected I show a Point of modern Delicacy. As for Beauties, there
> never can be found one in me which was not really intended; and for any
> Faults, they proceeded from too unbalanced Fancy, or too nice Judgement,
> but by no means from any Defect in either of those Faculties.[102]

The translator here is empowered, making choices, actively shaping the
translated text and fully confident in the combined capacities of his
'Fancy' and 'Judgement.'

The assurance is evident in the work of another eighteenth-century
Irish translator, Thomas Francklin, in his 1778 translations of Sophocles's
tragedies into English. We are informed in the 'Preface to the Reader' that
Sophocles's tragedies 'being now translated into English by the learned and
Rev. Dr. Francklin; the Reader is here presented with a Version of this
Work, equal, in every respect, to the great original'.[103] Although declarations of humility are common in eighteenth-century translation prefaces in
Ireland, they are increasingly less abject. There is a greater pride in the
translator's art and a greater confidence in the possibility of success. It is
hardly surprising that Irish translators should possess this new assurance for
they were conscious of translation as an international rather than exclusively national activity. The translators read translations in other languages
and compare these either at the level of production, as in the case of Ó

Maolchonaire's *Scáthán an Chrábhaidh,* or at the level of commentary, as exemplified by Arthur Murphy's 1793 translations of Tacitus. Murphy situates his work not in an Irish and British translation context but in a European framework:

> Almost all the nations of Europe have had the ambition to make Tacitus a denizen of their country, and to hear him in their own language. The Germans and the Dutch boast of good translations. Spain is proud of three translators, and Italy has a greater number; but the voice of Fame gives the preference to *Davanzati,* who is celebrated for a curious felicity of expression, that vies with the sententious brevity of the original.[104]

Murphy refers directly to Perrot D'Ablancourt, the seventeenth-century French translator, who along with Malherbe would play a decisive role in establishing greater autonomy for translators.[105] That this autonomy was often achieved at the expense of the meaning or indeed the style of the source text led to Ménage's notorious comment on D'Ablancourt's translations: 'Elles me rappellent une femme que j'ai beaucoup aimée à Tours, et qui était belle mais infidèle.'[106] Murphy notes that D'Ablancourt takes 'the liberty sometimes to retrench, and, occasionally to vary the sense of the original' but that the translation on the whole flowed with 'much ease and harmony'. The 'celebrated Rousseau' is specifically faulted by Murphy for the absence of such ease in his translation of the first book of Tacitus's History.[107]

The achievement of 'graceful ease' in translation is variously interpreted by translators in the seventeenth and eighteenth century. John Dryden claims that in his translation of Virgil's *Aeneid* 'I have endeavoured to make Virgil speak such English as he himself would have spoken, if he had been born in England, and in this present age.'[108] It is the figure of the author who is invoked here as the guarantor for Dryden's translation practice. Murphy, for his part, looks not to the author but to the potential reader of his translation. He declares that 'he has endeavoured to give a faithful transcript of the orginal, in *such English* as an *Englishman of taste* may read without disgust'[109] (his emphasis). By highlighting the centrality of target-language reception in evaluating translation success or failure, Murphy is simply making explicit the implicit aim of legibility behind Dryden's translation of Virgil into another language and time. The elements of reception are not only linguistic and cultural, they are also political. Murphy dedicates his four-volume translation of Tacitus to a fellow-Irishman, Edmund Burke. Burke is presented by Murphy as a latter-day Tacitus and the French revolutionaries as German legions fighting for anarchy rather than civilisation. Murphy, who identifies closely with England, sees Burke 'with a patriot spirit standing forth *the champion of Truth,* of your Country, and the British Constitution'[110] (emphasis in original). The Tacitus translations are thus politically encoded in two ways. Firstly, there is the specific historical moment in which they appear. In 1793, Louis XVI and Marie-Antoinette are beheaded and Robespierre and the Terror are on the ascendant. Therefore, the translations if they are presented in a particular light are likely to have greater impact than if they had appeared ten years previously. Secondly, there is the nature of the interpretation offered by the translator. In this instance, specific parallels are drawn between events described by Tacitus and contemporary political circumstances. Murphy is suggesting a deliberate interpretation of Tacitus's work where the Roman historian becomes retrospectively a precursor of Burke, and the ideological response of the Englishman of Taste is carefully delimited.

The importance of juncture for translation is apparent two centuries earlier in Ireland with the decision in 1577 to publish John Hooker's translation of the *Expugnatio Hibernica*, by Gerald of Wales, alongside Stanihurst's account of Ireland in Holinshed's Chronicles. In the propaganda war that was and would be fought to justify Tudor and Cromwellian policies in Ireland, a readily available translation of a work from the Middle Ages that offered a largely hostile depiction of the Irish was crucial in lending a historical legitimacy to the onslaught against the native population. Therefore, the decision to translate had a distinct political resonance and the consequences can be seen in the many references to Gerald's writings in the work of sixteenth and seventeenth-century propagandists. Again, the reception of the translation is linked to a specific set of political circumstances.

TRANSLATION, POETIC EXPRESSION AND FREEDOM

In his 1749 translations of the works of Horace, Philip Francis is aware of the standard repsonse to translation. Horace, it is generally claimed, is a difficult author to translate because of qualities that are inherent in Latin and do not survive transposition. Translation is a perilous exercise that can only end in the grief of poor approximation. In his Preface, Francis defends both translation and the English language:

But if we consider the Boldness and Copiousness of Expression, the Diversity and Harmony of Numbers in English, we shall impute the Failure of his Translators to somewhat [sic] injudicious in their Design, or careless in their Execution, rather than to any personal want of Abilities, or any weakness in their Language; to the Real Difficulty of the Work, not an impossibility of executing it with Success.[111]

Francis is, therefore, convinced of the capacity of his target language to render effectively a complex original. He does not accept, on the other hand, blind tribute to conventions that govern the stylistic possibilities of translators in that language. In a less than oblique reference to Pope, Dryden and their myriad imitators, Francis complains that 'the Misfortune of our Translators is, that they have only one Style, and that consequently all their authors, Homer, Virgil, Horace, Ovid, are compelled to speak in the same Numbers, and the same unvaried Expression'. The freedom of poetic expression is 'confined in twenty constant Syllables, and the Sense regularly ends with every second Line, as if the Writer had not Strength enough to support himself, or courage enough to venture into a third.'[112] The problem with making Horace speak as he would have in eighteenth-century England is that he ends up arguing in couplets, and the persons in his dialogues converse almost exclusively in epigrams. Francis exalts the skill of the translator, though not to the detriment of the stylistic variety or specificity of the source text. His attitude is similar in thrust to the Romantic theories of translation in the late eighteenth century that considered the preservation of the creative energy of the original to be of paramount importance[113] (Francis, in the case of Horace, talks of conserving that 'Force of Expression, in which his peculiar Happiness consists').[114] The concern with translating this energy into English does not lead Francis to eschew erudition. Though he warns translators against the dangers of disabling lyric poetry through the excessive explanatory zeal of scholarship, Francis is forthright in his defence of learning as a necessary preliminary to the act of translation:

It was esteemed a necessary Labour to consider the Text with the criticism of a Grammarian in View to the Purity of the Latin Tongue, and with the Care of an Editor in comparing the various Readings of Manuscripts and Editions. Such a Study is very little entertaining, but it often clears up Difficulties, that have perplexed the best Interpreters. It preserves us from authorising unknown Words; receiving defective Constructions for Elegancies, and Barbarisms for Beauties.[115]

Francis's statement begs the question as to who is capable of performing the task of translation. Is it to become the sole preserve of the professional scholars in the university or is there still a democracy of access based on intuition rather than erudition? Two years after the publication of Francis's translations, John Boyle, the Earl of Orrery, has his own translations of the *Letters of Pliny the Younger* published in Dublin. The translation is presented as an act of paternal devotion, dedicated to his son Charles. The tone of presentation is distinctly that of the dilettante and amateur scholar:

> the work itself proceeds from no vain ostentation of learning, or restless thirst of fame. On the contrary, I esteem it but as a trifle; the amusement of my leisure hours; the offspring of winter evenings passed in the country; and the effect of that retirement and inactivity from which I am scarce ever drawn, but with the utmost reluctance.[116]

Notwithstanding the affectation of casual ease which is belied by the scholarship of the copious notes accompanying the two-volume translation, it is significant that Boyle should still feel it possible to present his translations as an entertaining hobby. His dedication also suggests that despite the general confidence of Irish translators in the eighteenth century in the worthiness and high seriousness of their calling, there was still that lingering fear that translation might be a mere 'trifle'. The ambivalence towards translation that is reflected in the treatment and representation of translators over the centuries and in a frequent disregard for their contribution to Irish cultural life are inevitably, on occasion, internalised by translators themselves.

TRANSLATION CONTEXTS

Prefaces to translations in Irish, where they exist, are quick to stress the inadequacy of the translator to the task but are more concerned with the context or content of the translation than with the activity itself. In 1755, Tadhg Ó Conaill completed his translation of the French devotional text known as *La Trompette du Ciel* written by the southern French priest Antoine Yvan (1576–1653) a century earlier. Yvan preached in both French and his native Provençal.[117] Ó Conaill, a calced Carmelite, was prior of the Carmelite monastery in Kinsale when he produced his translation though the monastery as such was in reality a thatched mass-house located in the district. The Penal Laws were applied with greater or lesser severity depending on local circumstances, but the provision of devotional and catechetical works for Catholic clergy and people was problematic. As O'Rahilly notes: 'Many [books] were imported from the Continent at great personal risk, and seizure of such books was a common occurrence in the early eighteenth century.'[118] Translation became a necessity as one of the few means by which the clergy could provide devotional literature to Catholics in the eighteenth century. Priests who had been educated on the continent brought home religious works in foreign languages which they would then translate into Irish for the benefit of their parishioners. Ó Conaill also translated part of the Spanish work *Misterios del Monte Calvario* by Antonio de Guevara, a Bishop of Mondoñedo and court historiographer of Emperor Charles V.[119] In his dedication to James Butler, Archbishop of Cashel, Ó Conaill clearly states the aim of his poor work, his 'lagshaothar', is to remedy the widespread ignorance of the principles of Catholic teaching that is the result of religious oppression. The plight of Irish Catholic clergy and teachers who remain in Ireland is compared to that of the Jews in biblical history.[120]

The Irish translation tradition that Ó Conaill draws on, however, is both Protestant and Catholic. In passages taken from the Old Testament, Ó Conaill quotes the relevant passage in Latin from the Latin Vulgate and uses Bedell's version of the Old Testament for the Irish translations of these passages. In his Dedication, Ó Conaill acknowledges the inspirational work of the Louvain translators and scholars. He decided to embark on the translation:

> ar aithris mornuimhir d'aithreachaibh fiorfhoghllamtha d'Ord naomhtha Naomh Proinsias d'fhág mórán agus do chuir amach do leabhraibh deigh-theagaisg Criostamhla deigriartha i nGaoidheilge nó i dteangan ár máthar.[121]

The extent to which Ó Conaill operates in a particular translation tradition is evident in the very criticisms addressed to Ó Conaill by his twentieth-century editor, Cecile O'Rahilly. The latter praises Ó Conaill for the relative absence of gallicisms in his translation and his fidelity to the content of his French text. There are instances of mistranslations and inaccuracies, but O'Rahilly declares: 'The translator's chief fault . . . is not carelessness or inaccuracy. It is his inveterate habit of unnecessarily expanding his original, embroidering and adorning the simple French sentence so that its forcefulness is lessened not increased.' Ó Conaill's style is overloaded with verbal noun clauses, lists of adjectives and repetitive formulae. O'Rahilly argues that Ó Conaill 'often fritters away the effect of Yvan's French sentence by added epithets, by triplicated verbs, by lists of near-synonyms rendering one French noun, and in general by unnecessary fringes of phrases and expressions'.[122] These criticisms are remarkably similar to those that are directed at a number of medieval translators, and again there is distinct source-text bias in the evaluation of the translation and a failure to take into account the communicative context of the translation in the target language. O'Rahilly does concede that Ó Conaill's translation was to be used primarily for preaching to a people whose educational opportunities had been severely compromised by the Penal Laws. This function is, of course, quite crucial in explaining the translation policy adopted by Ó Conaill. The oral literature with which his audience would be familiar would contain much of the stylistic elaboration that O'Rahilly finds objectionable in the translation. In addition, the ornate language of the bardic period with its inevitable redundancies was part of the Irish literary tradition, so that it is only to be expected that a translator working in the Irish language would be influenced in some way by that tradition. There is a sense in which translators are taken to task by scholars who would prefer that literary history in Irish was other than it was.

Echoing Ó Maonaigh, O'Rahilly argues that Irish religious prose developed more rapidly in the seventeenth century because the large number of translations brought with them new metaphors and the imperative of efficient communication. This contrasted with native 'romantic literature' that remained a hostage to archaisms and stereotyped imagery.[123] There is a contradiction here, in that while O'Rahilly is absolutely right to stress the major contribution made by translation to the development of Irish, he appears to imagine translators as existing in cultural quarantine. For translators like Ó Conaill translating in Ireland, exposure to the native tradition of 'romantic literature' was inevitable and this would be one of the factors, in however attenutated a form, determining target-language acceptability of the translation. The 1762 Irish translation of Thomas à Kempis's *De Imitatione Christi* known as *Toruidheacht na Bhfireun air Lorg Chriosda* bears out the continuing influence of a specific form of language practice in Irish translation. Brian Ó Cuív is critical of the translator of à Kempis, claiming that he often tends to explain rather than translate and, what is more, 'the author of *Toruidheacht* constantly uses two or more words with similar meaning to translate a single word'.[124] Again, there is apparent confusion between semantic and communicative translation. In the case of the latter, the rhetorical impact of the translation is enhanced by an implicit appeal to stylistic conventions that are still present in the target language as happens in the two translations from French.

The close connection between translation and preaching is also apparent in the *Seanmóirí Muighe Nuadhad*. In a colophon to sermons one and five in volume two, Seán Ó Conaire states that he translated them from a collection of French Sermons by Claude Joli (1610–1678), the Bishop of Agen. The Maynooth volumes also include translations of sermons by two famous preachers of seventeenth and early eighteenth-century France, Louis Bourdaloue and Jean-Baptiste Massillon (1663–1742), the translations themselves dating from the eighteenth century.[125] However, it was not only devotional and homiletic material that exercised the competence of translators in Irish. Domhnall Ó Colmáin's satirical poem, *Párliament na mBan* has the women of Ireland gather together to discuss the shortcomings of Irish society (including their own marginalisation in that society), and it draws on a number of translation sources. The first two sessions of the Parliament are largely a translation of one of Erasmus's *Colloquia Familiaria* known as *Senatulus Sive*, and in English as 'The Parliament of Women'.[126] Erasmus had originally written the Colloquies as a textbook to be used by the sons of the rich whom he taught in his impoverished student days in Paris. Ó Colmáin's dedication of the late seventeenth century *Párliament* to his pupil, James Cotter, indicates, as Stewart points out, the pedagogical thrust of the text.[127]

The educational function of translation had, of course, been one of its primary justifications in the Renaissance period. When the Irish translator, John Hodges, in his Preface to his 1705 translation of the Second Satire of Persius into English, claims that 'I likewise think, such Translations [from classical languages] would be very serviceable to young Gentlemen at the Colledge', he is echoing Ó Colmáin's sentiments albeit in a more institutional context.[128] There is for Hodges a predictable tension between scholarship and instruction:

> I am of Opinion, that Authors (I mean the Poets) thus Translated, would save a great deal of time which Youth spends, to little or no purpose, in the long Windings and various Opinions of Voluminous Scholiasts; and that this Way the Thread, and Design of an Author, might be more clearly and easily comprehended by them.[129]

For centuries, translators in Ireland had concentrated mainly on translating foreign material into one of Ireland's languages. In the eighteenth and nineteenth century a new translation phenomenon would emerge, namely translation from Irish into English. This development would have profound implications for the relationship between the two languages on the island, and the change led eventually to fundamental changes in Irish self-perception.

Notes

1. John Dryden, 'To the Earl of Roscommon on his Excellent Essay on Translated Verse', l.41–48 in Wentworth Dillon, *An Essay on Translated Verse (1685) and Horace's Art of Poetry Made English (1684)*, Yorkshire, Scolar Press, 1971.
2. Dryden, l.7–10.
3. Knightly Chetwood, 'To the Earl of Roscomon on his Excellent Poem', l.14–16 in Dillon.
4. Dillon, p. 26.
5. J.E. Caerwyn Williams and Máirín Ní Mhuiríosa, *Traidisiún Liteartha na nGael*, Baile Átha Cliath, An Clóchomhar, 1979, p. 311.
6. Jacques Maurrais, 'Petite histoire des législations linguistiques au Royaume-Uni', *L'Action Nationale*, no. 80, 1990, p. 38.
7. Edmund Spenser, *A View of the Present State of Ireland*, ed., W.L. Renwick, Oxford, Clarendon, 1970, p. 68.
8. Spenser, p. 67.
9. Spenser, p. 75.
10. Spenser, p. 124.
11. Edmund Spenser, pp. 67–68. For other examples of what was perceived to be the malign influence of Irish wet-nurses see Sheila T. Cavanagh '"The fatal destiny of that land": Elizabethan Views of Ireland', Brendan Bradshaw, Andrew Hadfield and Willy Maley, eds., *Representing Ireland: Literature and the Origins of Conflict 1534–1660*, Cambridge University Press, 1993, pp. 123–4.
12. Andrew Hadfield and Willy Maley, 'Irish Representations and English Alternatives' in *Representing Ireland*, p. 9.
13. Raphael Holinshed, ed., *Chronicles of England, Scotland and Ireland*, Johnson, London, vi, 1807–8, p. 4.
14. Holinshed, vi, p. 4.
15. Cited in Edmund Curtis , 'The Spoken Languages of Ireland', *Studies*, vol. 8, 1919, p. 249.
16. For a discussion of the Keating/Stanihurst readings of language and conquest in Irish history see Brendan Bradshaw, 'Geoffrey Keating: Apologist of Irish Ireland' in *Representing Ireland*, pp. 181–184.
17. Richard Stanihurst, *On Ireland's Past: De Rebus in Hibernia Gestis* in Colm Lennon, *The Life of Richard Stanihurst the Dubliner*, Dublin, Irish Academic Press, 1981, pp. 144–145.
18. For a description of twelfth-century views on the alleged barbarity of the native Irish see John Gillingham, 'The English Invasion of Ireland' in *Representing Ireland*, pp. 26–28.

19. John Milton, *The Works of John Milton*, vol.6, New York, Columbia University Press, 1932, p. 245.
20. Norah Carlin, 'Extreme or mainstream? The English Independents and the Cromwellian reconquest of Ireland' in *Representing Ireland*, pp. 214–217.
21. *Irish Statutes 1310–1786*, Dublin, 1786, 124.
22. Nicholas Williams, *I bPrionta i Leabhar*, Baile Átha Cliath, 1986, p. 22.
23. 'If any learned expert should find fault with my expression or writing let him forgive me but my knowledge of Irish is that of the common person [my translation]', cited in Williams, p. 19.
24. Williams, p. 25.
25. Cited in William Bedell Stanford, *Ireland and the Classical Tradition*, Dublin, Allen Figgis, 1976, p. 45.
26. Williams, p. 33.
27. Williams, pp. 30–31.
28. *Tiomna Nuadh ar dTighearna agus ar slanaightheora Iosa Criosd*, ar na tarruing go fírinneach as Gréigis gu Gáoidheilg. Re Uilliam Ó Domhnuill. Ata so ar na chur a gclo a mbaile Atha Cliath, a dtigh Mhaighistir Uilliam Uiséir Chois an Droichid, ré Seón Francke. 1602.
29. H.R. McAdoo, 'The Irish Translations of the Book of Common Prayer', *Éigse*, vol. 2, 1940, p. 253.
30. Uilliam Ó Domhnuill , 'The Epistle Dedicatorie', n.p., *An Tiomna Nuadh*, 1602.
31. Ó Domhnuill, n.p.
32. *Leabhar na nurnaightheadh gcomhchoidchiond agus mheinisdraldachdha na sacrameinteabh, maille le gnathaighthibh agus le hordaigehibh oile, do réir eaglaise na Sagsan.* Ata so ar na chur a gclo a Mbaile atha Cliath, a dtigh Sheon Francke alias Franckton, Priontóir an Ríog an Eirin, 1608.
33. Williams, p. 34.
34. *Leabhar na nurnaightheadh gcomhchoidchiond*, n.p.
35. *Leabhar na nurnaightheadh gcomhchoidchiond*, n.p.
36. E.S. Shuckburgh, *Two Biographies of William Bedell*, Cambridge University Press, 1902; Gilbert Burnet, *The Life of William Bedell, bishop of Kilmore*, London, 1685, see also *Dictionary of National Biography* 105–108.
37. Williams, p. 54.
38. Cited in Williams, p. 109.
39. Brendan Bradshaw, 'Sword, Word and Strategy in the Reformation in Ireland', *Historical Journal*, vol. 21, 1978, p. 502.
40. John Richardson, 'The Dedication', *The Church Catechism Explained by Way of Question and Answer; And Confirm'd by Scripture Proofs*: Collected by John Lewis, Minister of Margate in Kent. And Render'd into Irish by JOHN RICHARDSON Minister of Belturbet in Ireland, Chaplain to His Grace James Duke of Ormond, and St. George Lord Bishop of Clocher, 1712, pp. iii–iv.
41. John Richardson, 'The Dedication', *Seanmora ar na Priom Phoncibh na Chreideamh ar na Ttaruing go Gaidhlig, agus ar na Ccur a Ccló a Lunnduin Tre Ebhlin Everingham. SERMONS upon the Principal Points of Religion*, Translated into Irish. London, Printed by Elinor Everingham, 1711, pp. iv–v.

42. Richardson, *Seanmora*, p. vii.

43. André Lefevere, *Translation, Rewriting and the Manipulation of Literary Fame*, Routledge, London, 1992, p. 15.

44. 'Texts were translated into Irish in Bohemia, Belgium, France, Spain and Italy, [my translation], Cainneach Ó Maonaigh, 'Scríbhneoirí Gaeilge an Seachtú hAois Déag', *Studia Hibernica*, vol. 2, 1962, p. 204.

45. See Brendan Jennings, 'The Irish Franciscans in Prague', *Studies*, no. 28, 1939, pp. 210–222.

46. Pádraig Ó Súilleabháin, ed., *Buaidh na Neamhchroiche*, Institiúid Ard Léinn Bhaile Átha Cliath, 1972.

47. Anselm Ó Fachtna, '"An Bheatha Chrábhaidh" agus "An Bheatha Dhiaga"', *Éigse*, vol. 10, 1961–63, pp. 89–95. Ó Fachtna claims, however, that we cannot be absolutely sure in our attribution of *An Bheatha Chrábhaidh* to Ua Raghallaigh.

48. Anselm Ó Fachtna, ed., *An Bheatha Dhiaga nó an tSlighe Ríoghdha*, Institiúid Ardléinn Bhaile Átha Cliath, 1967, p. xi.

49. In the chronicle of the Franciscan Order, the purchase of the printing press is recorded as follows: 'Pro communi Regni Hiberniae et animarum salute Hibernici idiomatis proprios characteres et impressionem, antea nunquam ob praedominantem Hereticam potestatem Catholicus ejus Regni permissum, anno 1611 erexit et aliquot ejusdem idiomatis libros fidelium utilitati impressit', Brendan Jennings, ed., 'Brevis Synopsis Provinciae Hiberniae', *Analecta Hiberniae*, 6, 1934, p. 43.

50. 'As the Catholic Church has a prayer book the heretics of Ireland saw to it that they had their own kind of prayer book called the Common Book and it is not a bad name if you added the word "false" to it. As this was not done, it is no misnomer to call it the Book of the Hell of Heretics. This book and a lot of the Bible were translated into Irish and they were written in the fullness of error',[my translation], Cainneach Ó Maonaigh, ed., *Scáthán Shacramuinte na hAithridhe*, Báile Átha Cliath, Institiúid Ardléinn Bhaile Átha Cliath, 1952, p. 5.

51. Williams, p. 41 and pp. 130–31.

52. Tomás Ó Cléirigh, *Aodh Mac Aingil agus an Scoil Nua-Ghaeilge i Lobháin*, Baile Átha Cliath, An Gúm, 1985, pp. 34–40.

53. Brian Ó Cuív, 'Flaithrí Ó Maolchonaire's Catechism of Christian Doctrine', *Celtica*, vol. 1, 1950, pp. 161–206.

54. Flaithrí Ó Maolchonaire, *Desiderius*, Thomas F. O'Rahilly, ed., Dublin, Stationery Office, 1941.

55. Seán Ua Súilleabháin, 'Sgáthán an Chrábhaidh: Foinsí an Aistriúcháin', *Éigse*, vol. 24, 1990, pp. 26–36.

56. 'Do mheasairme agus do mheasadar daoine eile . . . go mba tarbhach a chor a nGaoidheilg do thabhairt shoillsi don chuid dár nách tuigead theangtha eile, ar na neithibh naomhtha theagaisgeas. Agas gé nách fuil acfainn ná iomadumhlacht san nGaoidheilg aguinn, agus nach mó atáimuid, ó aois mhic fhoghluma anuas, a ngar do na seinleabhraibh, acht imchian uathu féin agus ón aois ealadhna ó a bhfuighimís ar sáith de sheanfhoclaibh snasdha, nách biadh ródhorcha agus do badh tarbhach do tharraing chum gnáthaighthe agus ó a mbeith an teanga saidhbhir so-gabáhla ar na neithibh maithi atá sna teangthaibh eile, agus ó a mbeith an labhairt líomhtha – ar a

shon sin má thig linn amháin, maille ré congnamh an Choimdheadh na neithi-se do chur síos go soilléir sothuisgi, saoilmíd go madh lia do na daoinibh deaghnaitheacha, deisgréideacho ghuidfeas oruinn ar son ár saothair, iná bhias ag iarroidh toibhéimi do thbhairt dár ndíthcheall ar son simplidheachta na sstíli in ar sgríobhamar go sonnradhach chum leasa na ndaoine simplidhe, nach foil géarchúiseach i nduibheagán na Gaoidhilge', Ó Maolchonaire, *Desiderius*, p. 1.

57. 'Our aim in writing is not to teach Irish but repentance and it is enough for us if this is understood even if our Irish is not correct', [my translation], Mac Aingil, *Scáthán*, p. 5.

58. 'European languages bringing new ideas into Irish and new terms and idioms to express them with the result that writing in Irish is reinvigorated. A lot of the old rules are cast off that had inhibited and blocked the development of the language in both prose and poetry', [my translation], Ó Maonaigh, p. 206.

59. J.F. O'Doherty, *Reflex Facs. iv, The 'Cathecismus' of Theobald Stapleton*, 1945, 31.

60. Ó Maonaigh, p. 201.

61. Ó Maonaigh, p. 186.

62. Pádraig Ó Súilleabháin, ed., *Rialachas San Froinsias*, Insitiúid Ard Léinn Bhaile Átha Cliath, 1953, p. xii.

63. 'Perhaps, the reason behind the archaism is that the translator may have tried in this life of Saint Francis to imitate the lives of the Irish saints so that it would have a native shape and feel about it', [my translation], Pádraig Ó Súilleabháin, ed, *Beatha San Froinsias*, Institiúid Ard Léinn Bhaile Átha Cliath, 1957, p. XLIV.

64. F.W. O'Connell and R.M. Henry, eds., *An Irish Corpus Astronomiae*, London, David Nutt, 1915, pp. xxii–xxvii.

65. Cainneach Ó Maonaigh, p. 199. The manuscript references are RIA MS 23 M3, pp. 1–56, 57–116, 23 M 10, pp. 121–86. Also TCD H.I. 10 f. 46.

66. Eleanor Knott, 'An Irish Seventeenth-Century Translation of the Rule of St. Clare', *Ériu*, vol. 15, 1948, pp. 1–187.

67. The material translated by Mac Fhir Bhisigh comprised of the following: *The Testament and Benediction of St. Clare; The Bull of Innocent IV concerning a grant by Gregory IX; Declarations and Constitutions of St. Colette, preceded by 2 letters addressed to Colette by Br. William Cassal, Minister-General of the Order of Friars Minor; An Exhortation by Fr. Benignus for the Better observance of these constitutions; The Obligation of the Rule of St. Clare as regards mortal sin; Praise of the Rule; An Examen of conscience for the religious; The 12 evils which come by venial sin; 9 ways by which we participate in the sins of others; 12 fruits of the Blessed Sacrament; 12 evangelical counsels; Malediction of St. Francis.*

68. Knott, p. 154. Knott's translation of the passage cited is: 'but from people's lack of knowledge of it, so that they find it easier to understand foreign words than the genuine Irish ones'.

69. Cited in Pádraig de Brún, 'A Seventeenth-Century Translation of the First Psalm', *Éigse*, vol. 17, 1977–9, p. 64.

70. *Dictionary of National Biography*, pp. 908–911.

71. *Dictionary of National Biography*, pp. 1063–64.

72. William Smith Clark, *The Early Irish Stage: The Beginnings to 1720*, Oxford, Clarendon, 1955, p. 64.

73. Clark, p. 67.
74. Williams, p. 108.
75. Edward Wetenhall, 'The Dedication', *The Wish being the Tenth Satire of Juvenal*. Periphrastically rendered in Pindarick Verse By a Person, sometimes Fellow of Trin. Col. DUBLIN, Printed by Benjamin Looke, Printer to the King's Most Excellent Majesty, n.p.
76. Theo Hermans, 'Images of Translation: Metaphor and Imagery in the Renaissance Discourse on Translation' in Theo Hermans, ed., *The Manipulation of Literature: Studies in Literary Translation*, London, Croom Helm, 1985, p. 106.
77. Ellis Walker, 'Epistle Dedicatory', *Epicteti Enchiridion* Made English in a Poetical Paraphrase. London, Printed by Ben. Griffin, for Sam Keble, and are to be sold at the Great Turks-Head in Fleet Street over against Fetter-Lane-End, 1692, n.p.
78. Will Peirse, 'To the Author on his Poetical Version of Epictetus his Manual' in Ellis Walker, n.p.
79. Dillon, p. 24.
80. Ezekiel Bristed, 'Acrostick on the ingenious Translator Mr. E.W.', in Ellis Walker, n.p.
81. Dillon, p. 23.
82. *Q. Horatii Flacci de Arte Poetica Liber ad Pisones*. Horace's Treatise Concerning the Art of Poetry together with Notes Critical, Historical and Poetical by the Earl of Roscommon. Dublin: Printed for William Heatly, Bookseller at the Bible and Dove on College Green, 1733.
83. Hermans, p. 115.
84. 'Advertisement', *A New Version of the Psalms of David*, Fitted to the TUNES used in CHURCHES by N. Tate and N. Brady. London. Printed by M. Clark for the Company of Stationers. 1696, n.p.
85. See *Dictionary of National Biography*, pp. 379–380, entry for Nahum Tate.
86. *The Satyrs of Persius*. Translated into English by Thomas Sheridan, D.D. Dublin. Printed by George Grierson, at the Two-Bibles in Essex-Street, 1728.
87. Dillon, pp. 14–15.
88. Dillon, p. 4.
89. Monck Mason, 1843, p. 286.
90. *Dictionary of National Biography*, p. 86.
91. Alfred Webb, *A Compendium of Irish Biography*, Dublin, Gill & Son, 1878, p. 475.
92. Thomas Sheridan, 'Preface', *Homer's Battle of the Frogs and Mice with the Remarks of Zolius*. To which is Prefix'd, The LIFE of the said Zolius. Printed for BERNARD LINTOT, between the Temple-Gates. 1727, n.p.
93. Sheridan, 'The Preface', *Homer's Battle*, n.p.
94. Sheridan, 'The Preface', *Homer's Battle*.
95. Sheridan, 'The Preface', *Homer's Battle*.
96. Sheridan, 'The Preface', *Homer's Battle*.
97. *The Institutio Oratoria of Quintillian*, vol. iv, trans. H.E. Butler. London, Heinemann, 1922, pp. 79–81.
98. *Institutio Oratoria*, n.p.

99. Hermans, p. 107.

100. Sheridan uses the metaphor in a more conventional fashion in his Dedication to Lady Cartaret that is prefixed to his translation of of Sophocles's *Philoctetes*: 'The Translation I have made is as close as the Propriety of our Language will admit, and your Ladyship will observe in it at least some traces of the Author's Genius. But as the lowest Painter in drawing Your Ladyship's Picture would be able to discover, that he at least designed to represent something extraordinary, and the best must need fall infinitely short of the Original; so I cannot but hope that Your Ladyship will observe in this Translation some faint Lineaments of the Author's great Genius, superior to that of all modern Tragedians.' Thomas Sheridan, 'Dedication', *The Philoctetes of Sophocles*. Translated from the Greek. Dublin. Printed by J. Hyde and E. Dobson, for R. Owens, Bookseller in Skinner-Row, 1725, n.p.

101. *Tiomna Nuadh*, n.p.

102. Sheridan, 'The Preface', *Homer's Battle of the Frogs*, n.p.

103. *The Tragedies of Sophocles from the Greek*; by Thomas Francklin, M.A. Fellow of Trinity College and Greek Professor in the University of Cambridge. In two volumes. Dublin. Printed by W. Sleater, No 51, Castle-Street, 1778.

104. Arthur Murphy, 'An Essay on the Life and Genius of Tacitus', p. xxxvi in *The Works of Cornelius Tacitus*; by Arthur Murphy, Esq. with an Essay on the Life and Genius of Tacitus; notes supplements and maps. In four volumes. London: Printed for G.G.J. and J. Robinson, Paternoster-Row, 1793.

105. See Roger Zuber, *Les 'Belles Infidèles' et la formation du goût classique*, Paris, Armand Colin, 1968.

106. Cited in Robert Larose, *Théories contemporaines de la traduction*, Québec, Presses de l'université du Québec, 1989, p. 4.

107. Murphy, *Tacitus*, pp. xxxvi–xxxvii.

108. John Dryden, 'On Translation', Rainer Schulte and John Biguenet, eds., *Theories of Translation*, Chicago, University of Chicago Press, 1992, p. 26.

109. Murphy, p. xl.

110. 'Dedication', Murphy, p. vi.

111. Philip Francis, 'The Preface', p. ii in *A Poetical Translation of the works of Horace*, with the Original Text and Critical Notes Collected from his best Latin and French Commentators by the Rev'd Mr. Philip Francis, vol. 1, A. Millar, London, 1749.

112. Francis, p. viii.

113. Kelly, p. 48.

114. Francis, p. vii.

115. Francis, p. xi.

116. John Boyle, 'The Dedication', p. lxxi, *The Letters of Pliny the Younger with Observations on Each Letter and an Essay on Pliny's Life*. Addresses to Charles, Lord Boyle by John, Earl of Orrery. Vol. 1. George Faulkner, Dublin, 1751.

117. Cecile O'Rahilly, ed., *Trompa na bhFlaitheas*, Dublin Institute for Advanced Studies, 1955, p. ix–x.

118. O'Rahilly, p. xii.

119. Antonio de Guevara, *Misterios del Monte Calvario*, trans. Tadhg Ó Conaill, 1755. The translation which dates from 1755 is in RIA 24 C 10.

120. 'An beagán do gach drong diobhso do fágbhag san / ríoghacht fá annródh, do bheith fá a ní bhus mó d'annsmacht, do chruadhtan, do mhoghsuine agus do sglabhadhacht ag na heirceidhibh reamhráidte ná do bhí Clann *Israel* faoi *Shalmanasar* nó an chine Iudaighe faoi *Nabuchodonozar*, ar mhodh nch féidir, faoi phéin báis, priosúntacht no dibiorrtha, nuimhir aco do theacht i bhfochair a chéile ar aonbhall chum fundaimeint a gcreidimh agus slighe a slanaigthe do chlosibid.', *Misterios*, pp. 2–3.

121. 'in imitation of the large number of the most learned fathers of the holy Order of Saint Francis who left us a lot and who published well-ordered books of good Christian teaching in Irish or our mother tongue [my translation]', *Misterios*, p. 3.

122. *Misterios*, p. xv.

123. *Misterios*, p. xxii.

124. Brian Ó Cuív, 'Irish Translations of Thomas à Kempis's *De Imitatione Christi*', *Celtica*, vol. 2, 1954, p. 271. There is some debate as to who is the author of the 1762 translation: see Séamus P. Ó Mórdha, 'Údar *Tonuidheacht na bhFireun air Lorg Chriosda*', *Studia Hibernica*, vol. 3, 1963, pp. 155–72; Anselm Faulkner, '*Tónuidheacht na bhFireun air Lorg Chríosda* (1762): The Translator', *Éigse*, vol. 15, 1973–74, pp. 303–11.

125. Pádraig Ó Súilleabháin, 'Varia', *Éigse*, vol. 9, 1958–61, pp. 233–242. For evidence of translation in Ulster sermons of the eighteenth century see Cainneach Ó Maonaigh, ed, *Seanmónta Chúige Uladh*, Institiúid Ard-Léinn Bhaile Átha Cliath, 1965.

126. James Stewart, 'Párliament na mBan', *Celtica*, vol. 7, 1966, p. 135.

127. Stewart, p. 140.

128. John Hodges, 'The Preface to the Reader', *The Second Satir of Aulus Persius Flaccus* grammatically Construed and Englished. By J.H. A.M. Dublin: Printed for the Author, and Sold by J. Ware Book-Seller in High-Street over against St. Michael's Church, 1705, n.p.

129. Hodges, n.p.

3

DIGGING UP THE PAST

IN 1717, HUGH MAC CURTIN published *A Brief Discourse in Vindication of the Antiquity of Ireland*. The *Discourse* was a response to the markedly partisan view of Irish history offered in *Hibernia Anglicana* (1689), by Sir Richard Cox, a former Chancellor of Ireland. Mac Curtin was known in Irish as Aodh Buí Mac Cruitín and came from a distinguished bardic family in County Clare. He came to Dublin around 1700 and was actively involved in scribal and translation work prior to the publication of the *Discourse*.[1] In the Preface Mac Curtin cites as his principal motive for going into print the malice and hatred towards the ancient inhabitants of Ireland and their posterity in the accounts of 'foreign writers':

> This is the Reason that moves me to give the following Account of the Antient Irish before the year above-mentioned. And tho' I confess myself not sufficient to write correctly in the English language, yet I promise my self the Favour of all serious indifferent Readers, that would value Truth in a plain poor dress; more than the fabulous Narrations of some Foreign Writers.[2]

LANGUAGE CHOICE, FACTS AND MEDIATION

Mac Curtin's readers were certainly not 'indifferent' in the modern sense of the adjective and he was subsequently imprisoned, though it is unclear whether his imprisonment was the direct result of his *Discourse* or of its intended publication or of a caustic poem on Cox that was attributed to him.[3] On his release from prison, Mac Curtin went to the continent, where in 1728 his *The Elements of the Irish Language, Grammatically Explained in English* was published in Louvain. Four years later, in collaboration with Conchubhar Ó Beaglaioch, he published an English–Irish dictionary. Mac Curtin's prefatory remarks signal the decisive shift in translation patterns in Ireland. In previous centuries, translations had largely been into Irish, with increasing numbers of translations into English appearing in the latter half of the seventeenth century. The eighteenth century opens with an admission by one of the most esteemed Gaelic scholars of the period that though he felt himself not 'sufficient to write correctly in the English language', he would have to do so in order to vindicate the reputation of his compatriots. His Irish grammar is explained in English, whereas this was not the case with the earlier Franciscan grammar of Irish from Louvain.[4] In his *Grammatica Anglo-Hibernica*, written in 1713, Francis Walsh claims in the Preface that 'I have done it [the grammar] in English, now the most common and most prevailing Language with the learned and unlearned of our Country.'[5] Walsh's claim is exaggerated in a country that was still substantially Irish-speaking, particularly in the case of the 'unlearned'. However, his choice of language, like Mac Curtin's, points to the linguistic consequences of political defeat for the native Irish.

The language of the public domain, of power and intellectual influence, was English. In translation terms, this implied that the major target language, the language of public, prestigious and politically effective translation, was English. As we shall see, there were translations into Irish, but they were dwarfed by the number of translations into English from Irish. The latter pointed to the core predicament of translators from Irish into English in the eighteenth and nineteenth centuries. In order to counter erroneous, Anglocentric views of Irish history and literature, it was felt necessary to demonstrate, using the evidence of Irish texts, that certain received notions with respect to Irish culture were based on misrepresentation and falsehoods. The language of public debate under the new dispensation was English and the evidence, therefore, had to be made available in English. A paradoxical consequence of translation activity in this colonial context was that the scholars and translators who were most to the fore in defending the intrinsic value of native Irish language and culture made a significant contribution, through translation, to the strengthening of the English language in Ireland and to the marginalisation of Irish in the public life of the country. Eric Cheyfitz argues that 'at the heart of every imperial fiction (the heart of darkness) there is a fiction of translation'.[6] The colonial Other is translated into terms of the imperial Self, with the net result of alienation for the colonised and a fiction of understanding for the coloniser.

The translators, however, were ultimately hostages to circumstance. In addition to the political and cultural efficacy of translation into English, there were the economic constraints of patronage. When patrons of Gaelic scholarship in the eighteenth century such as Anthony Raymond, John Stearne and Francis Stoughton Sullivan sought translations, they wanted them in English. Sometimes, as in the case of Raymond, the patron himself produced English translations, including a translation of much of Geoffrey Keating's *Foras Feasa ar Éirinn*.[7] The choice of Keating's work is significant, and the controversy surrounding Dermot O'Connor's translation of the work printed in 1723 provides a telling example of the political importance attached to translation in the Ireland of the period. Séathrún Céitinn, or Geoffrey Keating as he was known in English, was born in County Tipperary in 1580. He later went to Bordeaux, where he took a Doctorate in Divinity, but returned to Ireland to work on his major history of Ireland from the earliest times to the English conquest. In his work, he specifically attacks the writings of English commentators on Ireland. As Bradshaw points out, Keating addresses the contemporary concerns of the seventeenth-century Irish Catholic community in the context of a tradition of Counter-Reformation historical scholarship.[8]

The first translation of the *Foras Feasa* was begun as early as 1635 by Micheal Kearney of Ballyloskey in County Tipperary and was completed around 1688. John Lynch, the author of *Cambrensis Eversus*, translated Keating's text into Latin in France some time before 1674. In 1688, Timothy Roe O'Connor made a translation for Lord Orrery. These were all manuscript translations. In November 1721, Dermot O'Connor issued formal printed proposals for the publication of his translation of Keating's work and he duly attracted 300 subscribers for the London edition and 400 for the Dublin edition.[9] O'Connor appears to have based his translation on a manuscript copy of the *Foras Feasa* that he made for Maurice O'Connor, a wealthy London barrister.[10] O'Connor had previously worked as secretary to Anthony Raymond, who, as we noted, was making his own translation of Keating's work. Raymond was furious at the publication of O'Connor's translation, and was one of its most persistent and outspoken critics. Before considering the O'Connor translation controversy in more detail, however, it is worth examining the different and often conflicting motives that led to such intense pressure to translate Keating's historical writings.

The late seventeenth century saw the rise in England of a new historiography which sought to emulate the spectacular success of the physical sciences through the adoption of experimental methods. The new thinking eschewed the authority of the ancients in favour of scrupulous analysis of the 'facts' of history as found in documentary evidence. As Alan Harrison observes, 'In Éirinn is dócha gur spreag an sprid seo príomhscoláirí an *Dublin Philosophical Society* – leithéidí Narcissus Marsh, William King, Muintir Molyneux, John Madden agus John Stearne – le bunábhar faoi stair na hÉireann a bhailiú.'[11] Thus, though the new generation of scholars and patrons, who were almost exclusively members of the Protestant Ascendancy, would not be politically sympathetic to Keating's basic ideological stance in *Foras Feasa*, the interests of the new historical approach demanded that such an important documentary source not be overlooked. In eighteenth-century Dublin, there was no shortage of Gaelic scholars and translators to assist the new historians in their task. Muiris Ó Nuabha, Seán Ó Neachtain, Tadhg Ó Neachtain, Risteard Tiobar, Seán Ó Súilleabháin, Cathal Ó Conchubhair, Stiabhna Rís, Aodh Ó Dálaigh and Cathal Ó Luinín are just some of the scholars who were involved in scribal and translation work in the period. Unlike their patrons, they were usually Catholic, and if their religion was different so also were their motives in the early half of the eighteenth century.

For these translators, translating texts from Irish was further proof of the antiquity and distinction of the Gaelic tradition. The translation of historical and other materials was, for them, a direct challenge to the cruder caricatures of the seventeenth century with the presentation of the Irish as savage, uncivilised and uncouth. The notion that the Irish were bereft of learning and culture, thereby conferring superiority on the language and traditions of the conqueror, was challenged by Mac Curtin, among others, in his *Discourse*. From an economic point of view, of course, the native translators also benefited from this happy coincidence of motives. Harrison says of the Gaelic scholars:

> Bhíodh dúil faoi leith acu sna tuairiscí faoina sinsireacht a bhíodh le fáil i láimhscríbhínní cáiliúla na Gaeilge agus bhídís ar a ndícheall ag iarraidh teacht ar a leithéidí chun iad a chruinniú le chéile agus a chóipeáil. Ar ndóigh, ba fhreagairt nádúrtha ag Gaeil chloíte iarracht a dhéanamh ar uaisleacht, cráifeacht, léann agus sibhiltiacht a gcine a chruthú agus a dhearbhú as foinsí den chineál sin. Thuigeadar, freisin, go raibh a spéis sa stair ag teacht le himeachtaí árseolaíochta scoláirí Protastúnacha agus go mbeidís siúd sásta díol as lámhscríbhínní, agus as cóipeáil, aistriúchán agus míniú téacsanna stairiúla na Gaeilge.[12]

The differing perceptions of the translator, as a field-worker in the scholarly dig of antiquarianism or as the champion of an imperilled culture, have profound implications for the political appropriation of translated literature in the nineteenth century.

To some extent, it can be argued that precisely because the translators of the eighteenth century were *between* two cultures they would become increasingly aware of the specificity of their own indigenous culture, identity feeding on difference. When Diarmaid Ó Catháin notes that the history of the earlier part of the eighteenth century in Ireland needs to be revised because contact between the English-language and Irish-language traditions was much greater than previously thought, he draws particular attention to 'these shadowy figures, scholars from the Gaelic tradition earning their living within English-language culture'.[13] The choice of adjective is significant. 'Shadowy' suggests the near-invisibility of the translator, a retiring background figure, the silent mediator between the two competing cultures. The word also hints at the suspect, the vague, the underhand, and this implication can be variously interpreted. Translators could be seen as accelerating the decay of the language through making translations available and therefore dispensing with the need to learn the language in the first place. Furthermore, translators are never as innocent as they appear, and their motives can differ radically from those of their clients or sections of their target audience. Like the despised cosmopolitan of anti-semitic rhetoric, translators may indeed find themselves objects of suspicion because they are not wholly within one culture but occupy a space between cultures.

DERMOT O'CONNOR AND TRANSLATION POLITICS

This is the space in which we find Dermot O'Connor, who worked in both Dublin and London and was equally at ease in Irish and English. The appearance of his *General History of Ireland* provoked considerable controversy, the main critics being Anthony Raymond and Thomas O'Sullevane. Anthony Raymond was a Church of Ireland clergyman, a friend of Jonathan Swift, Thomas Sheridan and many of the Gaelic scholars living in Dublin at the time, who took a keen interest in Irish language and history. Thomas O'Sullevane was an Irishman living in London who had a reputation as an Irish language scholar.[14] O'Sullevane launched his attack on O'Connor's translation even before it appeared. In his preface to *The Memoirs of the Right Honorable the Marquis of Clanricarde* (1722), he dismisses Keating's work as a 'heap of insipid, ill-digested Fables' and claims that O'Connor has added material to the translation that was not in the source text: 'It is very strange, it being only to be translated by him [O'Connor], that he would give himself the Liberty to add to, or make any variation from the Original.'[15] O'Sullevane further alleges that the translator is merely a front-man for the devious heresies of the Donegal thinker and religious polemicist, John Toland:

> But the truth is, his Name is only made use of for a flourish, or outward shew, whilst others behind the Curtain are hard at Work, in licking this ill-born cub into some Shape, under the Direction of a certain Gentleman, who has already render'd himself famous by new Schemes of Doctrine and Religion.[16]

John Toland was a native Irish speaker and did, in fact, spend some time with the Irish Franciscans in Prague. His writings on natural religion, deism and pantheism caused considerable offence to more orthodox Christians in the eighteenth century.[17] O'Sullevane's objections are two-fold. Firstly, a printed translation gives credence to a view of history that he feels to be discredited. Implicit in his attack is the power of translation, the sense that translated texts can markedly alter or determine the reception of historical truth. Secondly, O'Sullevane's critique clearly demonstrates the rejection of a medieval notion of translation according to which the translator is at liberty to add or subtract material as s/he sees fit. The translator's task in matters of prose translation of historical material is one of scrupulous fidelity, a notion that would reach its apotheosis in the scholarly translations of Celtic scholars in the late nineteenth century. It is significant that O'Sullevane sees all manner of tendentious possibility in translation, the translator ghosted by the deist heretic, and denies it the innocence of transparency. O'Connor responded in detail to O'Sullevane's criticisms in his preface. Most notably, he claimed that 'It is certain that the Abilities of this Prefacer [O'Sullevane] in the Irish Tongue, extends no further than the Knowledge of a School Boy and a small acquaintance with the modern Characters of that Language.'[18]

Raymond, for his part, publicly criticised O'Connor's translation by way of a pamphlet, an open letter and a notice that he had inserted in the *Dublin Mercury* on the 13 July 1723.[19] He repeated O'Sullevane's charges of Toland's involvement in the translation and was similarly disparaging in his presentation of Keating's work. The latter feature of Raymond's argument is curious in that he himself expended a great deal of time and energy on his own translation of *Foras Feasa*, which was never published. Raymond, unlike O'Sullevane, dwells on the translation errors in his *Account of Dr Keting's History of Ireland, And the Translation of it by Dermot O Connor. Taken out of a Dissertation prefixed to the Memoirs of the Marquis of Clanricard lately published in London. With some specimens of the said History and Translation.* In both the first and second sections of the pamphlet, Raymond offers examples of O'Connor's erroneous translations and concludes that the translator had neither the learning nor the linguistic competence to undertake his task.[20] Raymond and O'Sullevane were successful in discrediting O'Connor's translation among scholars, but the translation itself was a publishing success and went through many editions. The extent of the animosity that the translation gave rise to can be judged from a diary entry by Thomas Hearne, a librarian in the Bodleian in Oxford. The entry is for the 5 April 1726:

> Mr. Scot told me Mr. Oconner's Translation of Dr. Keting's History of Ireland is a most horrid silly Performance, that Oconner is a most sad Blockhead, & wholly ignorant of all Learning, that he knows nothing of the old Irish History or Language, &, indeed that he is altogether unqualify'd for any such Undertaking . . . Oconner, it seems, hath been in prison, & his nose is eat of with the Pox, w[ch] he got by having two wives together, both it seems still living. This Oconner, therefore, by what I learn, is an Horrid Villain.[21]

Aside from questions of professional jealousy (both Raymond and O'Sullevane were working on histories of Ireland), the O'Connor translation controversy highlights trends in translation practice that will continue to grow in importance throughout the eighteenth and nineteenth centuries. Firstly, the direction of the O'Connor translation was Irish–English. Secondly, translation was implicitly political. Much of the controversy centred on whether Keating's historical writings had a valid historical basis. If they did, then the English conquest of the seventeenth century would be viewed as a negative development. If they did not, and were presented as hopelessly contaminated by fable and romance, it was possible to offer more sympathetic accounts of English involvement in Irish affairs. Thirdly, philological competence came to be seen as the yardstick of translation success or faliure.

GENEALOGY, THE CELTIC REVIVAL AND THE ELDER SISTER

The compilation of genealogies was an aspect of translation history in the eighteenth century that linked the economic self-interest of translators to the search for legitimacy on the part of the new Ascendancy class. In the seventeenth century, Sir George Carew, at one time President of Munster, noted for his military ferocity and his generally low opinion of the native Irish, nonetheless took an interest in collecting Irish manuscripts and constructing pedigrees for Irish families.[22] O'Connor's inclusion of genealogical and heraldic material in his translation was calculated to appeal to the desire of the new ruling class to acquire the imprimatur of antiquity through ingenious genealogies produced by the country's remaining Gaelic scholars. If flattering genealogies were a useful addition to the symbolic capital of the new Ascendancy, their function was little different from that of genealogy under the old Gaelic order, that of legitimising the right to power and possession. The principal difference in the eighteenth century lay in the perceived need to translate the documents that recorded the history of earlier ages.

Two events in the mid-eighteenth century combined to give an important fillip to translation activity in Ireland. The first was the enormous success enjoyed by the poem, 'The Bard' by Thomas Gray, based on an erroneous account of a massacre of Welsh poets by Edward I of England and published in 1757. The second event was the publication by James Macpherson of his *Fragments of Ancient Poetry Collected in the Highlands of Scotland and translated from the Gaelic or Erse Language* in 1760. Macpherson's poems turned out later to be apocryphal, but the publication was an instant success and along with Gray's poem was hugely influential in creating a 'Celtic Revival' in Britain in the 1750s and 1760s.[23] Macpherson's denigration of the Irish tradition, claiming that the Fenian cycle was a uniquely Scottish phenomenon, caused considerable upset in Ireland and had the effect of drawing the attention of English speakers to literature in Irish – if only to disprove the claims of Macpherson. The interest in contesting Macpherson's claims stemmed from a growing consciousness among sections of the Anglo-Irish Ascendancy of their cultural and economic separateness from their English counterparts. The perception of an internal threat was lessened by Ireland's inactivity during the 1715 and 1745 Scottish rebellions, and Protestant interest in the Irish language was also stimulated by work in comparative linguistics that was rooted in a tradition of study of the vernacular bible.[24] In 1782, the first volume of translations of Irish poetry in English appeared under the sober title, *Poems translated from the Irish Language into English*. The translations were by Charles Henry Wilson but there is no surviving copy of the work.[25] The first substantial body of widely available translated work did not appear in Ireland, however, until 1789. The *Reliques of Irish Poetry*, a selection of verse translations from Irish by Charlotte Brooke, is the first major translation work by an Irish woman translator that has come down to us. (At the beginning of the eighteenth century in Madrid, there was a large volume of writings in Irish on religious and historical topics by an Irish nun, Bonaventúr de Brún, but the manuscript has disappeared, so it is not possible to ascertain whether it contained copies of original texts or translations.[26]) Brooke is conscious of her entry into a domain that has been an exclusively male preserve. In her Preface to the *Reliques*, she quotes Sylvester O'Halloran on the importance of achievements in arms and the arts for the development of nationhood, and continues:

> But where, alas, is this thirst for national glory? when a subject of such importance is permitted to a pen like mine! Why does not some *son of Anax* in genius step forward, and boldly throw his gauntlet to Prejudice, the avowed and approved champion of his country's lovely muse?[27]

She insists on the 'limited circle of my knowledge' and compares herself unfavourably to O'Connor, O'Halloran and Vallancey, the antiquarians who helped her in her work: 'My comparatively feeble hand aspires only (like the ladies of ancient Rome) to strew flowers in the paths of these laurelled champions of my country.'[28] Brooke informs the reader that in her translations she is 'now, with extreme diffidence, presenting, for the first time, her literary face to the world'.[29] Protestations of inadequacy and humility were, of course, a standard feature of many translation prefaces in the sixteenth, seventeenth and eighteenth centuries, but Brooke is obviously foregrounding stereotypical female traits of weakness, shyness and what she presents as an avowed sense of inferiority to male achievement. In an illuminating passage where she calls for the reconciliation of Ireland and Britain through mutual understanding, Brooke questions her very right to speak and is ever-conscious of the patriarchal figure who, even dead, must not be made to feel threatened in any way by her ambition as literary translator:

> Let them [Britain and Ireland] come – but will they answer to a voice like mine? Will they rather not depute some favoured pen, to chide me back to

the shade whence I have been allured, and where, perhaps, I ought to have remained in respect to the memory and superior genius of a father – it avails not to say how dear! – But my feeble efforts presume not to emulate, – and they cannot injure his fame.[30]

Brooke's trepidation on entering the house of translated language is understandable when one considers the previous paucity of women translators in Irish translation history in both languages (and, indeed, this major under-representation would continue right throughout the nineteenth century). Brooke not only draws attention to the difficulty of translating herself into a traditionally male role but she is also quick to stress the political implications of her work. Her translations are conciliatory, being driven by the fraternal spirit of a Romanticism that will convince readers in Ireland and Britain of their shared humanity:

> As yet we are too little known to our noble neighbour of Britain; were we better acquainted, we should be better friends. The British muse is not yet informed that she has an elder sister in this isle; let us then introduce them to each other! Together let them walk abroad from their bowers, sweet ambassadresses of cordial union.[31]

Brooke's patriotism is not separatist. She does not see her belief in a political United Kingdom as irreconcilable with her Irish cultural patriotism. Translation characterises that harmonious and mutually beneficial exchange which she believes should obtain betwen the two islands. Translations from Irish will attest to the antiquity of Irish culture (Ireland is the 'elder sister') and to its degree of civility, contrary to the assertions of prejudiced critics. The English language will, in turn, benefit from a new voice and range of expressive possibility. Translation is both a means and a metaphor for mutual understanding and enrichment. The attributes of metaphor, similitude and difference ground Brooke's politics. Ireland is different, and she takes pride in this difference, but her unionism rests in a desire for similitude, the wish to see the emergence of a 'cordial union'. Translation, which is in essence metaphorical – making the foreign (difference) familiar (similitude) – is a perfect vehicle for Brooke's dual allegiance. The events of ten years later, when thousands of people would die in the 1798 rebellion, showed, however, that the utopia of reconciliation was remote. When the Dublin Parliament gave up its right to legislative independence in controversial circumstances and the two islands were joined by the Act of Union in 1800, the Act, as Robert Welch points out, 'was hardly the cordial union Charlotte Brooke had in mind'.[32]

Justifying the Irish poetry of earlier periods, Brooke claims that many of the poems breathe 'the true spirit of poetry' but they are also of interest to the 'Historian and Antiquary' as 'so many faithful delineations of the manners and ideas of the periods in which they were composed'. Brooke's motives are interesting in that they call into question facile distinctions between literary and non-literary translation in translation history. For the translator, the evidence of the poetry is not only literary but scientific, and indeed she describes her work as helping to prove Ireland's claim to 'scientific, as well as to military fame'.[33] Therefore, though Welch, for example, describes Brooke's *Reliques* as one of the 'fundamental "growth-points" for Anglo-Irish literature', it would be wrong to consider her translations as an exclusively literary enterprise. In many ways, her work is a continuation of the translation activity of the Dublin Gaelic scholars in the first half of the eighteenth century, with its antiquarian concern for historical evidence. The concerns that motivate the translations are not purely aesthetic and, like Hugh Mac Curtin, Brooke is anxious to 'vindicate, in part, its [Ireland's] history'.[34] Thus, though Brooke consciously seeks poetic effects in her verse translations, she does not see literature in reductive isolation from the mind-set and society which produced it. To this extent, then, good translation is not only a matter of aesthetic felicity but one of historical integrity (in intention if not always in result).

Brooke claims a theoretical innocence for her translations, saying that, 'unacquainted with the rules of translation, I know not how far those rules may censure or acquit me'.[35] She eschews a literalism that might have resulted from her antiquarian concerns by arguing that literal translations would betray the spirit of the original and not do justice to the 'many complex words that could not be translated literally without great injury to the original'. The frequence of synonymy in Irish and the difficulty of rendering Irish compound epithets in English are mentioned as specific translation problems by Brooke. More generally, she questions the adequacy of translation to its task:

> in the bolder species of composition, it [Irish] is distinguished by a force of expression, a sublime dignity, and rapid energy, which it is scarcely possible for any translation fully to convey; as it sometimes fills the mind with ideas altogether new, and which, perhaps, no modern language is entirely prepared to express.[36]

The identification of 'energy', 'force of expression' and metaphorical inventiveness ('it sometimes fills the mind with ideas altogether new')

with poetry in Irish is a common Romantic response to Celtic literatures in the eighteenth and nineteenth centuries. The association of natural
eloquence with native peoples also, as Cheyfitz suggests, determines Old
World responses to the New World in the age of discovery and conquest.
He describes an ideology of language for 'Europeans' which has metaphor
occupying the place of both 'nature and culture'.[37] Metaphor is 'at once,
the most natural of languages or language in its natural state and the most
cultivated or cultured'. Metaphor is emblematic of both the native genius
of the colony and the rhetorical excellence of the metropolis. The role of
Empire is to tutor 'natural' eloquence and effect the transition from barbarity to civility. However, the imperial culture itself has to pass through a
period of linguistic purification through the agency of translation. In the
case of English, this was done primarily through the translation of Greek
and Roman classical literature thereby proving that English was a fit
language for civilised discourse.[38]

In his *The Arte of English Poesie* (1589), George Puttenham argues nonetheless that English is not only equal to but superior to the classical
languages because it has retained the metaphoric speech and primitive
poetry of its origins.[39] In Ireland, the translation movement into English
from Irish that begins in earnest in the eighteenth century and continues
throughout the nineteenth century is a vast enterprise that aims to carry
the metaphorical energy and poetic eloquence of the older language into
English, the language of power and commerce. Anglo-Irish literature will
emerge as the most spectacular result of the translation process but whereas
Puttenham saw the origins of English linguistic superiority as intralingual
(coming from earlier forms of English), the origins of Irish inventiveness
are generally presented as interlingual. Cheyfitz's terminology oversimi-
plifies. 'Europeans' have radically different linguistic histories all of which
are intimately connected to questions of autonomy and subjugation. In
Ireland, a European country, the Old World met the New World, and
the search for Brooke's 'rules of translation' was a quest fraught with
political and aesthetic consequences.

HARDIMAN, CLASSICAL DIGNITY AND POLITICAL RIVALRY

The two volumes of James Hardiman's *Irish Minstrelsy* appeared in
1831. The introduction and notes to the translations in the collection

were supplied by Hardiman, and the translations were the work of Thomas Furlong, Henry Grattan Curran, William Hamilton Drummond, John D'Alton and Edward Lawson. Hardiman, a native Irish speaker, was a Catholic and sympathetic to O'Connell's campaign for the repeal of the Act of Union. His work appeared just two years after the granting of Catholic Emancipation, which finally removed all the disadvantages suffered by Catholics under the Penal Laws. The religious enmity of the period is apparent in a passage on the Penal Laws where Hardiman affirms: 'It was resolved to reduce the poor Catholics to a state of mental darkness, in order to convert them into enlightened Protestants.'[40] He differs from Brooke not only in religion and political outlook but also in his presentation of the Gaelic tradition. If Brooke's characterisation is Romantic, Hardiman's is avowedly Classical. Describing poetry in Irish from the pre Anglo-Norman period, he declares:

> They do not possess any of the wild, barbarous fervour of the Scandinavian Scalds; nor yet the effeminate softness of the professors of the 'gay science', the *Troubadours* and *lady-bards* of the period to which we are now arrived. The simplicity of expression, and dignity of thought, which characterize Greek and Roman writers of the purest period, pervade the productions of our bards.[41]

Hardiman reacts against the Celticist portrait of literature in Irish as the product of a wild, extravagant people possessed of natural Ossianic eloquence. As it was already civilised, Irish, he implies, did not require the civilising influence of English. Classical dignity, which English acquired through translation, was found in Irish from the earliest period. A century later, Robin Flower, in a similar reaction to Celticist stereotypes, stressed the sobriety and restraint of early Irish literature.[42] Hardiman's rejection of the inheritance of the eighteenth-century Celtic Revival is only partial. A primary motive for producing the *Irish Minstrelsy* was the success of Macpherson's pseudo-translations, which had appeared over seventy years previously. The success is interpreted politically as further evidence of the cultural deviousness of the neighbouring island. Hardiman claims that it is a matter of regret to him that the works of Irish bards 'should be consigned to obscurity at home, while a neighbouring nation derived so much literary fame from a few of those remains, boldly claimed and published as its own'.[43] Many translators in Ireland in the nineteenth century did not see their translations as independent of political and cultural rivalry with Britain. They were somewhat similar to translators in English in the seventeenth century who saw their translations in a competitive light, measuring their excellence against contemporary productions in French. This explains the seriousness of purpose that informs the translation prefaces.

William Hamilton Drummond, who likewise turned to translation as a result of the Ossianic controversy, declares in the preface to his *Ancient Irish Minstrelsy* in 1852 that the Lays he has translated 'are not to be considered as idle inventions or sports of imagination, but as records of interesting matter in the history of Ireland.'[44] Literary translation was not peripheral but central to debates about Irish history and culture which had obvious relevance for claims made on behalf of the legitimacy of conquest or autonomy. Indeed, rather than celebrating the superiority of the aesthetic over the political, Hardiman condemns former writers who 'have brought discredit on our history by injudiciously blending it with the fictions of romance'. The translator as commentator separates out the genuinely historical from the truly fictive. This is as much a question of patriotic duty as good scholarship.

THE ORIENT, ARCHAEOLOGY AND IRISH ANTIQUITY

If Celticism is a passion that is variously indulged in the latter half of the eighteenth century and throughout the nineteenth century, Orientalism achieves its apotheosis in the nineteenth century, the period of European imperial expansion.[45] A striking feature of Hardiman's preface is the analogies he draws between Irish and Oriental culture. Commenting on the early knowledge and progress of music in Ireland, Hardiman observes that the origin of this knowledge 'like that of our round towers, must be sought for in the East'.[46] In a footnote on the same page, he remarks that 'the native strains of several oriental nations have been observed to bear a close affinity to Irish music'. Hardiman explicitly appeals to the Orientalist vogue in advertising the particular virtues of the native tradition: 'In our poems and songs, but particularly in those exquisite old tales and romances, which for originality of invention, and elegance of expression, vie with the Eastern stories that have delighted Europe, the beauties of our language are fully displayed.' The alleged Scythian origins of the Irish language had long been a staple of native Irish historical writing, but the significance of Hardiman's Oriental identification lies in the set of attitudes to culture and translation that it implies. The Orient as presented to the

West in the nineteenth century was exotic, remote and ancient. Its exoticism among other things translated itself into a literature that was praised for its metaphorical ingenuity and musical vagueness. Its remoteness was both spatial and temporal.

Travel to the Orient was often presented as arduous and epic and the cultures encountered were almost invariably shown to bear the traces of their ancient origins. Archaeology, in this sense, was the indispensable complement of travel, the dig a diachronic trek through the history of chosen places. The temporal distancing that placed the Western observer on the progressive trajectory of the present, while the object of the traveller's gaze remained forever locked into past time, crucially determined interpretations of local cultures as well as providing a convenient Enlightenment rationale for the colonial enterprise.[47] Translation then becomes an act of recovery. The translator like the archaeologist rescues records from oblivion. The 'site' of translation is the patient unearthing of the language and literature of ancient civilisations whose past glories are translated into the idiom of the present.

In his preface to *Specimens of the Early Native Poetry of Ireland in English* (1846), Henry Montgomery explicitly situates translation activity in an archaeological framework:

> It seems a prominent characteristic of the present day, both in these islands and on the continent, that the popular taste is recurring to the productions of early times, and reviving the spirit of primitive literary ages. Of this, the institution of national Archaeological Societies, both in England and Ireland, would of itself afford sufficient evidence.[48]

William Hamilton Drummond, presenting his translations in 1852, remarks that 'here the archaeologist and the historian may find something, to gratify their taste, and to guide curious investigation'.[49] Drummond, in fact, sees translation as an alternative and competing form of archaeology:

> As reliques of the minstrelsy which once flourished in Ireland, these Lays have a claim to as much attention as any other objects of antiquity – as much, at least, as is paid to broken columns, illegible inscriptions, and cenotaphs abroad – or dilapidated round towers, fractured urns, trilithons, and ogham epitaphs at home.[50]

The archaeological motif would continue until the end of the century. In George Sigerson's *Bards of the Gael and Gall*, first published in 1897, the translator asks if a 'buried literature' may not have claims upon our attention, and continues: 'If it be of interest to delve and discover a

105

statue or a city, long concealed, should it not be more attractive to come upon a kingdom, where long-forgotten peoples live, love, and act?'[51] The recurrent emphasis on the antiquity of Gaelic literature was partly strategic. One of the effects of the Act of Union, as Welch observes, was an increasing attentiveness to 'marks of nationality, to the question of language, and to the difference between the English and Irish temperaments'.[52] He stresses that the aim of literature in Irish was to provide Irish people with a different history, a claim to ancient civilisation and to point up diversity rather than unity (though the extent to which translators highlighted difference depended on their political persuasion).

The archaeological approach to translation nonetheless had an effect which has had far-reaching consequences for language in Ireland. It is estimated that around 1801, fifty per cent of the five million people living in Ireland were able to speak Irish.[53] Due to the rapid growth in the poorer sections of the population, there were more Irish speakers in 1831 than ever before in Ireland.[54] The language, however, was severely affected by three developments in the nineteenth century. Firstly, the national system of education, which was introduced in 1831, forbade the teaching and speaking of Irish in primary schools funded by the National Board of Education. Irish was not admitted as a subject before 1878, and then only grudgingly. Secondly, the effects of the Great Famine of 1845–7 were most severely felt by the poorer, Irish-speaking population. Estimates vary greatly as to the numbers of those who actually died but it would appear to be around 800,000. Emigration, which had already existed before the Famine, was greatly accelerated by the events of 1845–7, and between 1846 and 1901 five million people left Ireland (the pre-Famine population was around eight million).[55] Many of the emigrants came from Irish-speaking areas and they emigrated to largely English-speaking countries.[56] Thirdly, unlike, for example, the situation in Quebec where the Catholic Church was to the fore in the defence of the French language, the Catholic Church in Ireland failed to support the maintenance of the Irish language. There were, of course, individual members of the clergy and hierarchy who were passionately committed to Irish, and a religious teaching order such as the Christian Brothers later became active in the promotion of Irish in its schools. However, the principal concern of the churches in Ireland in the nineteenth century was control of the educational system. Questions of language and culture were of secondary importance.

The translators working at the end of the eighteenth century and in the first half of the nineteenth century were working in a country where there were still millions of Irish speakers. Many of the poems and songs and stories that they translated were still part of the oral culture of Irish speakers. Drummond admits to this, although he immediately invokes the figure of imminent disappearance: 'In some parts of Ireland where Irish is still spoken, the custom of singing and reciting old lays is not yet altogether obsolete.'[57] Like the Romantic celebrating rural life, the Irish antiquarian celebrating Irish language and culture stresses its *pastness*. In this context, translation facilitates a process of aestheticisation whereby contemporary realities of language bound up with power and politics are obscured by what Johannes Fabian calls the 'denial of co-evalness', the distancing of a culture through the romantic figures of loss and nostalgia.[58] The themes of ruin, decay, decline and oblivion, core concepts in the Romantic apprehension of the present, are to be found in many of the nineteenth-century translation prefaces and have powerfully affected discourse on the Irish language to this very day. By positing translation as an act of retrieval, the implication is that the other language and culture is lost to the reader in its original form. They are lost both in the sense of coming from a very remote time and being condemned to the oblivion of obsolescence.

Hardiman does acknowledge, however, a contemporary political dimension to the question of language when he compares the treatment of Irish in Ireland to the situation in Wales and Scotland: 'What, it may be asked, is there in the Irish language to make worse men or worse subjects of those who speak it than are the Welch and the Highlanders, whose native dialects are cultivated and encouraged.'[59] He may be overly optimistic in his view of the treatment of other Celtic languages but he does not see language transition as a natural or innocent process. Indeed, he cites one of William Bedell's biographers, Heber, who characterised English policy towards Irish from Henry VIII onwards as a 'narrow and illiberal policy, which, though it has in part succeeded, has left a division in the national heart, far worse than that of the tongue'.[60]

CIVILISATION, SENTIMENT AND EMPIRICISM

Like Brooke, Hardiman renounces his plan of providing 'literal English translations' because of the 'widely different idioms of both languages'.[61]

He enlists the services of his previously mentioned 'literary friends' who produce translations that vary dramatically in quality. A translator who did not spare Hardiman's translations in his published criticism was Samuel Ferguson. He was born in Belfast in 1810 and became associated with the Ulster Gaelic Society which was established in 1830.[62] In 1834, he published a series of four articles on Hardiman's *Minstrelsy* in the *Dublin University Magazine*. The very existence of the articles and their detail is testimony to the importance attached to translation in early nineteenth century Ireland. Ferguson does not share Hardiman's nationalist views and he describes him as 'politically malignant and religiously fanatical', while acknowledging his 'pious labours' on behalf of Irish literature.[63] Ferguson's ideal is one of reconciliation between Irish Protestant and Catholic who would strive together for the common good of Ireland: 'We will not suffer two of the finest races of men in the world, the Catholic and Protestant, or the Milesian and Anglo-Irish, to be duped into mutual hatred by the tale-bearing go-betweens who may struggle in impotent malice against our honest efforts.'[64] Fergsuon resembles Charlotte Brooke in that his Irish patriotism situates itself within the context of continued union with Britain. He echoes nationalist interpretation of Irish history when he refers to Ireland's 'present civil degradation' and 'seven hundred years of outrage and outlawry', but sees Ireland's future as firmly within the empire: 'Eight millions of people cannot for ever remain in obscurity; sooner or later Ireland must rise into importance, perhaps as an emulator, perhaps as an equal, perhaps as a superior to the other members of our imperial confederacy.'[65] Ferguson sees the English conquest of Ireland as a necessary part of the civilising process. Commenting on internecine strife between the O'Neills and the O'Briens in 1252, he claims:

> Nor, as Irishmen, have we reason to be displeased, when we reflect that by such a disaster, English civilisation has been admitted with English conquest, and that, but for the insanity of such men as Tiege Caoluisce O'Brien, we still might be infinitely farther behind the rest of Europe in all the arts of peace and the best sinews of war.[66]

In translation, however, Ferguson is sceptical of attempts to 'civilise' the source language. He takes Hardiman's translators to task for their pursuit of mellifluous gentility:

> All the versifiers seem to have been actuated by a morbid desire, neither healthy nor honest, to elevate the tone of the original to a pitch of refined poetic art altogether foreign from the whole genius and *rationale* of its

composition. We are sorry to be obliged to add, that the majority of these attempts are spurious, puerile, unclassical – lamentably bad.[67]

Ferguson dismisses most of the translations by John D'Alton as victims of 'spurious pretension and bombastic feebleness'. He goes on to state that 'Mr. D'Alton's perversions are, however, mere petty larceny travesties compared with the epic grandeur of Mr. Curran's heroic declaration of open war against the original.' Ferguson condemns Henry Grattan Curran for introducing 'tropes, sentiments, or episodes' which are not present in the source text in order to ensure the translation's 'creditable Saxonisation'.[68] The trenchant criticism by Ferguson has two sources. The first is his scholarly concern to see translations reproduce what is actually in the source text. The second is his own uncertainty as to the literary merit of poetry in Irish. The chief interest of such poetry, for Ferguson, lies in the provision of essentialist evidence on the Irish character. He remarks that, from the translated samples of Irish verse that he has already given in his *Dublin University Magazine* articles, 'it must be plain to every reader that these pieces are more valuable as keys to Irish sentiment than as elegant additions to polite literature'.[69] Following in the tradition of the Celtic Revival of the 1750s and 1760s, and anticipating certain concerns of Arnoldian Celticism in the late nineteenth century, Ferguson considers 'sentiment' to be the 'one imprescriptible property of the common blood of all Irishmen'. The national songs of Ireland are distinguished from those of other nations by a 'wild, mournful, incondite, yet not uncouth, sentiment'.[70] The translator, then, must see his or her task as being faithful to this 'sentiment' rather than to the conventions of 'polite literature'. The implication for Ferguson is that he presents his translation work less as *literary* translation than as a form of applied ethnology. The translated texts will not enrich a literature in English, they are not 'elegant additions', but they will provide crucial evidence as to the nature of the Irish character.

Evidence for Ferguson comes in the form of facts and he is heir to the empiricism of the *Dublin Philosophical Society* of the late seventeenth century. He refers positively to seventeenth century scholars such as Ware, Davis and Ussher and to their taste for facts in an article in the *Dublin Penny Journal*. In the same article he goes on to defend the imaginative potential of the factual:

It is a most prejudicial error to suppose that matter of fact, however the term may have been abused, is necessarily dry or uninteresting: on the contrary, there can be no true romance, no real poetry, nothing, in a word, that will effectually touch either the heart or the imagination, that has not its foundation in the experience of existing facts, or in the knowledge of facts that have existed in times past.[71]

His translations then, driven by the facts of the source text, may indeed 'touch either the heart or the imagination', but their objectives must be not so much literary as empirical. They must register real differences between source and target languages and cultures at the risk of appearing deficient by the standards of the literature of the period (standards to which Ferguson subscribes). Thus, in his *Nationalism and Minor Literature*, David Lloyd is mistaken in attributing an 'ideal of transparent translation' to Ferguson.[72] For Ferguson, translation between the two languages was never straightforward, and the presence of irreducible difference stalked the conscientious translator from Irish into English. Commenting on the translation of *Tighearna Mhaigheo* in Hardiman's collection, Ferguson claims that the 'idiomatic differences of the two languages give to the translation an uncouth and difficult hesitation' that is not in the orginal poem.[73] In listing the difficulties of translating Irish verse, Ferguson draws particular attention to prosody where a 'multitude of words in the original' forms a 'measure which frequently does not afford room for more than half the English expressions requisite for their adequate translation.' The ellipsis of aspirated consonants and concurrent vowels means that three or four words are compressed into a single dactyl in Irish with predictable problems for the English translator.

On the question of metaphor, the translator has to avoid the 'perplexing vices of grotesqueness on the one hand, and of colloquial tameness on the other'. Discussing the appropriate register for the translations of songs attributed to the harpist Carolan, Ferguson points out that the sociocultural connotations of register in different languages rarely overlap: 'The classic language of Pope will not answer to the homely phrase of Carolan; but the slang of Donnybrook is equally inconsistent with the Bard's legacy.' The earnest faithfulness of the translator may paradoxically cast doubts on the usefulness of the enterprise. Ferguson observes that, while the rhythm and music of poetry in Irish may 'breathe the most plaintive and pathetic sentiment, the accompanying words, in whatever English dress they may be invested, present a contrast of low and ludicrous images as well as of an incondite simplicity of construction the most striking and apparently absurd'.[74] However, the images are only 'low and ludicrous' to the extent that they violate a sense of metaphorical decorum in English. It

110

is the very function of metaphor as defined by Aristotle to transfer a word from a familiar to a foreign place, to introduce an element of *strangeness* into the language.[75] Translation similarly involves taking texts from their familiar, home environment to the the foreign lands of other languages. Texts are displaced. Metaphors become refugees seeking asylum in the host language.

Ferguson's translations, later published in book form as *Lays of the Western Gael*, were highly praised and influential. Their success was due to those very uncertainties that compromised Ferguson's estimation of their poetic worth. It was precisely the metaphorical otherness, the metrical differences, the tension between prosody and image that attracted the makers of a new literature in English such as James Clarence Mangan to the translations. The translations were appreciated less for their insights into putative Irish emotional dispositions than for their destabilising effect on English. Unlike many of the translations in the volumes by Brooke and Hardiman, which opted for fluent strategies, making the texts acceptable to the literary tastes of English readers, Ferguson's unyielding empiricism produced translations that were distinct and different. An ironic political consequence for Ferguson is that it was the claims to difference as exemplified by translation that would provide an important impetus for cultural nationalists, the opponents of the 'imperial confederacy'.

LICENTIOUSNESS, METAPHOR, TRANSVESTISM

Translators can be viewed as revolutionaries or conservatives, dangerous subversives or reliable guardians of public morality. James Hardiman and Samuel Ferguson in the nineteenth century saw themselves very definitely as the latter, and a feature of translation activity in Ireland in the period is a close attention to matters of sexual morality. Hardiman is quick to point out that certain kinds of material will not be afforded the grace of translation in his *Irish Minstrelsy*:

> Aware of the influence of popular song on public morals, no verses, of even a doubtful tendency, have been admitted into the following pages; if some rigid moralist may not perhaps deem the *Chansons de boire* [sic] of our favourite CAROLAN exceptionable.[76]

Ferguson is less radical in his exclusion, but his presentation of material carries moral disclaimers. For example, commenting on the last lines of

the translation of Carolan's 'Song of Sorrow' he says that the 'con-
cluding stanzas rise into such a fervid frenzy of undistinguished desire
that we shrink from exhibiting them in their literal English. Yet there is
nothing impure, nothing licentious in their languishing but savage
sincerity'.[77] The orgasm is faked. The appearance of licentiousness is
based on a misapprehension of the purity of motive that Ferguson attributes to the forlorn lover in Carolan's poem. In Irish songs, Ferguson
observes, there are fervent expressions of love but 'little even of the
implied grossness of licentious desire'.[78]

The position of Hardiman and Ferguson can be seen as a simple
response to restrictive sexual mores, forestalling moral condemnation
through anxious reassurances. Their standpoint, however, is worth considering in the larger context of translation and sexual disorientation. In a
discussion of the English critic Puttenham's profound suspicion of metaphor, Eric Cheyfitz argues that 'what Puttenham refers to as the
Areopagites' ban on "all manner of figurative speaches" must be read as a
figure of the desire to domesticate the far-fetched, or alien, figure, all
"forraine & coulored talke"'.[79] Metaphor can be an act of transgression,
and metaphor in translation can be doubly transgressive. Though Cheyfitz
discusses the figure of dress as used to describe metaphor, he fails to see the
connection with translation where, as we observed in the last chapter, the
notion of garment or dress was commonly used to describe the translation
process. Indeed, Charlotte Brooke talks of her translations as 'clothing the
thoughts of the muse in a language with which they [the public] are familiar'.[80] If translation, like metaphor, carries with it the potential of foreign
contamination, it also, if the image of dress is taken into account, has the
transgressive possibility of transvestism. Transvestism here refers to dressing
in the clothes of another rather than in the specific sense of gender change
in dress.[81] If translation metaphorically involved a change of dress, there
was always the implicit sexual threat of disorientation. As in the Carolan
poem, appearances are not to be trusted. In James Clarence Mangan's
translations from Persian, Arabic and Turkish poetry (published in the
Dublin University Magazine as the series 'Literae Orientales'), he suggests in
prefatory remarks that appearances may be all there is. Mangan asks
whether it is in fact possible to translate Oriental poetry into English,
arguing that 'Oriental Poetry apparelled in western dress becomes essen-
tially unrecognizable, forfeits its identity, ceases to be an intelligent object
of apprehension to the understanding.'[82] The dress becomes a disguise that

ultimately disguises the subject from itself. The foreign dress of translation here conceals rather than reveals. Translation gives way to travesty.

Conversely, the translator may resemble the French Oriental traveller Isabelle Eberhardt, for whom transvestism offered the possibility of mediation. By dressing as a male Arab and speaking Arabic, she could gain access to areas of North African culture that would normally be out of bounds to a female Westerner. Cross-dressing invites understanding. But a disguise may be only that, a disguise, which hides real interests. As Ali Behdad points out in his *Belated Travellers: Orientalism in the Age of Colonial Dissolution*, Eberhardt's reports from North Africa played an important role in causing a shift in French colonial policy from assimilation to association in the latter half of the nineteenth century.[83] Eberhardt did not leave behind her French identity or the interests of the French colonial administration. Borrowing a term from Michel Serres, Behdad sees Eberhardt as a parasite, as the necessary noise in the French imperial system that allows it to restructure itself. To return to nineteenth-century Ireland, the passage of material from Irish into English has the potential to be doubly threatening. The threat in the political sense is obvious, though stressed by Hardiman rather than Ferguson. The foreignness and otherness of a culture that is largely identified with the politically oppressed majority is by definition unsettling for a ruling élite. The sexual menace is more oblique, lying in the possibility that wildness and sentiment might breach sexual decorum and introduce a troubling alterity. The translator as transvestite is Ó Catháin's 'shadowy figure', a necessary mediator, but suspect because of crossing sexual boundaries in one case and linguistic, cultural (and emotional) boundaries in the other. If, as Ferguson affirms, Irish song appeals more to the heart than to judgement, then the normative checks of reason are suspended and anything is possible.[84] Indeed, it is because anything is possible that translation is the parasite that will allow Anglo-Irish literature to restructure itself in the nineteenth century just as translation was to the fore in restructuring Irish language and literature in the seventeenth century. In the case of the translator as parasite, it is worth emphasising catalysis rather than dependency.

LINGUISTIC ASSIMILATION AND TRANSLATION READERSHIP

In the introduction to his *Irish Minstrelsy*, Hardiman acknowledges the help of the 'REVEREND DANIEL O'SULLIVAN of Bandon, who has enriched his native language with an inimitable translation of the "Imitation of Christ"".[85] This is one of the few references that we find in the English-language translators of the period to translators working in the Irish language. Daniel O'Sullivan's translation, entitled *Searc-leanmhain Chríosd* in Irish, was published in Dublin in 1822 and, as we saw in the last chapter, was not the first translation of Thomas à Kempis's work in Irish. Eleven years later, the Ulster Gaelic Society published an Irish translation of *Forgive and Forget* and *Rosanna* by Maria Edgeworth.[86] The two texts were translated by Tomás Ó Fiannachtaigh, who had founded an Irish-speaking school in Ballynascreen in County Derry in 1828 and later became a teacher of Irish at the Royal Belfast Academical Institution.[87] The decision to publish a translation in Irish of works by one of the important figures in an emerging Anglo-Irish literature is significant and demonstrates the changing balance of power between the languages.

Ulster had been one of the areas where the United Irishmen had been most active at the end of the eighteenth century, and in 1795 a publication known as *Bolg an tSolair: or Gaelic Magazine* appeared under the auspices of the paper of the United Irishmen, the *Northern Star*. The publication appeared only once and the *Northern Star* itself was banned by the authorities in May 1795. *Bolg an tSolair* contained translations into English (including, interestingly, translations by Charlotte Brooke) and into Irish. The Irish-language translations were of exclusively religious material: the Lord's Prayer, the Creed and extracts from Scripture. Thomas Russell, a United Irishman and librarian for the Belfast Reading Society (later to become the Linen Hall Library), was active in promoting Irish language and culture though it is probable that it was Pádraig Ó Loinsigh from County Down who actually produced the translations.[88] Whitley Stokes was friendly with Russell and worked with Pádraig Ó Loinsigh on producing Irish translations of Saint Luke's Gospel and the Acts of the Apostles, which were published in 1799 as *An Soisgéal Do Réir Lucais, Agus Gníovarha na nEasbal*.[89] However, non-religious books had been translated into Irish, and Stanford mentions the four books of Irish-language translations of passages from Greek and Latin poets which were produced by Lucas Smyth in Kilkenny between 1709 and 1721. The antiquarian Charles Vallancey included an Irish translation of the Punic speech from Plautus's *Poenulus* in his *Essay on the Antiquity of the Irish Language* in 1722.[90] John MacHale, the influential Catholic Archbishop of Tuam and one of the few senior Catholic clergymen to take an active interest in the Irish language in the nineteenth century, produced an Irish translation of Homer's *Iliad* which was completed in 1874. MacHale also produced a translation in Irish of *Moore's Melodies*. Like the Maria Edgeworth translation earlier in the century, MacHale's choice of text is interesting. Thomas Moore, who derived much of his poetic inspiration from the musical tradition in Irish, now found his verses being translated back into that language. In a letter to MacHale that is quoted in the Preface to the translations, Moore treats MacHale's translations as an act of restitution. The translation is the original. Moore declares: 'That these songs should be translated into what I may call their native language, is in itself a great gratification and triumph for me.'[91]

Given the numerical strength of Irish speakers, the paucity of printed translations into Irish is striking. Though translations, as we have seen, were published, many more translations, like much other literature in Irish, were still circulating in manuscript form throughout the eighteenth and the first half of the nineteenth century. The dissemination of translations in the period depended on literacy, the printing presses and a reading public which was usually concentrated in large urban centres and had the wherewithal to buy the translations. Though there were Irish speakers in most of Ireland's major cities, they were a minority and had no appreciable linguistic impact on the English-speaking public culture of the cities. The majority of Irish speakers were located in the countryside, many of them – though it is important to stress, by no means, all – were poor, and their access to education in their own language, despite the valiant efforts of certain hedge schools, was adversely affected by the Penal Laws. The economic incentives to learn English, whether for the purposes of economic advancement at home or emigration to Britain, the United States, Australia or Anglophone Canada, were compelling. One might have expected that the drift towards linguistic assimilation in the nineteenth century would have been checked by nationalist movements which would have championed the cause of language as irreducible evidence of difference. The Young Ireland movement in the 1840s did indeed stress the link beween language and cultural identity, but they were the exception rather than the rule for most of the century before the foundation of the Gaelic League.

Wolfe Tone was largely indifferent to questions of language and the preservation of Irish, though for the United Irishmen in Ulster in particular, the Irish language was an important meeting ground for Irish people of different religious persuasions.[92] Daniel O'Connell, leader of the mass movements for Catholic Emancipation and Repeal in the early nineteenth century, although himself a fluent Irish speaker, was decidedly unfavourable to the maintenance of Irish as a national language. When Anthony O'Connell took the manuscript of an Irish–English dictionary compiled by his uncle, Peter O'Connell, to the renowned political leader, Eugene O'Curry reported that 'Mr. O'Connell had no taste for matters of this kind, and he suddenly dismissed his namesake, telling him that his uncle was an old fool to have spent so much of his life on so useless a work.'[93] The Fenian movement in the 1860s was similarly uninterested, by and large, in issues of language and nationhood and was primarily concerned with developing physical force nationalism and breaking the link with England. Therefore, the Irish language for much of the eighteenth and nineteenth century was as conspicuously lacking in political allies as it was in economic supports. Even those movements which expressed concern for the fate of the language were beset by contradictions. Lloyd points to Mangan's translations for the *Nation*, the paper that became associated with the Young Ireland movement. He sees translation as embodying a duplicity that affects all nationalisms:

> Devoted to the reunification of a people by the revitalization of a hypothetical past unity, cultural or political, nationalism depends nonetheless on those forces that tend to deracinate a people and that, by instigating an uneven process of modernization, fragment those social structures which come to appear in retrospect as the expression of a coherent and unified national consciousness.[94]

The *Nation*, a paper written in the English language and printed in Dublin was, through its mass circulation, an important carrier not only of nationalist ideas but also, ironically, of the English language. In a sense, the Young Irelanders inadvertently undermined the very language and culture they sought to protect. Mangan's translations were contained within an organ that not only promoted his translations but also the *process of translation* itself. The *Nation* was yet another incentive for Irish speakers to translate themselves into the English language. Irish nationalism in the nineteenth century was a creature of circumstance. For reasons outlined earlier, the Irish language was continually under social and economic pressure, and most nationalist and republican movements appear to have accepted English-language assimilation as inevitable. Their faith in translation is strong because of an implied belief that an Irish nation can express its own distinctness in the English language. Learning and literature in the

Irish language can be carried across the language divide and used as building materials for a new Irish identity. As prime beneficiaries of this new order, translators were, in certain instances, more sceptical than anyone else. David Lloyd has demonstrated how Mangan consistently subverts notions of transparency in translation and the idea that the original text has an ideal equivalent in the target language. If translators such as Brooke, Hardiman, Ferguson and Drummond do not share Mangan's thoroughgoing radicalism or, in some cases, his political outlook, they nonetheless are not loath to point up real language difference and the limits to translation. Thus, whether translators are busy contributing to the pluralist project of empire (Ferguson, Brooke) or the emergent culture of the nation (Hardiman, Mangan), there are no seamless transitions: translation and tension are synonymous.

PREJUDICE, ORIGINALITY AND MENTAL MODERNITY

In *The Poets and Poetry of Munster*, published in Dublin in 1860 under the pseudonym 'Erionnach', George Sigerson underlines these tensions. Introducing a poem by Ó Lionáin in praise of Irish, he declares, 'The following is the production of O'Lionan, a man who could appreciate how much beauty and tenderness might be lost having the opportunity he had of hearing the inflexible, un-endearing language of the "porker" Saxons jarring upon the ear of his country.'[95] Sigerson attacks 'prejudiced foreigners, looking at the squalor in which their iniquitous laws have placed some of our people, and exaggerating basely and lyingly that misery'.[96] In his defence of the language and culture he translates, Sigerson contributes to an idealisation of Irish speakers that would soon harden to imperishable myth: 'In fact, in every rural district where the Irish is spoken, curious gems of quaint humour, flashing wit, and a keen knowledge of men and morals adorn that golden casket – a Celtic peasant's heart.'[97] However, despite the belligerent tone of some of his remarks, Sigerson is keen to emphasise the selfless, non-sectarian nature of his translation enterprise. If his opinions seem too 'favourable to these Celtic compositions', he points out that the 'translator is an Ulsterman and of Viking race' and that his only reason for publishing the translations is to gain an 'increase of respect and love for the delicacy, devotion and chivalry of a much-maligned people'.[98] The emphasis on inclusiveness rather than exclusiveness recurs in the introduction to the *Bards of the Gael and Gall* (1897), where Sigerson stresses the pluralism of the Gaelic tradition:

> Many bards bear foreign names. Their Fathers had crossed with the Normans, or with later settlers, yet they claimed the country's history as their heritage, and they make appeal to all its ancient traditions. So every generation fuses with the great Past, in the adopted land they love.[99]

Sigerson's celebration of the assimilative capacity of Gaelic culture can be read as an apologia for the act of translation itself. In producing these translations, he is offering to those in Ireland who do not speak Irish the possibility of fusing with 'the great Past'. Ferguson, for his part, had claimed sixty years earlier that 'to make Irishmen know themselves and one another; this is the want, this is the worthiest labour of the age'.[100] Thus, translation is not only an act of reconciliation between countries but also within a country. Violence and oppression stem from fear, and fear is predicated on ignorance. By disseminating knowledge of Gaelic culture, translation lessens ignorance and therefore robs prejudice of one of its most precious alibis. The cultural ecumenism of translation offers the possibility of a common ground that often proves elusive in a divided society. Writing on Arthur Brownlow – the Member of Parliament for Armagh in the House of Commons from 1692 to 1710 and a descendant of the planter, William Brownlow – Breandán Ó Buachalla notes Brownlow's keen interest in Irish language and culture and his patronage of Eoghan Mac Oghannain, the main Irish scribe in South-East Ulster in the last quarter of the seventeenth century. Ó Buachalla sees Brownlow's activities as an example of the manner in which cultural allegiances cut across social, political and religious alignments in Ulster.[101] Brownlow did, in fact, translate from Irish into English although only one of his translations has survived. The surviving translation is of a lament for Owen Roe O'Neill written by the County Down priest, Cathal Mac Ruairí, and deeply hostile to the English presence in Ireland. Thus, translation offered the possibility of an encounter with the other religion, language and culture that would have been unthinkable in other contexts. In stressing the political dimension to translation, it is always important to bear in mind the pedagogic and ecumenical objectives of translation activity in nineteenth century Ireland, as these were objectives close to the concerns of many of the translators themselves.

When Charlotte Brooke singles out the Irish language in 'the bolder species of composition' for its 'force of expression . . . sublime dignity, and rapid energy', she is like many succeeding translators emphasising the vigorous originality of the poetry she is translating. This poses an immediate problem for the translator, if the poetry *is* so original, so utterly different, how can it be translated without travesty into another language? In essence, does its very translatability not compromise its claims to originality? There is a less obvious problem with the use of romantic notions of originality which Lloyd highlights in the context of Orientalism. He argues that attributing 'originality' to Oriental peoples is quite ambivalent in its intent:

> The assertion that the Eastern races represent an earlier stage of human history than the Western races transforms easily into the assertion that they are accordingly more 'primitive' and, therefore, given an evolutionary model of human history that is at once racial, linguistic, and political, that they are susceptible of cultivation and development by Western powers.

Samuel Ferguson shares this ambivalence. His translations underscore the 'originality' of Irish poetry, but the society which produced these poems urgently needed the 'cultivation and development' that English conquest promised. Britain, according to Ferguson, was civilised through the feudal system and the revolution of 1688, whereas the Irish system of patriarchal loyalty did not admit of popular rights. Ireland, he claims, had finally been

> subdued by a people so far in advance of her own, that after centuries of fellow-citizenship, the two races are still unable to amalgamate from the want of these intermediate steps upon the civil state – steps forgotten by the one and never taken by the other.[102]

Although Sigerson initially presents an image of Irish literature that seems vaguely primitivist, comparing the 'picturesque forest' of the 'Literature of Ancient Erinn' to the 'Stately Parthenon' of classical literature, he goes on to declare that 'the reason why the Celts did not compose rimed epics was because of their extreme mental modernity'. Rather than seeing Ireland prior to English Conquest as shackled by backwardness and underdevelopment, he sees the society as anticipating the ferment of modernity:

> The activity and restlessness of our own days were in their blood in all known time. Their contemporaries sometimes noticed this trait and complained of it. It is vain to blame them for outrunning their age. They

119

were in truth, the Moderns of the Past – perhaps they are also fated to be the Moderns of the Future.[103]

His attempts, therefore, in *Bards of the Gael and Gall*, to reproduce the elaborate metrical structures of the original Irish poems in English could be seen not as self-indulgent archaism but as offering the reader poetic materials for the construction of a new Irish modernity. The fact that Austin Clarke, among others in the twentieth century, responded to the challenge of Gaelic prosody as presented by Sigerson, shows that the Ulsterman's ambitions were not totally without foundation.[104] He is also more explicitly indicating the meeting of tradition and modernity that will give rise to the dramatic changes in the fortunes of Irish writing in English through the works of Yeats, Synge and Lady Gregory.

THE CLASSIC CAMP AND CREATIVE EXPERIMENTS

Sigerson believes that the most distinctive feature of early Irish literature is that it is 'the sole representative . . . of that great world, which lived and thrived outside the classic camp'.[105] In nineteenth-century Ireland, there were still, however, a considerable number of translators who continued to work in the 'classic camp'. Visitors to rural Ireland in the eighteenth and nineteenth centuries were often surprised at the number of people they met who could speak Latin, and in 1868, a parish priest in Kerry was cheered by his congregation for saying, 'I make no apology for quoting Latin, for Latin is almost our mother-tongue.'[106] The Irish parliamentarian Isaac Butt, who founded what proved to be an important showcase for translations, the *Dublin University Magazine*, produced his own translation of the *Georgics* of Virgil in 1834.[107] Thomas Moore who is principally known for his *Melodies*, was also a classical translator, his translation of the *Odes* of Anacreon first appearing in 1800. Political and moral concerns are conspicuously present in Moore's preface to his translation. The religious discrimination of eighteenth-century Ireland is referred to when Moore describes his education: 'Born of Catholic parents I had come into the world with the slave's yoke around my neck; and it was all in vain that the fond ambition of a mother looked forward to the Bar as opening a career that might lead her son to affluence and honour.'[108] The obstacles to the translator's progress were not only political, however. When Moore as a student in Trinity College, Dublin, submitted a manuscript copy of his

120

translation to Dr Kearney, a senior fellow of the college who became Provost in 1799, he was informed by Kearney that the college board would find it difficult to sanction by means of a reward or prize, 'writings of so convivial and amatory a nature as were almost all those of Anacreon'.[109]

Moore notes ironically that standards for translation differ from those applicable to the original. When a monument to a former Provost of Trinity College arrived from Italy, two copies of Spaletti's facsimile of a manuscript in the Vatican library containing the Odes attributed to Anacreon were included along with the marble memorial. Both copies were gifts from the Pope that were presented to the Trinity College library and Dr Kearney by Dr Troy, the Catholic Archbishop of Dublin. Moore is alive to the multiple ironies of the gift:

> Thus, curiously enough, while Anacreon *in English* was considered – and I grant on no unreasonable grounds – as a work to which grave collegiate authorities could not openly lend their sanction, Anacreon *in Greek* was thought no unfitting present to be received by a Protestant bishop, through the medium of a Catholic archbishop, from the hands of his holiness, the Pope.[110] (emphasis in original)

Moore's fame rested on his achievements as a poet rather than as a translator. For William Maginn, another Irish translator of the nineteenth century, fame did indeed come with translation but it proved to be short-lived. Many classical scholars of the period were coming to the conclusion that the Homeric poems were composed primarily for popular audiences. Maginn translated the theory into practice by publishing his 'Homeric Ballads' in *Fraser's Magazine* in 1838 and they were subsequently published as a separate volume.[111] The 'Ballads' were sections of Homeric poems that were translated using popular ballad metres rather than the conventional iambic pentameter that was generally used in English to translate classical epic poetry. His translations were popular and praised by, among others, William Gladstone and Matthew Arnold, although a twentieth-century scholar has remarked: 'When one reads them now it is hard to see how they escaped instant condemnation.'[112] Neither fame nor fortune lasted, however, and after being imprisoned for debt, Maginn died a pauper in 1842. Maginn had obtained a doctorate from Trinity College in 1819, so his translations cannot have been the fruits of a reckless ignorance. They do show, however, a willingness to experiment that is a feature of one strand of Irish translation activity from Stanihurst through Maginn to

Ciaran Carson in the late twentieth century. Translation is as much a domain of creative experiment as of dutiful service. In Maginn's case, responding to the speculations of classical scholars, both are combined. It was deference to the original context of the Homeric compositions that led to the jettisoning of the iambic pentameter in favour of the ballad form.

The other Irish classical translators of the nineteenth century tended on the whole to be less extravagant in their formal initiatives. Translators such as S.H. Butcher, Jebb, Ridgeway, Godley, T.W. Rolleston, Henry McCormac and Thomas Talbot published translations that were readily accepted as part of the canon of classical translation in English. These individual talents were part not only of a broader English-language tradition of classical translation but also of an existing tradition in Ireland itself where translation into both Irish and English had been practised for centuries. When Louis Kelly, in *The True Interpreter*, describes the use of modulation by classicists 'in England', he takes an example from the translations of 'Robert Tyrell of Dublin'. Apart from the geographical confusion, Kelly's comment rests on the mistaken assumption that translation traditions in Ireland and England were in all points similar.[113]

THE MASKS OF TRANSLATION

There were, of course, source languages other than English, Irish, Greek and Latin for Irish translators to work from in the nineteenth century. James Clarence Mangan, for example, made a number of significant translations from German.[114] Many of these translations appeared in the *Dublin University Magazine* in March 1836 under the heading 'Anthologia Germanica', and others appeared in publications like the *Nation* and the *Irish Penny Journal*. Mangan translated work by Heine, Schiller, Novalis, Goethe, Jean Paul, Justinus Kerner, Friedrich De La Motte Fouqué and others. In addition to genuine translations, however, Mangan also produced a number of bogus translations of poems attributed to 'Drechsler' and 'Selber', poets who, in fact, never existed. In the issue of the *Dublin University Magazine* where the Drechsler and Selber translations appeared, there is also high praise for John Anster's translation of Goethe's *Faust*.[115] In 1849, the year of Mangan's death, he described Anster in the *Irishman* in the following terms:

Dr. Anster has not merely translated *Faust*: he has done much more – he has
translated Goethe – or rather he has translated that part of the mind of
Goethe which was unknown to Goethe himself . . . he has actually made
of Goethe the man whom his German worshippers claim him to be . . .
he is, in short, the *real author of Faust*.[116] (Emphasis in original)

The 'authorial' theory of translation that Mangan is proposing inverts
conventional hierarchies of writer/translator, primary/secondary, original/
derivative that inform received ideas on the translation process. The
production of fake translations could be seen as the logical outcome of a
radical version of the authorial theory. The translator is the real author of
the text because there is no original. The translation is the original. The
attractions of Mangan for post-structuralist critics are obvious, but his
deconstructionist malleability should not obscure the historical significance
of his treatment of the translator. As we saw in Chapter One, the medieval
Irish translators were active shapers of the translated text, often adopting a
highly interventionist practice and 'authoring' sections of the translation as
they saw fit. There is also the tradition of Stanihurst and Maginn, to name
but two Irish translators in English. Therefore, Mangan is not so much
creating a radical new translation practice as simply making explicit the
creative role of the translator that was already implicit in certain specific
approaches to translation in Ireland. He is also emphasising the responsibility of the translator. If the translator is to assume authorial power, then
abdication of responsibility for the final result ('I was only doing my job'),
is no longer possible. Self-effacement has its own securities (or, more
properly, insecurities).

The unwillingness to efface or erase the self draws the translator into
another set of paradoxes. Robert Welch argues that for Mangan as Proteus
(Mangan had so described himself), 'the mask of translation' allowed the
exercise of a plurality, a degree of objectivity 'which freed him from the
tremors of his private grief and agony'.[117] The implication is that translation
allows for the multiplication of selves, a costume drama in language.
However, it could equally be argued that an authorial theory does not so
much lead to a multiplication of selves as a multiplication of self. It is
Mangan's presence, not his absence, that is distinctly felt in his translations.
It is the fact that they are unmistakably his translations that makes them so
different from the translations of, say, Samuel Ferguson or James
Hardiman. Just as Mangan baulks at the general notion of transparency in
translation, so too is he resistant to a transparent self. It is the very opacity

of the translator that inflects the direction of the translation and ensures that no two translators will ever translate a poem in exactly the same way.

Nations, like individuals, can be seen as opaque, and where this view is widely held, the challenge for translation can be formidable. Lloyd claims that 'It is only when those specificities of language that render it radically *untranslatable* come to be recognized as representative of the unique spirit of any culture or national language that the problem of equivalence comes to the fore.'[118] There is nothing unusual or exceptional about this point of view. Nations derive their existence from those aspects of their culture that make them irreducibly different. To translate is to suggest that the differences are not fundamental, that they can be converted into the common currency of humanity. Herein lies the basic conflict about the nature of translation in Ireland that has continued right up to the present day. On the one hand, there is the view shared by Brooke, Ferguson and others that translation promotes mutual understanding, that it stimulates interest in past achievements and that, just as translation is a bridge between languages, it can also act as a bridge between cultures. Equivalence is difficult but possible. A later variation on this view is that the literature of Ireland produced in one language could be subsumed into a new literature in another language through the good offices of translation.

The other view would be articulated with greater force towards the end of the nineteenth century and was heavily influenced by Humboldtian linguistic relativism, that is to say, the view that languages were different and that they generated different world-views. These world-views in turn gave rise to cultures that constituted the legitimate basis for the claim to nationhood. In these circumstances, translation is coercive. It is a strategy by the coloniser to assimilate the language of the colonised and deny their right to be different and free. There was no readily available political shorthand to assign these opposing viewpoints to identifiable political persuasions. Many nationalist translators were sympathetic to the need for information and understanding that was stressed by the unionist translators, Brooke and Ferguson. These nationalist translators, by virtue of the very fact that they translated from Irish into English, obviously did not feel that they were undermining their claim to cultural and political separateness. The dominant objective in many of the nineteenth-century translations into English was the same as Hugh MacCurtin's: to vindicate the antiquity of Ireland. The war with Tudor and Cromwellian propagandists was not over. The evidence of past greatness undermined the legitimacy of conquest and exposed the Union as an unwanted fiction. Differences in habit, belief and outlook could survive transfer into a new language environment. It was the translators, then, who would lay the cultural basis for this new nationhood.

Translation activity continued in Irish throughout the eighteenth and nineteenth centuries and it is important to stress the continuity. However, it is undoubtedly true that the adverse political and economic circumstances greatly hampered the emergence of translation into Irish on a large scale. The selection pressures strongly favoured translation into English, and those who might have worked as competent translators in Irish, had circumstances been different, found themselves producing translations in English. For example, Pól Ó Longáin, the son of the poet Mícheál Óg Ó Longáin, was one of the most industrious Gaelic scribes of the nineteenth century. William Newell, a Head Inspector, visited the school in White-church, outside Cork City, where Ó Longáin was schoolmaster and noted in his report to the educational authorities: 'He is pretty constantly employed in translating Irish manuscripts which may interfere with his proper vocation of schoolmaster.'[119] Like most literary or academic translators to this day, Ó Longáin had a day-job, but the financial rewards were for translation into English, not Irish. Ó Longáin was only one of the hundreds of scribes in nineteenth-century Ireland who earned part of their income from either copying Irish-language manuscripts or translating them. They worked in a translation tradition that had begun in the antiquarian interests and empirical curiosity of the late seventeenth and eighteenth century.

Jonathan Swift was a close friend of Anthony Raymond, one of the prominent figures in the revival of interest in Irish learning. 'The Description of an Irish Feast', a translation of the Irish poem, 'Pléaráca na Ruarcach' is attributed to Swift in the second volume of his work, published in 1735. Alan Harrison expresses doubts as to whether Swift had sufficient command of Irish to undertake the translation without assistance and surmises that help may have come from Raymond. In popular folklore, another version of the genesis of the translation has the great satirist meet the blind harpist Carolan, who gives him a prose version of the poem in English:

> The Dean admired Carolan's genius, had him frequently at the Deanery House in Dublin, and used to hear him play and sing the *pléaráca*. He was particularly struck with the happy and singular onomatopoeia in several

passages of the original, particularly that which represented the sound of the
wet in the dancers' shoes, 'glug glug i n-a mbróg'. This was thought to be
inimitable by English words, till Carolan bade him send his servant to walk
in shoes over a pool of water and dance before him. This coincided with the
Dean's own whimsical fancy. The experiment was made, and the Dean
caught the sound and expressed it by 'Splish Splash in their pumps'.[120]

It is significant that two major figures of Ireland's English-language and
Irish-language traditions should meet on the common ground of
translation. As the nineteenth century drew to a close, the inheritors of
both traditions were to look once again to translation as the catalyst for
renewal and invention.

Notes

1. Alan Harrison, *Ag Cruinniú Meala*, Dublin, An Clóchomhar, 1988, pp. 49–51. See
   also Vincent Morley, *An Crann os Coill*, Baile Átha Cliath, Coiscéim, 1995.
2. H. Mac Curtin, *A Brief Discourse in Vindication of the Antiquity of Ireland,* Dublin,
   Printed by S. Powell at the Sign of the Printing-Press in Copper-Alley, for the
   Author, 1717, pp. ix–x.
3. Harrison, p. 50. Morley, pp. 34–62.
4. Parthalán Mac Aogáin, ed., *Graiméir Ghaeilge na mBráthar Mionúr*, Baile Átha
   Cliath, Institiúid Ardléinn Bhaile Átha Cliath, 1968.
5. Cited in Harrison, p. 34.
6. Eric Cheyfitz, *The Poetics of Imperialism: Translation and Colonization from The
   Tempest to Tarzan,* Oxford University Press, 1991, p. 15.
7. Harrison, p. 112.
8. Brendan Bradshaw, 'Geoffrey Keating: Apologist of Irish Ireland', Brendan
   Bradshaw, Andrew Hadfield & Willy Maley (eds.), *Representing Ireland: Literature
   and the Origins of Conflict 1534–1660*, Cambridge, Cambridge University Press,
   1993, p. 166.
9. Diarmaid Ó Catháin, 'Dermot O'Connor, Translator of Keating', *Eighteenth-
   Century Ireland: Iris an dá chultúr*, vol. 2, 1987, pp. 67–87.
10. Ó Catháin, p. 75.
11. 'In Ireland it is likely that it is this spirit which prompted the leading scholars of
    the *Dublin Philosophical Society* – the likes of Narcissus Marsh, William King, the
    Molyneux brothers, John Madden and John Sterne – to collect material on Irish
    history' (Harrison, p. 46).
12. 'They were particularly interested in the reports on their antiquity that were to be
    found in the famous old Irish-language manuscripts and they made every effort to
    find them so as to collect and copy them. Of course, it was a natural reaction of
    the defeated Gaelic Irish to attempt to prove and affirm the nobility, sanctity and
    civility of their race from these sources. They also understood that their interest in
    history was in keeping with the antiquarian activities of Protestant scholars and

that the latter would be happy to pay for manuscripts, and for the copying, translation and interpretation of historical texts in Irish' (Harrison, p. 51).

13. Ó Catháin, p. 87.

14. Harrison, p. 86.

15. *An Account of Dr. Keting's History of Ireland and the Translation of it by Dermod O'Connor. Taken out of a Dissertation prefixed to the Memoirs of the Marquis of Clanricard, lately published in London. With some specimens of the said History and Translation*. Dublin, Edwin Sandys, 1723, p. 4; see also Brian Ó Cuív, 'An Eighteenth-Century Account of Keating and his *Foras Feasa ar Éirinn*', *Éigse*, vol. 9, 1958–61, pp. 263–269.

16. *An Account*, p. 11.

17. J.G. Simms, 'John Toland (1670–1722), a Donegal Heretic', *Irish Historical Studies*, vol. XVI, no. 63, 1969, pp. 304–20.

18. Dermot O'Connor, 'Preface by the Translator', *The General History of Ireland*. Collected by the Learned Jeoffry Keating. Faithfully translated from the original Irish Language by Dermod O'Connor, 2nd edn, London, Creake, 1726, p. iii.

19. Harrison, p. 96.

20. *An Account*, p. 18.

21. Cited in Harrison, p. 115.

22. Nessa Ní Shéaghdha, 'Collectors of Irish Manuscripts: Motives and Methods', *Celtica*, vol. 17, 1985, pp. 1–28.

23. See Robert Welch, *A History of Verse Translation from the Irish 1789–1897*, Gerrards Cross, Colin Smythe, 1988, pp. 19–24.

24. Aodán Mac Póilín, '"Spiritual Beyond the Ways of Men"– Images of the Gael', *The Irish Review*, no. 16, 1994, p. 14.

25. Welch, pp. 25–6.

26. Cainneach Ó Maonaigh, 'Scríbhneoirí Gaeilge an Seachtú hAois Déag', *Studia Hibernica*, vol. 2, 1962, p. 191.

27. Charlotte Brooke, *Reliques of Irish Poetry*, Dublin, Georges Bonham, 1789, p. iv.

28. Brooke, p. iii.

29. Brooke, p. viii.

30. Brooke, p. viii.

31. Brooke, p. vii.

32. Welch, p. 5.

33. Brooke, p. v.

34. Brooke, p. v.

35. Brooke, p. v.

36. Brooke, p. 6.

37. Cheyfitz, p. 121.

38. See Julia G. Ebel, 'Translation and Cultural Nationalism in the Reign of Elizabeth', *Journal of the History of Ideas*, vol. 30, 1969, pp. 593–602; J. Matthiesen, *Translation, an Elizabethan Art*, Cambridge, Harvard University Press, 1931.

39. George Puttenham, *The Arte of English Poesie (1589)*, Gladys Doidge Wilcock and Alice Walker, eds., Cambridge University Press, 1936, p. 154.

40. James Hardiman, *Irish Minstrelsy, or Bardic Remains of Ireland with English Poetical Translations*, 2 vols., London, Joseph Robins, 1831, p. xxxii.

41. Hardiman, p. xvi.

42. Robin Flower, *The Irish Tradition*, Oxford, Clarendon Press, 1947, pp. 109–110.

43. Hardiman, p. xxxviii.

44. William Hamilton Drummond, *Ancient Irish Minstrelsy*, Dublin, Hodges and Smith, 1852, p. xxvii.

45. For a discussion of Orientalism and translation see Richard Jacquemond, 'Translation and Cultural Hegemony: The Case of French-Arabic Translation', Lawrence Venuti, ed., *Rethinking Translation*, London, Routledge, 1992, pp. 139–158.

46. Hardiman, p. viii.

47. Mary Louise Pratt, *Imperial Eyes: Travel Writing and Transculturation*, London, Routledge, 1992, p. 64.

48. Henry R. Montgomery, *Specimens of the Early Native Poetry of Ireland in English*, Dublin, James McGlashan, 1846, p. iii.

49. Drummond, p. xxvii.

50. Drummond, p. xxviii.

51. George Sigerson, *Bards of the Gael and Gall*, 2nd edn., London, Fisher Unwin, 1907, p. 3.

52. Welch, p. 5.

53. Cathal Ó Háinle, 'Ó Chaint na nDaoine go dtí an Caighdeán Oifigiúil', Kim McCone et al., eds., *Stair na Gaeilge*, Maigh Nuad, Coláiste Phádraig, 1994, p. 746.

54. J.E. Caerwyn Williams and Máirín Ní Mhuiríosa, *Traidisiún Liteartha na nGael*, Baile Átha Cliath, An Clóchomhar, 1985, pp. 311–12.

55. Williams and Ní Mhuiríosa, p. 315.

56. See Jeffrey L. Kallen, 'Language maintenance, loss, and ethnicity in the United States: Perspectives on Irish', *Teanga*, vol. 13, 1993, pp. 100–111.

57. Drummond, p. xviii.

58. Johannes Fabian, *Time and the Other: How Anthropology Makes its Object*, New York, Columbia University Press, 1983, p. 35.

59. Hardiman, p. xxxii.

60. Hardiman, p. xxx.

61. Hardiman, p. xxxix.

62. The life and work of Samuel Ferguson have attracted a lot of interest in recent years. See Welch, pp. 90–101; Gréagóir Ó Dúill, *Samuel Ferguson: Beatha agus Saothar*, Baile Átha Cliath, An Clóchomhar, 1993, esp. pp. 68–90; Terence Brown and Barbara Hayley, eds., *Samuel Ferguson: A Centenary Tribute*, Dublin, Royal Irish Academy, 1987; and Peter Denman, *Samuel Ferguson: The Literary Achievement*, Gerrards Cross, Colin Smythe, 1990.

63. Samuel Ferguson, 'Hardiman's Irish Minstrelsy No. II', *Dublin University Magazine*, vol. 4, no. 20, August 1834, p. 153.

64. Samuel Ferguson, 'Hardiman's Irish Minstrelsy No.I', *Dublin University Magazine*, vol. 3, no. 16, April 1834, p. 457.

65. Samuel Ferguson, 'Hardiman's Irish Minstrelsy No. III', *Dublin University Magazine*, vol. 4, no. 22, October 1834, p. 447.

66. Ferguson, 'Irish Minstrelsy No. III', p. 450.

67. Ferguson, 'Irish Minstrelsy No. III', p. 453.

68. Ferguson, 'Irish Minstrelsy No. III', p. 455.

69. Ferguson, 'Irish Minstrelsy No. III', pp. 453–4.

70. Ferguson, 'Irish Minstrelsy No. II', p. 154.

71. Samuel Ferguson, 'The Dublin Penny Journal', *Dublin University Magazine*, vol. 15, no. 85, January 1840, p. 115.

72. David Lloyd, *Nationalism and Minor Literature: James Clarence Mangan and the Emergence of Irish Cultural Nationalism*, Berkeley, University of California Press, 1987, p. 84.

73. Ferguson, 'Irish Minstrelsy No. III', p. 460.

74. Samuel Ferguson, 'Hardiman's Irish Minstrelsy No. IV', *Dublin University Magazine*, vol. 4, no. 23, November 1834, p. 529.

75. Aristotle, *On the Art of Poetry*, trans. T.S. Dorsch, Harmondsworth, Penguin, 1978, pp. 61–62.

76. Hardiman, p. xxxvii.

77. Ferguson, 'Irish Minstrelsy No. II', p. 154.

78. 'Irish Minstrelsy No. II', p. 160.

79. Cheyfitz, p. 93.

80. Brooke, pp. vi–vii.

81. It is worth pointing out, however, that one of the features of Irish culture stressed in Celticism is precisely its feminine quality, and translation from Irish into English would therefore involve transvestism in the more restricted sense of dressing in the linguistic clothes of the opposite sex. For Celticist notions of the feminine see Catherine Nash, 'Embodying the Nation: The West of Ireland, Landscape and Irish Identity', Barbara O'Connor and Michael Cronin, eds., *Tourism in Ireland: A Critical Analysis*, Cork, Cork University Press, 1993, pp. 86–112.

82. James Clarence Mangan, 'Literae Orientales no. iv', *Dublin University Magazine*, vol. 15, no. 88, April 1840, p. 377.

83. Ali Behdad, *Belated Travellers: Orientalism in the Age of Colonial Dissolution*, Cork, Cork University Press, 1994, pp. 113–132.

84. Ferguson, 'Irish Ministrelsy No. II', p. 155.

85. Hardiman, p. xxxviii.

86. *Maith agus Dearmad, Sgeul beag d'ar b'ughdar Maria Edgeworth. Rosanna ón ughdar chéadna.* Air na d-tarruing go fírinneach ó Bhéarla go Gaoidheilg air iarratas & fa thearmonn na Cuideachta Gaoidheilge Uladh a m-Beul-ferrsaide le Tomás Ó Fíannachtaigh, Oide Gaoidheilge a m-Beul-ferrsaide. Clodh-bhuailte a m-Baile-ath-Cliath, 1833.

87. Breandán Ó Buachalla, *I mBéal Feirste cois cuain*, Baile Átha Cliath, An Clóchomhar, 1968, pp. 85–6.

88. Williams and Ní Mhuiríosa, p. 325.

89. Ó Buachalla, pp. 37–8.
90. William Bedell Stanford, *Ireland and the Classical Tradition*, Dublin, Allen Figgis, 1976, p. 87; Charles Vallancey, *Essay on the Antiquity of the Irish Language*, Dublin, Powell, 1772.
91. John Mac Hale, *A Selection of Moore's Melodies*, Dublin, Duffy, 1871, p. vi.
92. Marianne Elliott, *Wolfe Tone: Prophet of Irish Independence*, New Haven, Yale University Press, 1989, p. 418; Brendán Ó Buachalla, 'The Gaelic Background', Brown and Hayley, eds., *Ferguson*, pp. 28–9.
93. Cited in Ní Shéaghdha, p. 22.
94. Lloyd, p. 94.
95. Erionnach (George Sigerson), *The Poets and Poetry of Munster*, Dublin, John O'Daly, 1860, p. viii.
96. Sigerson, p. xx.
97. Sigerson, p. xxiii.
98. Sigerson, p. xxvii.
99. Sigerson, *Bards*, p. 91.
100. Ferguson, 'Irish Minstrelsy No. III', p. 451.
101. Breandán Ó Buachalla, 'Arthur Brownlow: A Gentleman more Curious than Ordinary', *Ulster Local History*, vol. 7, no. 2, 1982, pp. 24–28.
102. Ferguson, 'Irish Minstrelsy No. III', p. 451.
103. Sigerson, *Bards*, p. 2.
104. Welch, p. 169–170.
105. Welch, p. 2.
106. Quoted in Stanford, p. 27.
107. Isaac Butt, *The Georgics of Virgil*, Dublin, Curry and Company, 1834.
108. Thomas Moore, *Odes of Anacreon* in *The Poetical Works of Thomas Moore*, vol. 1, London, Longman, 1840, p. xv.
109. Moore, p. xxiv.
110. Moore, p. xxv.
111. William Maginn, *Homeric Ballads*, London, Parker, 1850.
112. Stanford, p. 170.
113. Louis Kelly, *The True Interpreter: A History of Translation Theory and Practice in the West*, Oxford, Basil Blackwell, 1979, p. 151.
114. Mangan's German translations are the subject of a particularly penetrating chapter by David Lloyd and my purpose here is not to repeat his arguments but to concentrate on an aspect of Mangan's work that relates more broadly to translation activity in Ireland. For his analysis see Lloyd, Chapter 5, pp. 129–158.
115. James Clarence Mangan, 'Anthologia Germanica', *Dublin University Magazine*, vol. 7, no. 39, March 1836, pp. 278–302.
116. Cited in Welch, p. 105.
117. Welch, p. 111.
118. Lloyd, p. 105.
119. Cited in Ní Shéaghdha, p. 12.
120. Cited in Harrison, p. 117.

4

TRANSLATION AND THE EMERGENCE OF A NEW IRELAND

TRANSLATION HAD BECOME a fine art. This was the conclusion of Robert Tyrrell writing in the Trinity College journal, *Hermathena*, in 1887. He delighted in the perfection of Jebb's translations of Sophocles and declares that 'happily for the learners of the present day, bald translation is no longer in fashion. Every editor at least aims at making his versions not only accurate but adequate.'[1] Tyrrell's enthusiasm was understandable if ahistorical. Every generation is convinced that they translate better than the previous one if only because language changes and the idiom of one age seems archaic to the next. Less obvious to Tyrrell was the revolutionary potential of this fine art in Ireland.

The late nineteenth century in Ireland was a period of accelerated political change. The successes of the Land League, the emergence of Parnell, the conversion of Gladstone to Home Rule, and the foundation of the Gaelic Athletic Association, in 1884, were signs of growing political and cultural confidence. Curiosity about the past was an expression of an interest in the future. Questions of language and cultural self-confidence were central to the emerging definitions of Irishness in the period, but without translation it is unlikely that the questions could even have been formulated. Translation cannot be ignored in an analysis of the founding moment of Irish modernity. Furthermore, to understand the role of translation in the emergent cultural movements of the century is also to understand many of the limits, difficulties and paradoxes of these movements. Translators were hugely influential in this period, but their influence has often been overshadowed by their discretion. Brief prefatory appearances and dense thickets of footnotes concealed rather than revealed the unsung makers of a new culture.

DANGEROUS POLITICS, TRANSLATION AND SCHOLARSHIP

The Irish language in early nineteenth-century Ireland was studied but feared. The associations that emerged to promote scholarship in the language publicly eschewed any political intentions. The Dublin Gaelic Society, founded in 1807, had a rule expressly proscribing discussions of politics: 'no religious or political Debates whatever shall be permitted, such being foreign to the Object and Principles of the Society'.[2] The Iberno-Celtic Society, founded in 1818, had a similar rule. Political questions were also ignored by later societies such as the Ulster Gaelic Society (1830), The Irish Archaeological Society (1840), The Celtic Society (1845) and The Ossianic Society (1853). Cathal Ó Háinle notes that, 'These societies confined themselves to resurrecting ancient texts from the manuscripts and publishing them: this was safe. To show interest in preserving the living language, however, would be dangerous, as it could revive old enmities and fears.'[3] The association of language with dangerous politics was reflected in the tendency of mainstream nationalism to play down cultural demands for much of the nineteenth century. Agrarian violence, the bloody outcome of the 1798 rebellion, the enormous success of O'Connell's repeal movement, the ravages of landlordism did not make for a country at peace with its temporal rulers. As Leerssen points out:

> It was only by explicit agreement to exclude the political implications of their pursuits from their collective consciousness that these societies were able to steer a precarious middle course between Scylla and Charbydis – to avoid participation either in the sectarian enmity between Gael and Gall, or in the national enmity between Ireland and Britain.[4]

Translations of manuscript materials figured prominently in the transactions of the different societies and were produced by both Catholic and Protestant scholars. Antiquarianism was a middle ground and so, by extension, was translation. The societies continued the antiquarian tradition of the eighteenth century, which allowed an exploration of cultural identity, namely the antiquity of Irish 'civilisation', but studiously avoided contemporary parallels. The activity was not, however, as innocent as it seemed. From the mid-eighteenth century onwards, the Anglo-Irish felt an increasing sense of cultural separateness from England.[5] The work of the antiquarians could only be fully appreciated by most members of the Ascendancy class in translation, so translated materials were of crucial importance in providing alternative accounts of Irish history, language and learning. The exclusion of political considerations from the activities of the antiquarian societies was effective in that little was done to protect the living language. At another level, the exclusion was wholly ineffective in that the very substance of separate cultural identity in the nineteenth century would be drawn from the translations and studies of the Celtic scholars. The act of Irish–English translation remained inescapably political.

The long-term political effects of scholarly activity should not be confused, however, with popularity and easy access. A certain translation tradition in Celtic scholarship in the nineteenth century prided itself on a forbidding literalism that saw exactness, not felicity, as the reward of erudition. W.K. Sullivan, the Professor of Chemistry at the Catholic University in Dublin edited Eugene O'Curry's *On the Manners and Customs of the Ancient Irish*. The three-volume work appeared posthumously in 1873. The fact that a professor of chemistry would edit such a work is itself eloquent testimony to the interaction between the two cultures (science/arts rather than Catholic/Protestant) in nineteenth-century Dublin. Sullivan as editor supplies references to manuscripts and to the originals of translations used in the text. He is mildly critical of O'Curry's translation strategy, finding that 'some of Professor O'Curry's translations were only free renderings of the original text, more or less paraphrased, but always sufficiently close and correct for the purposes for which they were used'.[6] Although 'anxious' to correct some of the translations, Sullivan refrains from doing so out of respect for his colleague's memory. He discusses the difficulties in translating names and technical terms from Old and Middle Irish and the specific problems of changing orthography. Sullivan's policy is clearly stated:

> [. . .] to spell them [names] as they are spelled in the oldest manuscripts avoiding especially the modern system of corrupt aspiration, which renders Irish so barabarous looking. I have not used *ea* for the long Irish *e*, as is invariably done by most Irish writers, because I believe that any deviation whatever from the original form, is a mistake.[7]

The original is sacrosanct, and deviation in matters of translation or orthography is suspect. The scholarly attention that was brought to bear on the original in the translated texts of the period was formidable. In John O'Donovan's seven-volume translation of the *Annals of the Four Masters* published in 1851, many footnotes run on for pages, dwarfing the text and its translation on the printed page.[8] The dutiful concern with formal equivalence in translation was further reinforced by the involvement of foreign scholars such as Ernst Windisch, Thurneysen, Strachen, de Jubainville and Kuno Meyer in Celtic Studies. These scholars, trained in the rigorous traditions of continental philology, were not primarily concerned with translation as a fine art. As with their compatriots working in Oriental studies, the emphasis was on exactness and the production of texts acceptable to other scholars. Standish Hayes O'Grady in *Silva Gadelica*, first published in 1892, acknowledges the intimidating translation environment. His opening remarks in the Preface to his translations are defensive, and O'Grady claims that:

> The work is far from being exclusively or even primarily designed for the omniscient impeccable leviathans of science that headlong sound the linguistic ocean to its most horrid depths, and (in the intervals of ramming each other) ply their flukes on such audacious small fry as even on the mere surface will ply within their danger.[9]

The analogy he uses to describe his own labours is explicitly Orientalist. O'Grady claims that he hopes to see his work 'occupy the rank which Orientalists agree in according to the products of the native presses of Stamboul, Cairo and Boulaq: that of a good and careful manuscript'.[10] The native scholars were to produce good copy for the visiting linguists. O'Grady does not present himself, as others did in the century, as an 'archaeologist' but as a 'humble quarryman who painfully gets the rough stuff'. The rough stuff is to subsequently serve as 'raw material for "keltologue" and "philologue", for folklorist, comparative mythologist and others'.[11] The inverted commas suggest a residual scepticism on the part of the native quarryman, but the list of beneficiaries of his work appears to our eyes curiously incomplete. There is no mention of writers. The benefits of translation are cognitive not aesthetic. The translation enterprise feeds philology, folklore, comparative mythology, Celtic studies but not art. Already, however, the teleology of translation was changing.

A NEW LITERARY VERNACULAR

In 1890, a collection of prose translations entitled *Beside the Fire* was published.[12] The translator was the future President of Ireland, Douglas Hyde. The collection included translations of some of the folk-tales contained in his own *Leabhar Sgeuluigheachta*, published in 1889, and the other sources were Irish-language material collected by folklorists such as

William Larminie and Patrick Kennedy. The translations by Hyde were into a distinctive Hiberno-English. They were idiomatic, unpretentious and conveyed energy and difference without descending into parody. In the year that the folk-tale translations were published, Hyde's translations of poetry were being published in the *Nation* newspaper (between April and November). When that newspaper ceased publication, further translations of poetry appeared in the *Weekly Freeman* in 1892. A year later, a number of these translations were published in book form as *Abhráin Grádh Chúige Connacht* or *The Love Songs of Connacht*. In his introduction to a modern edition of the *Love Songs*, Mícheál Ó hAodha claims that the translations 'marked a turning-point in the Irish Literary Revival and revealed a new source for the development of a distinctive Irish mode in verse and poetic prose'.[13] Hyde pursued the translation policy adopted in *Beside the Fire*. The prose translations of the poems were in the English vernacular of the Irish countryside. In the way that biblical translations in earlier centuries had conferred a new status and legitimacy upon European vernaculars, Hyde's bold step in translation opened up the possibility of using Hiberno-English as a new literary vernacular. W.B. Yeats emphasised the liberatory effects of Hyde's translation strategy in a preface to a limited edition of the *Love Songs* published by Dun Emer Press:

> This little book . . . was the first book that made known to readers that had no Irish the poetry of Irish country people. There have been other translators but they had a formal eighteenth century style that took what Dr. Hyde would call the 'sap and pleasure' out of simple thought and emotion. Their horses were always steeds and their cows kine, their rhythms had the formal monotony or the oratorical energy of that middle class literature that comes more out of will and reason than out of imagination and sympathy . . . His [Hyde's] imagination is indeed at its best only when he writes in Irish, or in that beautiful English of the country people who remember too much Irish to talk like a newspaper, and I commend his prose to all who can delight in fine prose.[14]

Yeats felt that Hyde's prose translations were superior to his verse translations. These were victims of an anxiety of influence that compromised their novelty. Hyde was aware of the translation tradition, however, and saw his own individual talent invested in the attempt to reproduce the vowel rhymes as well as the exact metres of the original language. He is modest in his claims for the prose translations: 'My English prose translation only aims at being literal, and has courageously, though no doubt ruggedly, reproduced the Irish idioms of the original.'[15] Hyde's translations mark a transition from translation as an act of exegesis to translation as an agent of aesthetic and political renewal. Translations no longer simply bore witness to the past, they were to actively shape a future. The threshold that was being crossed was clearly marked by the translator. In his preface, Hyde claims that the work contained in the collection was originally in Irish and he continues:

> but the exigencies of publication in a weekly newspaper necessitated the translation of it into English. This I do not now wholly regret; for the literal translation of these songs will, I hope, be of some advantage to that at present increasing class of Irishmen who take a just pride in their native language, and to those foreigners who great philologists and etymologists as they are, find themselves hampered in their pursuits through their unavoidable ignorance of the modern Irish idiom which can only be correctly interpreted by the native speakers, who are, alas! becoming fewer and fewer every day.[16]

The old and new audiences for translation, foreign philologists and native readers, are juxtaposed. Translation that down the centuries has featured in periods of political change in Ireland is once more present. Taking a just pride in one's native language has political implications that are made explicit in Hyde's Irish 'Fuagradh' to the collection where he calls on God to free Ireland – 'go saoraidh Dia Éire'.[17] The political caution of the antiquarians is no longer in evidence. However, it is interesting to note that in one sense Hyde's translation theory does not represent a radical break with his scholarly predecessors. Hyde himself was a much respected scholar and when he offers a 'literal translation' to his readers, he is echoing Sullivan's belief that any deviation from the original form is a mistake. Patrick Rafroidi failed to realise this when he discussed the birth of a new literature in English through translation:

> The criterion used [to judge success in literary translation] is the exact opposite of the one used by the Celtic scholar. The necessary prerequisite – though not in itself always sufficient – is at the very least a certain distance with respect to the original if not unfaithfulness.[18]

The criterion used by the Celtic scholar and the literary translator may, in fact, be remarkably similar. Thus, literalism in translation can be seen to have both a conservative and a subversive function. The literal translation of texts into the functional prose of formal English can minimise the aesthetic effects of the original, while scrupulously respecting meaning. The translation contains the source language and conserves the target language. Literalism becomes subversive when, as in Hyde's case, the target language itself is undermined or altered by a different syntax, sound-system or lexicon. In both cases, the translations are driven by similar concerns to be faithful to the original, but it is the fate of the target language rather than fidelity to the source language that will determine the outcome of the translation effort.

It is important to remember the factor of patronage in assessing the impact of translation. The transactions of learned societies were read by a cultivated few. The publications did not enjoy a large readership. In an address to the Irish Literary Society in London in July 1892, Charles Gavan Duffy wondered aloud, 'how much of the wealth of our ancient Gaelic literature still lies buried in untranslated MSS., or in the transactions of learned societies'.[19] The appearance of Hyde's work in weekly newspapers like the *Nation* and the *Weekly Freeman* meant that his work was reaching a wide audience. To this extent, he was realising the ambition of the Dublin bookseller and publisher, John O'Daly, who as Cathal Ó Háinle puts it, wanted 'not to reach into the English drawing room, but into the cabins of the Irish peasantry'.[20] O'Daly published *Reliques of Irish Jacobite Poetry* (1844), *Irish Popular Songs* (1847) and *The Poets and Poetry of Munster* (first series, 1849; second series, 1860) in cheaper editions in the hope of reaching a reading public that was not predominantly Ascendancy. Popularity for Hyde was not without contradiction. The paradox of dissemination is expressed by Hyde himself when he says that the decison to translate was dictated by the 'exigencies of publication in a weekly newspaper'. Newspapers that were sympathetic to cultural nationalism were powerful agents of anglicisation. The full extent of the linguistic change in nineteenth-century Ireland is evident in the need for translation of Irish work into English if it is to reach a popular audience. Hyde implicitly identifies one reason for translation in his lament for the rapidly disappearing native speakers of Irish. It is precisely his concern for the state of the living language that led Hyde along with Eoin MacNeill and others to found the Gaelic League on the 31 July 1893. In *Synge and the Irish Language*, Declan Kiberd expresses the tension between the intention and effects of Hyde's translation activity:

> The translation was included simply to help the student who found difficulty with the Irish, for the object of the work was to popularise the spread of Irish literature. It soon became clear, however, that the main appeal of the book to Yeats and his contemporaries lay in Hyde's own translations, and especially in those translations written in Anglo-Irish prose rather than in verse. The very success of the book caused the defeat of its primary purpose. Instead of popularising Irish literature, it made the creation of a national literature in English seem all the more plausible.[21]

Hyde's translations were not so much pedagogical as proseletysing in their intent, but Kiberd is correct to identify the unintended effects of the translations. They did set in train a new movement in Irish writing in English. In his attempts, however, to prove the pre-eminence of what he refers to as the 'Anglo-Irish dialect', Kiberd is less convincing. The work of Hyde was not only responsible for the emergence of a new literary movement in English. It would also, through the agency of *Conradh na Gaeilge* or the Gaelic League, lay the foundation for the emergence of a new literature in modern Irish. The *Love Songs* did succeed in their primary purpose, to make a wider public aware of the literary riches of the Irish language. The difference lay in the response to his translations. For Yeats, Synge and others the translations were the beginnings of a new literature in English. For other writers such as Patrick Pearse, the translations pointed to the excellence of the original and were an incentive to rediscover the language and create a new literature in Irish. Thus, the two literatures of modern Ireland can be said to emerge from the translation moment in the nineteenth century.

TRANSLATION AFTERLIFE AND THE LITERARY REVIVAL

The influence of the works of Standish James O'Grady on the Irish Literary Revival was considerable. A classics scholar from Trinity College, he had become interested in Celtic studies after reading Sylvester O'Halloran's *History of Ireland*, first published in 1778. O'Grady's *History of Ireland: Heroic Period* appeared in 1878, to be followed three years later by *History of Ireland: Cuchulain and his Contemporaries*. For Yeats, 'every Irish imaginative writer owed a portion of his soul' to O'Grady.[22] Synge was reading him as early as 1892.[23] Standish James O'Grady had, however, only a scanty knowledge of Irish and his work was heavily based on translations. His real achievement was to turn what Yeats called 'the dry pages of O'Curry and his school' into a dramatic, highly-coloured narrative.[24] O'Grady's role as literary catalyst was only conceivable because translation existed. In the absence of translated materials, he would have had no option but silence. O'Grady demonstrates the importance of the afterlife of the translation itself. The translation work of O'Halloran, O'Curry and others was in a sense recreated for a wider audience. O'Grady was the link between the antiquarianism of the eighteenth and

138

nineteenth centuries and the Literary Revival, a link that was forged in translation. Lady Gregory was another prominent figure of the Revival who, like O'Grady, acted as mediator for the translation scholarship of earlier generations. Though considerably more proficient in Irish than O'Grady, she had recourse to English translations when preparing *Cuchulain of Muirthemne* (1902), her influential version in Anglo-Irish dialect of the stories of the Red Branch knights.[25] Though criticised by Synge, Hyde, O'Grady and Meyer for the scholarly shortcomings of the text, and particularly for bowdlerisation, the value of Gregory's work was vindicated by its aesthetic importance for Synge among others.[26] Her adoption of Hiberno-English crucially strengthened the case for a literature in that language. In his review of the translation, Synge mentioned Hyde's translations of the *Love Songs* as well as articles by Yeats on folklore written 'with this cadence in mind', and concludes:

> The intellectual movement that has been taking place in Ireland for the last twenty years has chiefly been a movement towards a nearer appreciation of the country people, and their language, so that it is not too much to say that the translation of the old MSS. into this idiom is the result of an evolution than of a merely personal idea.[27]

Translation, for Lady Gregory, was not simply a tale of two languages. She successfully introduced Molière to Abbey Theatre audiences. The *Doctor in Spite of Himself*, *The Rogueries of Scapin* and *The Miser* were produced between 1906 and 1909. All three plays were translations into Gregory's 'Kiltartan' or Anglo-Irish dialect of the French originals. Her translation of *Le Bourgeois gentilhomme* was produced as *The Would-Be Gentleman* in 1926. In her edition of Lady Gregory's translations and adaptations, Ann Saddlemyer is somewhat uncritical in her assessment of foreign-language translations in Gregory's *oeuvre*, 'She [Lady Gregory] never really considered translations to be "creative work"; instead, as she explains in *Our Irish Theatre*, they were simply part of her responsibility to the Abbey.'[28] The presentation of translation as a secondary, uncreative activity is depressingly familiar and Gregory's own analysis needs to be challenged. If Tudor England and Romantic Germany were eager to translate the Greek and Roman classics into their language, it was because translation was a part of nation-building. Making Homer or Virgil available in English or German showed that the vernacular languages were capable of the highest levels of poetic expression and, also, that the literatures of past civilisations could be confidently absorbed into new national cultures. These cultures gained through the associated prestige of past greatness.[29] Translating Molière into 'Kiltartan' is an act of cultural self-confidence. It implies that Hiberno-English is a fit vehicle for one of the greatest playwrights of the European literary tradition. If the language of Synge or Lady Gregory's 'Kiltartan' is the translated speech of a rural population whose syntax and speech habits are Gaelic, translation is obviously central to the genesis of this new literary language. However, not only translation process but translation product is important in the construction of cultures. The translation of Molière into Hiberno-English, rather than British English, is replicating the initial Tudor 'conquest' of the classics through translation that is at the heart of rising linguistic self-confidence in sixteenth and seventeenth-century England. When the Irish Free State embarked on a translation scheme in the Irish language in the 1920s to form the basis for a new literature in that language, it echoed what had already been happening in the English language in Ireland since the early years of the century.

A fellow translator and collaborator with Lady Gregory in translation from French was John Millington Synge.[30] He published translations of both French and Italian poetry.[31] In Declan Kiberd's words:

> Synge had a genius for translation. His literary sensibility found its truest expression in the manoeuvre between two languages, Irish and English. His own poetry, composed in English, seems all to often to be a pastiche of second-rate contemporary styles, whereas the brilliant translations from continental languages into Anglo-Irish dialect give us a sense of the man himself. The dialect in which he finally found his desired medium was the bilingual weave produced by this manoeuvre between two languages.[32]

Synge as the unhoused, the extraterritorial, wandering between two languages is a figure who is both translator and translated. He translates but, like so many other Anglo-Irish writers of the nineteenth century, he is translating himself into the language and culture of the other. It is no wonder that he finds himself drawn to the process of translation as it externalises and in a way resolves his divided linguistic allegiances. Synge not only embodies the centrality of translation to the Revival, but he also points to the literary future of twentieth-century Ireland which lies under the sign of translation. Patrick Pearse, Brendan Behan, Eoghan Ó Tuairisc, Flann O'Brien, James Joyce, Samuel Beckett, Austin Clarke, Liam O'Flaherty and Frank O'Connor are but some of the writers in modern Irish literature who are caught between languages and cultures. They will in a sense assimilate the lesson that Eric Cheyfitz sees as underlying a post-imperialist politics of translation:

We must be in translation between cultures and between groups within our own culture if we are to understand the dynamics of our imperialism. For our imperialism historically has functioned (and continues to function) by substituting for the difficult politics of translation another politics of translation that represses these difficulties.[33]

Synge studied Irish while in Trinity College from 1888 to 1892. In his early years, his vision of Irish was mainly antiquarian, but during his period as a student in Paris he became passionately interested in Breton literature, and this eventually brought him back to Ireland and to the living reality of Irish on the western seabord. Among other texts he translated were poems by Keating, a folk poem from Aran called *Rucard Mór* and the *Oidhe Chloinne Uisnigh* or *The Fate of the Children of Uisneach*. Synge was acutely aware of the fact of translation intertextuality, of the translator working in a particular tradition. He was particularly scathing on much of the Irish verse translation produced in English in the nineteenth century: 'There is probably no mass of tawdry commonplace jingle quite so worthless as the verse translations that have been made from it [Gaelic poetry] in Ireland during the last century.'[34] Part of the contempt he directed against the translators was born out of self-loathing, as he had previously been drawn to the work of such translators. In view of the fact that Synge's studies in Trinity and Paris were strongly philological in orientation, it is not surprising that his initial exercises in translation were guided by a literal caution.

Examples of this early translation work are to be found in his review of J.C. MacErlean's edition of the poems of Geoffrey Keating, *Dánta, Amhráin is Caointe Sheatrúin Céitinn*.[35] An Aran Islander who was dissatisfied with Archbishop MacHale's translations of Moore's *Irish Melodies* had told Synge that 'a translation is no translation unless it will give you the music of the poem along with the words of it'.[36] The translator as writer, or the writer as rewriter, saw that the challenge was to convey the excitement and beauty of the source language in the target language. To do this, he would have to abandon the artifice of fluency and allow the target language, the language of the coloniser, to be colonised in its turn by the language of the colonised. Synge felt this was now possible for the first time in centuries: 'the linguistic atmosphere of Ireland has become definitely English enough, for the first time, to allow work to be done in English that is perfectly Irish in essence'.[37] Synge was to realise what Paul Hiffernan had hoped for in his 1754 pamphlet, *The Hiberniad*, the use of Irish subject matter in a national literature in the

English language.[38] Translation of a language and a culture on the scale envisaged by Synge was a heroic enterprise. Translation is not merely a matter of texts, however, it is also to do with contexts and traces. The Great Famine had certainly cleared the 'linguistic atmosphere' but translation would be haunted by the lost source, the problem of origin. The uncertainty as to the exact role of translation is evident in Yeats's shifting allegiances. In 1892, Yeats had argued that translation not (language) revival would be the way forward for a new national literary movement:

> Can we not keep the continuity of the nation's life, not by trying to do what Dr. Hyde has practically pronounced impossible, (i.e. saving Gaelic), but by translating and retelling in English, which shall have an indefinable Irish quality of rhythm and style, all that is best in the ancient literature.[39]

In 1900 in another letter to the editor (this time of the *Leader*), Yeats claimed that 'the mass of the people cease to understand any poetry when they cease to understand the Irish language, which is the language of their imaginations'.[40] By this definition, Yeats would have excluded himself from the appreciation of poetry and he would, in later life, argue that 'no man can think or write with music and vigour except in his mother tongue . . . Gaelic is my native tongue but it is not my mother tongue.'[41] Yeats's uncertainties were symptomatic rather than exceptional. Seamus Deane sees language as a distinguishing feature of European Romanticism as it affected Ireland: 'Irish literature tends to dwell on the medium in which it is written because it is difficult not to be self-conscious about a language which is simultaneously native and foreign.'[42] Translation is the fault-line that runs between the native and the foreign, and Irish writers since the Literary and Language Revival in the 1890s have been divided as to whether translation is indeed possible. Is translation an act of pillage and conquest, or is it a bisociative shift towards a newer, more exciting synthesis? In his study of Synge, Kiberd argues that the latter's Anglo-Irish dialect revitalised the inert clichés of the source language and in so doing reinvigorated the English language.[43]

In a preface to a new edition of the work, Kiberd invokes the notion of death and transfer: 'The potency of Synge's idiom derived in great part from the reported death of Irish; and the deader (or, at least, the more doomed) that language, the more vital the semantic energies that passed into Hiberno-English and the more magnificent that language seemed.'[44] Translation here is a form of necrophilia. Hiberno-English communes with the corpse of the dead language and draws a sustenance that nourishes: the translator becomes Dracula (a character who interestingly was the fictional creation of an Irishman, Bram Stoker). Seamus Deane employs the image of the nutritional remains of the departed language in a discussion of the work of another translator and writer, Thomas Kinsella. Deane describes the creative but violent energy in Kinsella's post-1973 poetry and gives as an example of this – 'the English language which revives itself in his own work on the corpse of the Irish language it destroyed'.[45] The ambiguity that is present in the image of the parasite is a key to the ambivalence felt towards translation itself.[46] The parasite feeds on another organism, breaks it down, destroys it. It is the symbol of aggression, rot, decay. The parasite also transforms, recycles and ensures the continuity of the cycle of life. Our assessment of the value and contribution of the translation enterprise to Irish modernity partly depends on how we respond to these metaphors of translation.

MISTRANSLATION AND THE STAGE IRISHMAN

The decision to use the English language of Irish people in written prose and on the stage represented a strategic change in the translation fortunes of the Irish. A standard attribute of the Stage Irishman from the seventeenth century onwards was a strong accent or 'brogue'.[47] Andelocra, an English character in a play by Thomas Dekker entitled *Old Fortunatus*, disguises himself at one stage in the play as an Irish costermonger and, later, as a French quack doctor. In both instances, the characters are distinguished by outlandish speech mannerisms and accents.[48] In Beaumont and Fletcher's comedy, *The Coxcomb* (1609), the protagonist, Antonio, disguises himself as an Irish footman. His object is to uncover his wife's infidelity by delivering a love-letter to her. Antonio jibs at having to speak an uncouth English: 'This rebell tonge sticks in my teeth worse then a toughe hen; sure it was nere knowne at Babell, for they soul'd no apples, and this was made for certaine at the first planting of Orchards, 'tis so crabbed.'[49] In his discussion of another seventeenth-century English play, Robert Howard's *The Committee*, Joseph Leerssen describes the appearance of a feature in the play that would enjoy a long life on the English stage. Teg is the name of the Irish character in the play:

> A new comical trait is his [Teg's] propensity to make verbal blunders, that is, statements which, though their intended meaning is clear and straightforward,

are so infelicitously expressed as to be self-contradictory. When ascribed to Irish-men, such blunders became known as 'Irish Bulls' and came to occupy a place alongside the brogue as standard markers of an Irish character's nationality.[50]

Leerssen describes the stereotype but fails to situate it in a translation context. A foreign accent and infelicitous expression are obvious consequences of unsuccessful translation, of the failure to master the language of the master. The notion that foreigners speaking one's lan-guage are irresistibly funny is, of course, common to many languages. However, in the Irish case, differences in language and expression became equated not only with the comic but with the inept. If Irish people after the conquest of the country were to become English speakers, then the same standards would be applied to them as to other English speakers. If they expressed themselves in strange or unusual ways or used different modes of intentionality, then they were classed with chlidren and the insane as quaint but dim. Paddy the Irishman is above all the archetype of mistranslation. By concealing the labour of translation, the difficulties that many Irish people faced in learning English as a foreign language, coupled with mother tongue interference and with apparent idiosyncrasies of accent and idiom, were presented as the undisguised hallmarks of stupid-ity. Depending on the state of relations between Ireland and England, the dullness was cast as sinister or endearing. Therefore, the decision by Synge, Hyde, Yeats and Lady Gregory to positively champion the English language spoken in rural areas was to make an aesthetic virtue of a translation necessity. The unwitting translation process that had sustained ridicule in jokes and on the stage was now consciously cultivated as a marker of specificity rather than shunned as a brand of inferiority. Instead of concealing translation, the process was now foregrounded in the public search for a new Irish literary idiom.

INFECTED AREAS

The solution to Ireland's language problems advocated by certain writers of the Literary Revival did not meet with unqualified approval. Pearse believed that the notion of an Irish literature in English was a contradiction in terms, and devoted his energies to creating a modern literature in the Irish language.[51] Another translation response to the language question came from the Reverend Timothy Corcoran in 'How English may be taught without Anglicising', an article published in the *Irish Monthly* in 1923. Corcoran believed that there was a danger from 'the general influence of works steeped in English thought in Irish schools of wide general service'.[52] Writing a year after Independence, Corcoran advocated the removal of 'English-hearted literature' from the school curriculum. His definition of this literature included works by Wordsworth, Byron and Macaulay. However, he did not see a role for Anglo-Irish literature in this purge:

> The removal is not meant to afford a wider field for 'Anglo-Irish literature': the cure would nearly be as bad as the disease; in some ways it would be definitely worse in its effects. A command of English and of English expression is essential for Ireland and for Irish education: but the need of it should not be a ground for tolerating either English thought, or the expression of Irish thought in English, in any enduring way or secured position intimately affecting our ideas and lives.[53]

The problem then was to reconcile the educational pragmatism of knowledge of the English language with the pernicious effects of its literature. Corcoran's answer was translation. Irish students would read English-language translations of masterpieces by Catholic writers from the European continent. History, literature and art would no longer be seen through the medium of the English mind and pupils and students would see what contemporary Catholic writers had to say on these activities. Corcoran's image of English culture, underpinning his commitment to the translation project, draws heavily on the Romantic origins of Irish cultural nationalism:

> If in very large proportion, this literature in English, but not English literature, is of the first quality, opening up to us not the products of a narrow insularity, of a repellent materialism, and of chronic indifference to what is of real worth in life, then the case for its use as a medium of full education in command of English expression is complete.[54]

Corcoran points specifically to modern French Catholic literature as a splendid source of inspiration for a new literature that was not to be in English, however, but in Irish. The purpose of learning English was exclusively utilitarian and only indirectly aesthetic, in that translations in that language might prove beneficial to Irish. There is a certain irony in Corcoran's advocacy of translation from French, as an earlier cultural nationalist, Charles Gavan Duffy, had viewed translation from French with alarm. We have already seen that Duffy was anxious for translations of Irish literature in English to be made available. His chief concern, like Corcoran's, was the minds of the young: 'I have made inquiries, and I am assured that the books chiefly read by the young in Ireland are detective and other sensational stories from England and America, and vile translations from the French of vile originals.'[55] Inventing 'stimulating stories of our own' would 'drive out the impure and aetheistical but sensational literature borrowed from the French'.[56] Translation, therefore, is a prophylactic, in one case against the vileness of French literature and, in the other, against the disease of English thought. Corcoran speaks of the 'infected areas of English thought' and concludes gloomily, 'Practically, all its areas are infected.'[57] To translate or not to translate, therefore, in the case of Duffy and Corcoran is guided by a gamut of political, linguistic, religious, educational and aesthetic reasons. The language choice provides an interesting glimpse into the shifting images of French literature, from godless atheism in the 1890s to exemplary Catholicism in the 1920s.[58] In both cases, however, translation is accorded considerable power and influence, notably in corrupting or improving the minds of the young. For this reason, the question of translation was never very far from the minds of writers and educators in Ireland.

PEADAR UA LAOGHAIRE AND THE SPEECH OF THE PEOPLE

If a new literature was to be created in Irish, what was to be the role of translation? One of the most influential figures in the birth of the new literature was Canon Peter O'Leary or, as he was known in Irish, An t-Athair Peadar Ua Laoghaire. He held strict views on translation which were expressed in a number of articles that were subsequently published posthumously as *Papers on Irish Idiom*. In two articles published in *Fáinne an Lae* in January 1899, Ua Laoghaire gives 'Some Hints as to How English Literary Matter should be Translated into Irish'. He starts with translation history, examining the 1833 Irish translation by Tomás Ó Fiannachtaigh of the Maria Edgeworth tale, *Forgive and Forget*. Ua Laoghaire is not convinced by the literal translation of the title, *Maith agus Dearmad*, and goes on to argue for the importance of dynamic equivalence in the translation of figurative language. The difference between Irish and English is absolute: 'It may be laid down as a general rule, such is the innate antagonism between the two languages in every phase, that so surely as a word is used figuratively in one it is certain to be taken literally in the other, and to express outrageous nonsense.'[59]

Figurative language is the site of opposition, the source of dissent in the meeting between two languages. Like the English-language translators we saw in the last chapter who were sensitive to the doubly transgressive qualities of metaphor in translation, Ua Laoghaire counsels extreme caution in dealing with the figurative:

> Read over the English matter carefully. Take all the ideas into your mind. Squeeze the ideas clean from all English *froth*. Be sure that you allow none of that oozy stuff to remain. English is full of it. You must also get rid of everything in the shape of metaphor. Take instead of it the true idea which the metaphor is intended to convey. When you have the ideas cleared completely of foreign matter, put them into the Irish side of your mind and shape them in the Irish language, just as you would if they had been your own ideas from the start.[60] [emphasis in original]

Ua Laoghaire is, in fact, restating a position that has had a long history in translation theory and practice, namely, that the translator must produce the text as if s/he were writing an original, contemporary text in the language. The seventeenth-century translator produces a translation of Virgil that reads like a text that Virgil would have produced in English had he been a seventeenth-century writer in that language. A striking difference between Dryden's and Ua Laoghaire's formulation, however, is the subtext of linguistic relativism.[61] The Romantic and Humboldtian identification of language with the specific *weltanschauung* of a people is evident in Ua Laoghaire's distinction between the 'Irish side of your mind' and the English ideas that are full of 'oozy stuff'. The distinction is made even more explicit in an article on the translation of the English passive voice published in 1900. Ua Laoghaire takes the example of the autonomous form of the Irish verb 'Dúntar' where the agent of the action does not have to be specified and argues:

> The Irish mind and this capability of the Irish verb have interacted on each other throughout all the time of the existence of both. When I think in Irish, I can let my verbs work in a mode entirely independent of the agents or objects of the actions which the verbs express. When I think in English I find I cannot do that.[62]

At one level, Ua Laoghaire's advice to translators is eminently sensible. The two languages are very different, and there is considerable metaphorical modulation between the two. Irish, on the whole, is more noun-centred and favours concrete images in expressing abstractions. Inductive generalisations and moral/political values are merged nonetheless in Ua Laoghaire's observations, and there is a distinctive value judgement in the disparaging reference to English '*froth*'. Translation is clearly separatist in orientation. The 'innate antagonism' between the two languages is a reflection and expression of political hostility between the two peoples. Ua Laoghaire is in fact unhappy with the very term, translation, and declares with regard to 'English matter', '*reproduce* the matter; don't *translate* it' (emphasis in original).[63] Implicit in his thinking on translation is a practice that is strongly teleological, the stress firmly on the target language. Ua Laoghaire explicitly advocated a strategy of fluency, the 'reproduction' of texts in recognisably idiomatic Irish. In order for his translation theory to take effect, it was important that his ideas on language also be taken seriously.

In his preface to *Mion-Chaint. An Easy Irish Phrase-Book*, Ua Laoghaire was dismissive of much of the printed material available in Irish. He felt that using texts that dated from the seventeenth century, the century of Geoffrey Keating, was 'many degrees worse than useless'.[64] These texts could only be deciphered by those with considerable willpower: 'Fortunately we have in considerable abundance persons of that stamp. Persons whom even a sensation like intermittent lock-jaw cannot frighten from the work.'[65] Ua Laoghaire offered the reader the picture of the learner of Irish who stolidly advanced through Easy Lessons in Irish, then 'through the Ossianic volume, lock-jaw and all'. Antiquarian zeal is only for the few and, for most people, a living language should not induce the enforced silence of lock-jaw. Ua Laoghaire declares: '*For a living language, the books and the speech of the people should go hand in hand*. What is printed in the books should be the exact representation of what comes out of the people's mouths' (emphasis in original).[66] His views were shared by Eoin MacNeill, one of the founders of the Gaelic League. He had written in the *Gaelic Journal* of 1897 of 'the absolute necessity of basing all literature on the living usage'.[67] To this end, the *Gaelic Journal* published Ua Laoghaire's novel, *Séadna*, between 1894 and 1897, demonstrating that literary work could be produced in the everyday language of modern Irish speakers. This emphasis on *caint na ndaoine*, the contemporary spoken vernacular, had two obvious consequences for the subsequent development of translation in Irish. Firstly, the language of translation was to be the language of the people. The text would be 'naturalised' in translation, rendered in the idiom of Gaeltacht speakers. Secondly, those who were most familiar with *caint na ndaoine* were obviously native speakers themselves. Therefore, the question of who was translating into Irish became more important. Ua

Laoghaire warns of the dangers of incompetence: 'It is an outrage upon common sense for any person to attempt to translate from one language to another unless he has a thorough knowledge of both.' He goes on to say: 'A person can translate fairly well *from* a language he has learned into his native language, if he knows his native language well. No man can translate *into* a language which he knows imperfectly' (emphasis in original).[68]

The implications of Ua Laoghaire's remarks were far-reaching. Many of the scholars, though by no means all, who had become interested in Irish in the nineteenth century were not native speakers of Irish. The translation direction had been predominantly Irish-English rather than the reverse. As the language revival movement gained momentum, translation into Irish became more commonplace. The danger lay in misguided amateurism, enthusiasm being a poor substitute for competence. Translators whose mother tongue was not Irish ran the risk of producing texts that were syntactically and idiomatically beholden to English. Hence the ambivalence towards translation that has been a feature of writing and criticism in Irish from the late nineteenth century onwards. Ua Laoghaire, in the very articles where he dispenses advice to would-be translators in Irish, expresses grave doubts about the possible outcomes of the translation process. If translators can produce translations that read like original texts in Irish, 'we shall be delighted to read your efforts'. However, 'If you are not able to do it yet, aim at it and you very soon will. But do not torture us with your translations. They are by far the most deadly element in the disease which is killing our language. They effectually disgust and repel the most courageous of native Irish speakers.'[69] If Synge and Lady Gregory were trying to capture the traces of Irish in English, the concern of Ua Laoghaire was to eradicate the traces of English in Irish. In a population of just over four million where the number of Gaelic monoglots was reported in the census to number just 38,192 in 1891, the balance of linguistic power had shifted massively to English.[70] The threat of uncontrolled 'béarlachas' (anglicisms) overwhelming the minority language in a radically asymmetrical situation was real. Translation therefore was an activity that was both necessary and questionable. Ua Laoghaire had the signal merit of being one of the first writers in Irish to self-reflexively analyse the translation process. The analysis was not immensely sophisticated, but in drawing the attention of Irish-language translators to questions of metaphor, syntax and reader-response, he foregrounded differences that might otherwise be ignored in unreflective translation.

Ua Laoghaire knew that translators do not translate in a linguistic vacuum. The language situation in Ireland was one of diglossia, with circumstances favouring the rapid expansion of one language and the decline of the other. Ua Laoghaire did not adopt a voluntarist policy of wishing away this state of affairs but constantly points out to the translator that s/he is translating in an environment that is predominantly Anglophone. A negative consequence of Ua Laoghaire's policy was that a justifiable suspicion of excessive 'béarlachas' could, in the minds of purists, shade into paranoia. Instead of allowing a language to evolve through the contribution of translation, the temptation was to put it in quarantine and ignore the impact of English on *caint na ndaoine* in Gaeltacht areas. Theoreticians of translation in Irish were and have been rare. Ua Laoghaire's reflections on translation had a decisive influence on the translation policy that was pursued by the Irish state after Independence. Pragmatic in intent, the reflections were pragmatic in their effects. More general, speculative thinking on translation and the Irish language did not come until much later into the twentieth century. The result has been that the contribution of translation to the development of Irish literature and language in the twentieth century has been generally ignored.

THE SUBALTERN IN TRANSLATION

Tejaswini Niranjana has described the impact of English education after 1835 and the decline of indigenous learning on the relationship that Indians had to their own past. This past became inaccessible, and could only be recovered through the translations and histories produced by the colonisers. She observes that the 'subaltern . . . exists only "in translation", always already cathected by colonial domination'.[71] Intellectuals in Ireland at the end of the last century were acutely aware of this particular dilemma, and translation was the focus of their concerns. In a letter to Lady Gregory after the publication of *Cuchulain of Muirthemne*, Eoin MacNeill commented ruefully:

> A few more books like it, and the Gaelic League will want to suppress you
> on a double indictment, to wit, depriving the Irish language of her sole right
> to express the innermost Irish mind, and secondly, investing the Anglo-Irish
> language with a literary dignity it has never hitherto possessed.[72]

Indeed, MacNeill had already expressed his reservations about translation in *An Claidheamh Soluis*, where he said that what he most feared
was the success of the enterprise:

> Reading translations exposes to the danger of looking at things from the
> English standpoint; and it might be said that the better and more faithful a
> translation is the worse it is, for it will keep people from going to the
> original where alone the literature can be judged for what it is really worth.[73]

To create a new literature in Irish, it was considered important to make
the texts from the Irish tradition available to readers in Modern Irish.
However, only a tiny minority of speakers of Modern Irish could read
texts in Old Irish. Hence, as Philip O'Leary points out, 'for a knowledge
of their own literary tradition, many fluent in the modern language were
forced to consult the translations, especially those in English, accompanying the editions prepared by their countryman Whitley Stokes or by
foreigners like Meyer, Thurneysen, Windisch, de Jubainville and Mars-
trander'.[74] The translation responses to the situation took two forms. The
first was to argue the pre-eminence of relativism and the impossibility of
equivalence. Discussing the *Táin Bó Cuailgne*, Father Richard Henebry
notes in 1909 that:

> To a person whose mind is charged with English it is strange, uncouth and
> foreign. To one reared through Irish it is the same tune he has always heard;
> he knows it. But how to define its tone, its atmosphere for foreigners? It
> cannot be done, it is the other way, it differs in everything and entirely from
> the way of the strange people. Nor can it be translated.[75]

The second was to advocate intralingual translation. The texts of the
Irish classics would be made available in modern Irish language editions.
The effect of this second solution was to displace the translation debate.
The issue was now whether the translations should offer the 'literal text'
or try to capture 'the ineffable and elusive spirit of the early tales'.[76]
Peadar Mac Fhionnlaoich favoured the scholarly prudence of earlier
interlingual translators: 'In rendering Old Irish into modern I conceive
the best way to be to change as little as possible.'[77] An tAthair Peadar Ua
Laoghaire, on the other hand, favoured communicative translations. His
liberal handling of the source materials was primarily dictated by the
desire to produce readable narratives in the contemporary vernacular:

> Often reliant on English translations because of his lack of training in Middle
> Irish and always far more interested in providing colloquial and
> unadulteratedly 'Irish' entertainment for native speakers than in meeting the

scholarly criteria of academicians, Ua Laoghaire made no coherent or consistent effort to capture either the letter or spirit of his originals.[78]

It is ironic in the light of Ua Laoghaire's comments on translation that he himself should find his translation practice in Irish shaped by the translation strategies of English-language translators. Bowdlerisation of the ancient texts was widely practised by Ua Laoghaire and others, and Philip O'Leary sees the changes as corresponding to a number of ideological imperatives; firstly, the representation of ancient Irish prose as free from foreign influence and, secondly, the protrayal of ancient Irish heroes in a manner that would be inspirational for contemporary readers. There was the further wish to rebut the charge made by Professor Robert Atkinson of Trinity College, Dublin, in 1898 that many passages in ancient Irish literature were fatuous or indecent.[79] Though Philip O'Leary is correct in noting that changes in translation are rarely innocent and that ideological pressures shape its practice, it is also important to examine translation in its own context.

Ua Laoghaire's intralingual translations were not unusual or unprecedented, the hapless creatures of circumstance. We have already commented in Chapter One on the strong bias towards communicative translation in elements of the medieval translation tradition in Ireland. Ua Laoghaire, in his explicit concern with target language and audience, stands within rather than outside that tradition. The translator is, of course, also an interpreter. His or her interpretations of the needs and outlooks of the target audience are rooted in the translator's own ideological orientation. Though freedom in the use of earlier texts has an obvious echo in nationalist myth-making, the element of bowdlerisation, also present in Lady Gregory's translations, is particularly interesting in that the translator's signature is everywhere. The audience is literally the target in a crusade for sexual propriety. Transforming readers of Irish into members of the English Victorian urban middle class, while at the same time extolling the virtues of a ruggedly independent rural Ireland, is one of the more familiar contradictions of nationalism in Ireland.[80] From the point of view of translation, however, the modernisation movement in Irish is notable for the use of a target-oriented, communicative practice that is highly directive i.e., the translators decided for themselves what the opinions of their audience would be in respect of sexual matters and translated accordingly. The translator, unlike a conference interpreter, does not have an audience that s/he can hear and see. In this respect, the translator is like the writer;

the audience is invisible, unpredictable, imaginary. In all teleological translation, the translator sees this imaginary audience as corresponding to a real one. That they rarely coincide is hardly surprising and even less desirable. It is precisely in that distance between the real and the imaginary that the figure of the translator emerges, and that the presence of alterity makes itself felt in the target language. This alterity is manifested in two ways. Firstly, there are the traces of the other language, culture and text that make their way through the translation into the other language despite the naturalising efforts of communicative translators. Secondly, there are the value-systems of the translators who construe the image of the target audience in the translators' own likeness. In concentrating on questions of audience in communicative translation, the imaginary dimension to translation practice can be forgotten. Between semantic and communicative translation we may need a third term such as *proactive translation*. This is translation that is communicative in terms of adaptation to the target language, and exercises a relative latitude with regard to elements of the source language and culture, but is interventionist in that changes to texts are strongly driven by the specific values of the translator in question. Proactive translation is as much an attempt to create an audience as it is to find one.

TRANSLATION POLICY AND THE NEW STATE

In 1918, the Sinn Féin party was victorious in the general elections in Ireland. As part of its policy to secure Irish independence its members did not to take up their seats in the Westminster parliament and established their own parliamentary assembly in Dublin. The first meeting of the Irish parliament, *Dáil Éireann*, was held on the 21 January 1919 in Dublin. There was no need for translation on that day as all the proceedings were in Irish. However, the linguistic realities of a bilingual Ireland soon dictated a change in policy, and, in June of that year, Mícheál Ó Loinsigh was appointed the first official translator to the Dáil. In September 1922, a Standing Order of Dáil Éireann stipulated that the texts of all legislation be available in Irish and English. This stipulation led to the setting up of the Translation Section of Dáil Éireann, Rannóg an Aistriúcháin.[81] The translation policy of the Dáil was part of the commitment by the new Irish Free State to the revival of the Irish language as the vernacular language of the Irish people. The two other main areas of translation activity were the educational system and literature.

The nature and necessity of translation in the early years of the state indicated that the task of revival was subject to many contradictions, though the important successes should not be ignored in the scramble to demythify. The direction of the translation work undertaken by Rannóg an Aistriúcháin from its inception was largely English–Irish. The majority of the TDs (members of the Irish parliament) addressed the Dáil in English. Legislation was drafted first in English and only later translated into Irish. In a state where Irish monoglots were becoming increasingly rare, it was easy to be dismissive of the efforts made at official level to make the texts of laws passed by the state available in Irish, laws that were drafted and largely debated in English. However, such a criticism tends to conceal the enabling contribution that translation makes to the development of a national language. Rannóg an Aistriúcháin used Roman rather than Gaelic characters from the outset, and worked actively on a simplified and coherent spelling system for Irish. The system was adopted by the government, and, in 1931, government departments were informed of the new system in a circular from the Department of Finance entitled *Spelling of Irish in Official Documents*. The arrival of the Fianna Fáil party in power in 1932 resulted in the use of Gaelic rather than Roman characters in printed translations. However, five years later Eoin MacNeill chaired a committee that explored proposals for simplifying the spelling used in the draft Constitution. In 1945, the Taoiseach, Eamon de Valera, realised the need for a simplified spelling system that would be acceptable as a standard in modern Irish. Tomás Page from the Rannóg was largely responsible for the production of this standard, and a booklet was produced in July 1945 entitled *Litriú na Gaeilge: lámhleabhar an chaighdeáin oifigiúil*. The translators in the Rannóg claimed subsequently that the publication of *Litriú na Gaeilge* led to a demand from teachers, writers and other interested parties for a standard grammar of Irish.[82] The standardisation of Irish grammar would not only facilitate the work of schoolteachers, journalists and official bodies but it would also give the Irish language a status similar to that enjoyed by other European languages.[83] In 1953, the Rannóg published *Gramadach na Gaeilge: caighdeán Rannóg an Aistriúcháin*. The *Gramadach* contained the standard grammar that the Rannóg was recommending for general use. The recommended standard was based on internal discussions within the Rannóg itself and consultations with teachers and writers. The purpose of the 1953 publication was to obtain the opinions of the general public and interested parties on the proposed standard and incorporate these where relevant into a more definitive document.

In May 1957, de Valera asked Séamas Daltún, the Chief Translator in the Rannóg, to proceed with producing a definitive standard grammar of Irish. Opinions on the standard were sought from speakers from different Gaeltacht areas as well as from those who had a particular knowledge of or interest in the language. *Litriú na Gaeilge* and the new standard grammar were published together in 1958 as *Gramadach na Gaeilge agus Litriú na Gaeilge: An Caighdeán Oifigiúil.*[84] The aim of the publication was to act as a standard for official state business and a guide for teachers and the general public.[85] The principles guiding the *Caighdeán* were not radically different from the principles enunciated decades earlier by Ua Laoghaire: rules or grammatical forms that were not in common use in the living language of the Gaeltacht were to be ignored; the most commonly used forms in the Gaeltacht were those adopted as standard forms; due recognition was given to the history and literature of Irish and the compilers of the *Caighdeán* were guided by the need for consistency and simplicity.[86] Translators were thus intimately involved in the standardisation of Irish orthography and grammar which was essential if Irish was to function as a working language in a modern society. The extraordinary difficulties faced by those wishing to learn Irish or to write in the language prior to the emergence of broadly accepted orthographical and grammatical standards are too easily forgotten.[87] The policy adopted by the state drew more on a Gallic rather than an Anglo-Saxon model, but it did not necessarily have the historical leeway that would have allowed for the more organic emergence of consensual norms. The promoters of a minority language that accedes to the status of an official or national language can find themselves using a degree of accelerated interventionism that is concealed by the more gradual and long-term changes in major languages. The continual translation demands on the Irish language in the Rannóg and elsewhere meant that common standards and guidelines similar to those for other modern languages had to be established so that, irrespective of national or regional background, speakers could learn to read and write a widely understood version of the language.[88]

Standardisation is inevitably a reductive as well as an enabling process. The ascendancy of one dialect over others and the consequent impoverishment of dialectical differences are charges that have frequently been directed at Standard Irish over the years.

TRANSLATION SCHEMES AND CONTROVERSY

It would be mistaken, however, to see Irish-language translators as adopting a purely instrumental view of dialect and acting as ardent apostles of standardisation. On the contrary, the translation scheme of the publications branch of the Department of Education, An Gúm, favoured the publication of translations that drew heavily on specific dialectical resources. Translation had already figured as a concern of the first Dáil as we have seen in the appointment of Mícheál Ó Loinsigh. This concern was also evident in the allocation by the Dáil of five hundred pounds for the provision of reading material in Irish. The money was to be 'spent in publications urgently required such as text books on all subjects and Irish translations of standard works'.[89] Nothing much came of the scheme, and in 1926 Coiste na Leabhar was established to examine the provision of reading material in Irish. Douglas Hyde was a member of the Coiste. Another committee, known as An Coiste Foillsiúcháin, was established in 1927. The brief of the latter related more explicitly to the commissioning of translations, but as translation was also implicit in the guidelines issued to Coiste na Leabhar, the two committees were amalgamated under the one name, Coiste na Leabhar, in 1928.[90] A competition was organised in 1928 where translators were invited to submit sample translations in Irish of a chapter of English prose. Those drafting the official notice of the competition assumed general ignorance in the wider community about the nature of translation, claiming that there might be 'people who were unaware of the fact that they were able to do this work [i.e. translation]'.[91] The government minister responsible for the translation scheme inspired by existing Welsh and Flemish models, Earnán de Blaghad, was however convinced of its necessity:

> In the Galltacht . . . there must be made available great masses of reading matter in Irish and reading matter to suit all tastes. The quantity that is required can only be obtained in time by translation. Therefore, we must translate English novels and detective stories in much greater numbers than had been thought of heretofore.[92]

156

The decision to embark on the extensive translation of works in foreign languages into a language in order to consolidate its literary base, or to make a wider range of material available to readers in that language, has not been unusual in the development of most languages. This is precisely the major contribution of translation to the spread of civilisation. The Irish situation was somewhat different in that diglossia was extensive and that literate monoglots in Irish were a rarity. Thus, Irish people who could read the English original were less likely to read the Irish translation. As English was the only other language that most of the successful translators in the translation competition possessed, the tendency was inevitably to translate English-language works into Irish. Hence, in their desire to lay the foundations for a new literature, translators in Irish found that they were bound to the literary culture of the major language. Citing the statistics for the translations produced by An Gúm, Roibeárd Ó Faireacháin stated in 1937 that, 'there are good reasons for the preponderance of translation over original writing. But what reasons could justify a scheme by which four times as many books are translated from English as from all other foreign languages put together?'[93] The dominance of English as a source language should not obscure, however, the existence of translations from other languages in the period. Works by René Bazin, Louis Hémon, Henri Bordeaux, Alphonse Daudet, Émile Erckmann, Pierre Alexandre Chatrian, Wilhelm Hauff, Felix Von Luckner, Thomas Mann, Hector Malot, and Adam Mickievicz, among others, were translated into Irish as a result of the scheme.[94] By 1937, ninety-nine novels had been translated from other languages into Irish by the translators working in An Gúm.

The state translation enterprise gave rise to considerable controversy. One of the translators involved in the scheme, Seosamh Mac Grianna, felt that it was born out of a lack of faith in the value of contemporary writing in Irish. In his view, the architects of the scheme assumed that 'Níl litríocht ar bith sa Ghaeilge is fiú a léamh. Níl scríbhneoir ar bith Gaeilge againn ar fiú scríbhneoir a thabhairt air. Taobh thall den fharraige Ghaelaigh atá gach rud a bhfuil tairbhe ar bith ann.'[95] In Mac Grianna's view, the impulse to translate was driven by a cultural inferiority complex that failed to take seriously the literary possibilities of the living language. Seán de Beaumont, one of the editors of *An t-Éireannach*, the weekly newspaper that appeared between 1934 and 1937, claimed in 1939 that the translation scheme was an insult to people living in Gaeltacht areas implying that they were incapable of producing their own literature.[96] A later historian of the period, Éamon Ó Ciosáin, claimed that creative writing in Irish was adversely affected by the time and effort devoted to translation, 'bhí lag trá áirithe i "nua"-scríbhneoireacht na Gaeilge i rith na mblianta úd mar gheall ar pholasaí aistriúcháin an Ghúim, a d'fhág cuid mhór den dream ba chumasaí i mbun conamar a thiontú ón mBéarla'.[97] General disenchantment with the scheme led to its gradual abandonment after the Second World War, with An Gúm concentrating on the translation of school textbooks and children's literature. The scheme lacked focus and there was no explicit policy, for example, with respect to the works translated. The translators themselves chose works that appealed to them, and the result was a curious eclecticism in the titles that were translated. The translations were not subject to any form of translation editing or revision and were only checked for consistency in spelling.

The legitimate criticism that was directed at the translation scheme has tended to overshadow the nature of its achievments. It was unfortunate that at the time of the scheme no proper provision was made for the support of contemporary writing in Irish. Translation became the target by default for writers who were deeply unhappy with state indifference to the plight of the Irish-language writer. In his study of the novel in Irish, Alan Titley is generous in his praise for the much-maligned scheme:

> Is é oighear an scéil é gur luachmhaire agus gur fiúntaí cuid de na haistriúcháin . . . ná go leor den bhunshaothar a bhí á fhoilsiú ar chomhuain leo. Más é *David Copperfield* a d'aistrigh Seán Ó Ruadháin an leabhar is toirtiúla ar fad díobh, is saothar máistriúil aistriúcháin agus scríbhneoireachta é san am céanna. Is maise ar scríbhneoireacht na Gaeilge é go bhfuil úrscéalta le Joseph Conrad, le Thomas Mann, Henri Bordeaux, Alexandre Dumas, Ivan Turgenev agus Geroge Eliot le fáil ar a fud, gan ábhar níos éadroime nó níos coitianta a bhac in aon chor. Caighdeán ard teanga, friotail agus íogaireachta tá le fáil sa chuid is mó ar fad díobh seo in ainneoin an dothíos a bhraith scríbhneoirí lena gceird.[98]

In a round table discussion on translation, Titley claimed that the translation scheme had an influence that was positive if rarely acknowledged and the policy of An Gúm 'may, however, have had a more beneficial effect than we realize, in that it provided for both translator and reader alike some sorts of models and an appreciation of the disciplines and literary conventions which certain genres entailed, things which were helpful to them in their original writing and their appreciation of literature'.[99] He goes on to suggest that the poor state of prose in Scottish Gaelic may be related, in part, to the absence of a similar translation scheme for that language. The very eclecticism of the scheme was arguably one of its strengths. Stories for children, detective novels, tales of adventure, literary fiction (both in the form of short stories and the novel) and philosophical and theological works were among the different kinds of writing that were published in translation under the auspices of the scheme. The generic possibilities of writing in Irish were made obvious. Through translation the language demonstrated its ability to handle very different genres, in particular genres where contemporary works were scarce or non-existent. In addition, the considerable output of the An Gúm translators dramatically changed the publishing scene in Irish. Prior to Independence, the number of printed books available in Irish was quite limited, a fact that is often overlooked in retrospective judgements of An Gúm's activities. The annual appearance of new translated titles in Irish in the 1930s arguably created a critical mass of printed literature which would be indispensable for the post-1945 renaissance in writing in Irish.

Criticisms levelled at the translation scheme were not only prompted by concern for the living writer. More conservative critics saw translation in Irish as a filter, a form of pre-emptive censorship, that would cleanse the Irish mind of foreign impurities. The watchword was moral vigilance. Aodh de Blácam articulates this position in 'The World of Letters: Poison in the Wells', an article which appeared in the *Irish Monthly* in 1937. The article is a forthright condemnation of 'intellectuals' and literary modernism and praises Kipling, Conan Doyle and the operation of Ireland's censorship laws which 'shows a readiness in our government to use its powers to check the rot in civilisation'.[100] He deplores his students' lack of interest in G.K. Chesterton and adds that their 'Gaelic, fed with translated detective stories, and forgotten altogether as soon as they go into the university or into the world, is no bulwark'.[101] He asks why Chesterton has not been translated into Irish and claims that

> the State has lavished money on the translations of vulgar American tales of crime but nothing on Chesterton. It has published the translation of a novel in which the hero is an Irish Catholic who deserts his religion and who stands out as the one fine, honest character before a tribe of drunken, treacherous, murderous Papists, while his English servant is contrasted with the torturing Spanish inquisitors; and yet this book is branded as officially approved for Irish children! Yet Chesterton the orthodox is not translated.

For de Blácam, translation was a means of building up a national culture and therefore needed special attention. Translation represented a dangerous source of the 'rot' that censorship was designed to check. The danger is presented as all the more real because of the threat to 'Irish children' from immoral American tales of crime. The fact that the novel in question is inoffensive by today's standards is less important than the significance de Blácam attaches to translation and his morally explicit and voluntarist conception of what should constitute the translation policy of the state. He divides the target audience of translations into two groups, adult men ('the widely-read man, who offsets the bigotry by his experience') and impressionable children ('it is educationally bad for children to read books of such a bias').[102] De Blácam praises the work of the translator, ('the translation is better than the original'), but the very success of the translation makes its effects all the more permanent in the case of one section of the target audience, schoolchildren. Policing translation was an element in a larger ideological project aimed at using Irish to create a more conservative national culture. Indeed, de Blácam argues that 'All great writing is conservative. After all, the very purpose of the writing is to conserve.'[103]

The translations of An Gúm were indeed conservative in de Blácam's sense of writing as conservation. They conserved dialectical variety. The translators in the 1930s were not expected to choose one dialect of Irish over another; they were at liberty to draw on all the resources of their native dialect, whether it was Donegal, Mayo, Munster or Connemara Irish. The translations from the period are, as a result, storehouses of dialectical difference.[104] In employing many native speakers as translators for the scheme, and allowing them to write in the dialects of their own region, An Gúm was primarily directed by the translation philosophy of Peadar Ua Laoghaire. The fidelity to Ua Laoghaire's principles was not without problems. As Máirtín Mac Niocláis has pointed out in his study of Seán Ó Ruadháin's translation of Charles Dickens's *David Copperfield*, the expression of differences of formal and colloquial register in English and, in particular, the attempt to capture the specificity of colloquial urban idiom in Dickens's work, are made difficult, if not impossible, by the deliberate choice of rural *caint na ndaoine*.[105] The problem of the translator was paradoxical. S/he was able to produce dialectically-rich translations in the absence of a standard form of the language, but the very absence of that form meant that representing more formal varieties of the language became a daunting task for the translator. In addition, the number of Irish speakers in urban areas has grown considerably since the 1930s so that establishing equivalents for urban speech in Irish is easier now than then, though finding urban colloquial equivalents is still quite problematic.

The An Gúm translators were particularly anxious to respect Ua Laoghaire's prescription against anglicisms or *béarlachas*. The result was inventiveness and variety in the exploration of their own linguistic resources in Irish, but also an extreme reluctance to import different, unusual or foreign forms into Irish. Consequently, the translations themselves did not occupy a primary, iconoclastic role in the invention of new literary idioms in Irish. Though it would be easy to tax the translators with being conservative and ethnocentric in their rejection of linguistic otherness, it is important to remember that languages and their circumstances differ. Irish was then, and still is, under pressure from English. In producing a corpus of printed literature in Irish, the translators of the 1930s sought to consolidate the linguistic specificity of the language. They were anxious, above all else, to avoid producing a pidgin Irish that would confirm Synge's worst fears about language revival, namely, that linguistic disorder would leave the bewildered Irish 'semi-literate in both languages'.[106]

James Joyce's passion for literature and languages was also a passion for translation. He used translation as a means of learning Norwegian and German, translating Ibsen and Gerhart Hauptmann into English.[107] In 1904, he sent his translations of Gerhart Hauptmann's *Vor Sonnenaufgang* and *Michael Kramer* to W.B. Yeats in the hope that they might be performed at the Irish Literary Theatre. Yeats rejected them and informed Joyce that he was not as accomplished a German scholar as he imagined himself to be.[108] The figure of Joyce in his teens already applying himself to the translator's task is emblematic. He completed the *Vor Sonnenaufgang* translation in 1901 at the age of nineteen. Joyce's activity paralleled the intense translation ferment in Ireland at the beginning of the twentieth century. Two national literatures would emerge from the ceaseless movement between languages, a birth that would have been literally and figuratively inconceivable without the long gestation of translation. As Louis Kelly notes: 'Approach to another is not the peaceful process of legend, but often a violent assessment of self in relation to another person.'[109] Translation in late twentieth-century Ireland would come out of, and provoke violent assessment of, what were to be the island's cultures, languages and identities at the end of the century.

Notes

1. Robert Tyrrell, 'Translation as a Fine Art', *Hermathena*, vol. 6, no. 13, 1887, p. 148.
2. Joseph Leerssen, *Mere Irish and Fíor-Ghael: Studies in the Idea of Irish Nationality, its Development and Literary Expression prior to the Nineteenth Century*, Amsterdam, John Benjamins, 1986, p. 436.
3. Cathal Ó Háinle, 'Towards the Revival. Some Translations of Irish Poetry: 1789–1897', Peter Connolly, ed., *Literature and the Changing Ireland*, Gerrards Cross, Colin Smythe, 1982, p. 38.
4. Leerssen, p. 439.
5. See Leerssen, chapter 6, pp. 325–444, for a detailed examination of this phenomenon.
6. Eugene O'Curry, *On the Manners and Customs of the Ancient Irish*, 3 vols., W.K. Sullivan, ed., London, Williams and Norgate, 1873, p. 9.
7. O'Curry, p. 14.
8. John O'Donovan, ed., *Annals of the Kingdom of Ireland*, 3rd ed., 7 vols., Dublin, de Búrca, 1990.
9. Standish Hayes O'Grady, *Silva Gadelica*, vol. 2 (1892), New York, Lemma, reprinted, 1970, p. v.
10. O'Grady, p. xxv.
11. O'Grady, p. xxv.
12. Douglas Hyde, *Beside the Fire* (1890), reprinted Dublin, Irish Academic Press, 1978.
13. Mícheál Ó hAodha, 'Introduction', Douglas Hyde, *Abhráin Grádh Chúige Connacht: The Love Songs of Connacht* (1893), Shannon, Ó hAodha, Irish University Press, reprinted, 1969, p. v.
14. William Butler Yeats cited in Ó hAodh 'Introduction', p. vi.
15. Douglas Hyde, *Abhráin Grádth Chúige Connacht*, n.p.
16. Hyde, ibid.
17. An Chraoibhín Aoibhinn, 'Fuagradh' in ibid., n.p.
18. Patrick Rafroidi, *L'Irlande et le romantisme*, Paris, Éditions Universitaires, 1972, p. 247. My translation.
19. Charles Gavan Duffy, 'What Irishmen may do for Irish Literature' in Charles Gavan Duffy, George Sigerson, Douglas Hyde, *The Revival of Irish Literature* (1892), New York, Lemma, reprinted, 1973, p. 16.
20. Ó Háinle, p. 50.
21. Declan Kiberd, *Synge and the Irish Language*, 2nd ed., Dublin, Gill and Macmillan, 1993, p. 197.
22. William Butler Yeats, *Autobiographies*, London, Macmillan, 1955, p. 220.
23. Kiberd, p. 106.
24. Yeats, *Autobiographies*, p. 221.
25. Lady Gregory, *Seventy Years*, Gerrards Cross, Colin Smythe, 1974, p. 392.
26. Kiberd, pp. 89–91.
27. John Millington Synge, *Collected Works*, vol. 2, Oxford University Press, 1966, p. 367.

28. Ann Saddlemyer, ed., *The Translations and Adaptations of Lady Gregory and her Collaborations with Douglas Hyde and W.B. Yeats*, Gerrards Cross, Colin Smythe, 1970, p. vii.

29. See Eric Cheyfitz, *The Poetics of Imperialism: Translation and Colonization from* The Tempest *to* Tarzan, Oxford University Press, 1991, p. 101; and Louis Kelly, *The True Interpreter: A History of Translation Theory and Practice in the West*, Oxford, Basil Blackwell, 1979, pp. 49–51.

30. Saddlemyer, p. viii.

31. See Marco Sonzogni, 'Courtly Love in Ireland: Synge's Translations of Petrarch', *Translation Ireland*, vol. 9, no. 1, pp. 7–11.

32. Kiberd, p. 88.

33. Cheyfitz, p. xvi. It is unclear here whether the implied reader ('our') is American or a generic Westerner.

34. Synge, p. 371.

35. See discussion of Synge's translations of poetry and prose in Kiberd, pp. 61–76.

36. Synge, p. 149.

37. Synge, p. 384.

38. Leersen, p. 409.

39. William Butler Yeats, Letter to the Editor, *United Ireland*, 17 December 1892.

40. William Butler Yeats, Letter to the Editor, *Leader*, September 1900.

41. William Butler Yeats, *Essays and Introductions*, London, Macmillan, 1951, p. 515.

42. Seamus Deane, Introduction, *Celtic Revivals*, London, Faber and Faber, 1985, p. 13.

43. Kiberd, p. 202.

44. Kiberd, p. xv.

45. Deane, p. 144.

46. Michel Serres in particular has devoted much attention to the notion and role of the 'parasite'; see Michel Serres, *Le parasite*, Paris, Grasset, 1980.

47. For an account of the origins and metamorphoses of the Stage Irishman see Leersen, pp. 85–168.

48. Fredson Bowers, ed., *The Dramatic Works of Thomas Decker*, Cambridge, Cambridge University Press, 1953, vol. 1, pp. 112–205.

49. Fredson Bowers, general ed., *The Dramatic Works in the Beaumont and Fletcher Canon*, Cambridge University Press, 1966, Act II, scene iii, p. 297.

50. Leerssen, p. 101.

51. Patrick Pearse, Letter to the Editor, *An Claidheamh Soluis*, 20 May 1899.

52. Timothy Corcoran, 'How English may be taught without Anglicising', *Irish Monthly*, vol. 51, June 1923, p. 269.

53. Corcoran, p. 270.

54. Corcoran, pp. 270–71.

55. Duffy, 'What Irishmen may do', p. 12.

56. Duffy, p. 49.

57. Corcoran, p. 272.

58. The exemplary Catholicism was not, however, seen as extending to all French literary productions. Countless translations of French works in English were banned for decades in Ireland.

59. Peter O'Leary, *Papers on Irish Idiom*, T.F. O'Rahilly, ed., Dublin, Browne and Nolan, 1929, p. 90.
60. O'Leary, p. 92.
61. John Dryden, 'On Translation', Rainer Schulte and John Biguenet (eds.), *Theories of Translation*, University of Chicago Press, 1992, p. 26.
62. O'Leary, p. 83.
63. O'Leary, p. 92.
64. O'Leary, p. 86.
65. O'Leary, p. 86.
66. O'Leary, p. 86.
67. Cited in Brian Ó Cuív, 'MacNeill and the Irish Language', F.X. Martin and F.J. Byrne, eds., *The Scholar Revolutionary: Eoin MacNeill (1867–1945) and the Making of the New Ireland*, Shannon, Irish University Press, 1973, p. 9.
68. O'Leary, p. 91.
69. O'Leary, p. 92.
70. J.E. Caerwyn Williams agus Máirín Ní Mhuiríosa, *Traidisiún Liteartha na nGael*, Baile Átha Cliath, An Clóchomhar, 1985, p. 345.
71. Tejaswini Niranjana, *Siting Translation: History, Post-Structuralism and the Colonial Context*, Berkeley, University of California Press, 1992, p. 43.
72. Cited in Gregory, p. 402.
73. Cited in Philip O'Leary, '"The Greatest of the Things Our Ancestors Did": Gaelic Adaptations of Early Irish Literature, 1891–1916', Cyril J. Byrne, Margaret Henry and Pádraig Ó Siadhail, eds., *Celtic Languages and Celtic Peoples*, Halifax, St Mary's University, 1990, p. 479.
74. O'Leary, pp. 463–64.
75. Richard Henebry, 'Revival Irish', *The Leader*, 16 January 1909.
76. O'Leary, p. 465.
77. Peadar Mac Fhionnlaoich, Letter, *An Claidheamh Soluis*, 2 May 1903.
78. O'Leary, pp. 466–67.
79. O'Leary, p. 461.
80. See Maurice Goldring, *Faith of Our Fathers: The Formation of Irish Nationalist Ideology 1890–1920*, Dublin, Repsol, 1982.
81. Séamas Daltún, 'Scéal Rannóg an Aistriúchain', *Teangeolas*, 17, 1983, pp. 12–14.
82. *Gramadach na Gaeilge agus Litriú na Gaeilge: An Caighdeán Oifigiúil*, Baile Átha Cliath, Oifig an tSoláthair, 1958, p. vii.
83. *An Caighdeán Oifigiúil*, p. viii.
84. Daltún, pp. 14–16.
85. For a close analysis of the 1953 and 1958 documents see Cathal Ó Háinle, 'Ó Chaint na nDaoine go dtí an Caighdeán Oifigiúil', Kim McCone, et al., eds., *Stair na Gaeilge*, Maigh Nuad, Coláiste Phádraig, 1994, pp. 782–91.
86. *An Caighdeán Oifigiúil*, p. viii.
87. Kiberd, for example, is eloquent on the difficulties faced not only by Synge but by native Irish speakers themselves in attempting to master the written language in the absence of accepted conventions governing usage. See Kiberd, pp. 19–53.

88. For a consideration of state language policy in general including the role of Rannóg an Aistriúcháin see Seán Ó Riain, *Pleanáil Teanga in Éirinn 1919–1985*, Baile Átha Cliath, Carbad, 1994.

89. *Miontuairiscí Díospóireachtaí an Chéad Dála 1919–1921*, p. 273.

90. Máirtín Mac Niocláis, *Seán Ó Ruadháin: Saol agus Saothar*, Baile Átha Cliath, An Clóchomhar, 1991.

91. The original text of the advertisement that appeared in the *Irish Independent* on the 9 February 1928 was as follows: 'Tá an Coiste Foillsiúcháin ag lorg sgríbhneoirí chun leabhartha do thionntódh go Gaedhilg ó theangacha eile. Chítear don Choiste gur féidir daoine do bheith ann i ngan fhios dóibh a bheadh i n–inmhe an obair sin a dhéanamh, agus, i gcaoi go bhfaghfaidh gach uile duine cothrom na féinne, táthar 'gha iarraidh ar sgríbhneoirí sompla dá gcuid oibre do chur ar triall orthu. Is é sompla atá ceaptha i gcomhair an chomórtais seo ná aistriúchán go Gaedhilg ar an gcéad chaibidil d'úirsgéal áirithe a thoigh an Coiste chuige.

An duine is fearr a dhéanfaidh an t-aisdriúchán san, toghfar é chun leabhair iomlán d'aisdriú do réir na gcoinngheallacha agus na rátaí san ach sgríobhadh chun Rúnaidhe an Choisde 'ghá lorg.

Caithfear na hiarrachtaí do sheoladh chun an Rúnaidhe, An Coiste Foillsiúcháin, Sráid Hiúm a haon, Baile Átha Cliath, i gcaoi go bhfagfaidh sé iad roimh an gcéad lá de mhí na Bealtaine 1928.'

92. Cited in Mac Niocláis, p. 111.

93. Roibeárd Ó Faireacháin, 'Regarding an Gúm', *Bonaventura*, Summer 1937, pp. 175–6.

94. For publication details of translations published before 1937 see Risteard de Hae and Brighid Ní Dhonnchadha, eag., *Clár Litridheacht na Nua-Ghaeilge*, Vol. 1, Baile Átha Cliath, Oifig an tSoláthair, 1938.

95. 'There is no literature in Irish worth reading. Everything worthwhile is on the other side of the Gaelic Sea' [my translation], Seosamh Mac Grianna, *Filí agus Felons*, Cathair na Mart, Foilseacháin Náisiúnta, 1987, pp. 75–76.

96. Seán de Beaumont, 'Litridheacht na Gaeilge – Céard tá i nDán di?', *The Irish Times*, 4 November 1939.

97. 'there was a certain ebb in the fortunes of "new" writing in Irish during those years because of an Gúm's translation policy that meant many of the most able writers were involved in translating worthless bits and pieces from English' [my translation], Éamon Ó Ciosáin, *An t-Éireannach 1934–1937: Páipéar Sóisialach Gaeltachta*, Baile Átha Cliath, An Clóchomhar, 1993, p. 183.

98. 'The problem is that some of the translations were of a higher quality and more worthwhile than the original works being published around the same time. If Seán Ó Ruadháin's translation of *David Copperfield* is by far the longest, it is also a masterful piece of writing and translation. Irish is better off for having novels by Joseph Conrad, Thomas Mann, Henri Bordeaux, Alexandre Dumas, Ivan Turgenev and Geroge Eliot available in the language without bothering with more lightweight or commonplace material. There is a high standard of language and expression in most of the translations and a great finesse despite the churlish attitude of certain

writers to their trade as translators' [my translation], Alan Titley, *An t-Urscéal Gaeilge*, Baile Átha Cliath, An Clóchomhar, 1991, p. 46.

99. Alan Titley, 'Thoughts on Translation', *Poetry Ireland Review*, No. 39, Autumn 1993, p. 69.

100. Aodh de Blácam, 'The World of Letters: Poison in the Wells', *Irish Monthly*, vol. 65, p. 280.

101. de Blácam, p. 278.

102. de Blácam, p. 281.

103. de Blácam, p. 280

104. Mac Niocláis, p. 120.

105. Mac Niocláis, pp. 122–147.

106. Kiberd, p. 219.

107. Colin Walker, 'Literary Translation of Dialogue in German Dilaect into Anglo-Irish Dialect', Peter Skirne, Rosemary E. Wallbank–Turner and Jonathan West, eds., *Connections: Essays in Honour of Eda Sagarra on the Occasion of her 60th Birthday*, Stuttgart, Verlag Hans-Dieter Heinz, 1993, pp. 275–283.

108. Jill Perkins, *Joyce and Hauptmann. Before Sunrise*. James Joyce's Translation, with an Introduction and Notes by Jill Perkins, San Marino, Huntington Library, 1978, pp. 9–10.

109. Louis Kelly, p. 62.

5

THE STATE OF TRANSLATION: REVIVAL RENEWAL AND CONFLICT

IN HIS *LITERATURE IN IRELAND* (1916), Thomas MacDonagh saw translation as a sketch of possibility, the ante-chamber of change:

> This is an age of beginnings rather than of achievements; for a hundred years now writers in this land have been translating, adapting, experimenting – working as the writers of the sixteenth century worked in many countries. The translations which have survived are those most in consonance with the genius of the country. An age of beginnings: what the next age or the ripeness of this may bring, one can only guess at.[1]

A signatory to the 1916 Proclamation and subsequently executed for his part in the Easter Rising, MacDonagh did not hold with the view that translation was, at best, a compromise and, at worst, a form of betrayal. On the contrary, he argued *ante* Derrida that the test of excellence in a literature was its degree of translatability. Quoting John Dryden, 'A thing well said will be wit in all languages', MacDonagh stresses the importance of the *überleben* or afterlife in translation:

> The high things of the Scriptures, the words of Our Lord about considering the lilies of the field, are still poetry in all languages. When the language of their first expression is dead and the day of its most gracious felicities is over, they still live. If Shakespeare's phrases refuse to translate beautifully into some tongues, it is that their beauty consists rather in felicity of words than in high poetry. All that is great in his dramatic power, in his creation of character, in his philosophy, will be great in other languages, only indeed less great for that want of Shakespearean diction.[2]

Translations can, in fact, surpass the original. He cites the examples of Arthur O'Shaughnessy's translations of Sully Prudhomme and Douglas Hyde's translations from the Irish. For MacDonagh, a dead image in one language can come alive in the new context of translation. This metaphorical resurrection energises the poetic idiom of Hyde. MacDonagh's generous belief in the possibilities of translation is shared by many commentators on contemporary Irish culture, but it is a belief that is not without its dissenters. Translation in modern Ireland is as much a hostage to controversy as it has been in previous centuries, though polemic can occasionally obscure the extraordinary scale and range of translation activity in both of the languages of late twentieth-century Ireland.

FIXATION AND DISCONTINUITY

Robert Welch, a historian of translation, considers translation to be a pervasive and necessary procedure in all cultures:

> All legitimate intellectual enquiry is translation of one kind or another: it takes a text, a phase of history, an event, an instant of recognition, and proceeds to understand it by reliving it in the process of re-creating it. In doing so it renews the unpredictability of the event or text by subjecting it once again to the challenges and opportunities of contingency. The thing is lived again, and it re-enacts its completeness in the new context. There is a state of change, but the thing, in the course of the re-enactment, reveals itself more completely than ever before.[3]

In the Irish context, translation is not simply a historic fatality resulting from massive language shift in the nineteenth century, but is vital in freeing the culture from obsessive concerns with continuity and purity. Welch takes the Cyclopean fixation of Joyce's Citizen as a warning against treating any culture as static and immutable. Translation is a mode of creative evolution that allows a culture to preserve what is valuable, while leaving itself open to the creative intervention of change.[4] Translation is both the product and champion of discontinuity. If the condition of Ireland is the condition of modernity – discontinuity, fragmentation, self-doubt – then it is only to be expected that translation will emerge as a dominant feature of contemporary Irish culture.

Translation is not, however, in the Irish case uniquely the cultural consequence of language shift. Other factors must be taken into account in situating the tremendous growth in translation activity from the mid 1980s onwards. The abandonment of economic protectionism and the adoption of new, export-oriented, free trade policies by the Lemass government from 1958 onwards led to a period of strong economic growth in Ireland. The industrial sector in the economy grew, emigration declined and urbanisation increased. In 1973, Ireland became a full member of the European Economic Community, and a majority of the electorate has consistently supported moves towards greater European integration. The period of rapid economic and social transformation of the Irish Republic was accompanied by armed conflict in Northern Ireland, which left thousands dead and injured. The effects of these economic and political developments were two-fold. Firstly, Irish contact with Europe led to a growing awareness of the European dimension of Irish culture. Secondly, the equation of Irish ethnic identity with rural, pre-modern, Catholic culture and an exclusivist nationalism was repeatedly challenged as the conflict in Northern Ireland became increasingly violent in the 1970s. As fixed identities were being questioned both north and south of the border, it was not surprising that translation itself became a privileged mode of interrogation. It was also seen as a form of release, a creative opportunity that would open up different areas of Irish culture to each other and to the rest of the world.

CULTURAL SELF-REPRESENTATION

In 1984, Goldsmith Press published *Tacar Dánta/Selected Poems*. It was a bilingual collection of Máirtín Ó Direáin's poems translated into English by Douglas Sealy and Tomás Mac Síomóin.[5] The publication of the translations represented a decisive change in cultural policy in Ireland. There had, of course, been many earlier collections of Irish–English translations such as the highly successful *An Duanaire: Poems of the Dispossessed*, published in 1981.[6] The novelty of *Tacar Dánta* was, firstly, that it contained English translations of work by a contemporary as opposed to a long-dead Irish-language writer and secondly, that the publication was assisted by the Arts Council as part of a new policy to encourage bilingualism in five areas of its work: the writer; literary organisations; publishers; literary magazines; and participation. This policy was explicitly formulated in a 1985 Arts Council publication, *Services to Literature: Seirbhísí don Litríocht*. Laurence Cassidy, the Arts Council's Literature Officer, claimed that the motivation for the policy initiative in the translation area 'arose from the Council's conviction that many of the finest writers of Irish literature were writing in Irish but had little or no impact on their English-speaking compatriots'.[7] Irish-language writers had complained informally to the Council that they received little recognition in the wider literary world in Ireland and that, consequently, their income from writing was low and, in some cases, negligible.[8] The second title that illustrated the Arts Council's new translation policy was *The Bright Wave: An Tonn Gheal*, edited by Dermot Bolger and published by Raven Arts Press in 1986. *The Bright Wave* contained poems by many leading Irish-language poets accompanied by translations produced by writers in the English language. Raven Arts Press also published in that same year Nuala Ní Dhomhnaill's *Rogha Dánta: Selected Poems*, English translations of Ní Dhomnaill's Irish-language poetry by the poet herself and Michael Hartnett. The translation initiative was a commercial success, *The Bright Wave*, for example, going through several reprints. Cassidy's opinion in retrospect, was that the contemporary Irish–English translations were an 'idea whose time had come'.[9]

Collections of translations from contemporary Irish-language poets continued to appear throughout the late 1980s and early 1990s, but translations from Irish prose, though equally encouraged, were much rarer.[10] An exception was Seán Mac Mathúna's *The Atheist*, published by Wolfhound Press in 1987, which contained many of his own translations of stories that had originally appeared in his 1983 collection *Ding agus Scéalta Eile.*[11]

The second phase of the Arts Council's translation policy was to promote the translation in Ireland of foreign-language works into English. Bord na Leabhar Gaeilge, the Irish-language book board, was already responsible for grant-aid to assist the translation of foreign-language titles into Irish. The Bord granted assistance on the basis of the number of words in the translation and had different rates for poetry, prose and drama. The second phase of the Arts Council's policy was contemporaneous with its bilingual initiatives, and the main instruments of policy were direction publication assistance and the author's royalty scheme, which allowed publishers to recoup the translation fees of a title. The policy was largely a response to the cultural implications of growing European integration. The Cultural Activities Division of the European Commission (DGX) had begun to develop a cultural policy for the European Community in the late 1980s. An outline statement entitled *A Fresh Boost for Culture* was published in 1987 to be followed in 1989 by *Books and Reading: A Cultural Challenge for Europe.*[12] The latter document paid particular attention to the translation process, and the result was the establishment in 1990 of the European Community Pilot Scheme to provide financial aid for the translation of contemporary literary works. The EC also decided to fund two annual prizes, the Aristeion-European Literary Prize and the Aristeion-European Translation Prize. There was a realisation on the part of the Arts Council that 'the multiplicity of languages found in the EC places a demand upon the translation process, both generally and within the literatures of each country'.[13] The logic was not only cultural but economic. Irish publishers could profit from translation by signing up major foreign writers and selling English-language translations in the larger and more lucrative British and American markets.[14]

The end of the 1980s saw a strong upsurge in the number of English translations of foreign-language titles published in Ireland. Examples of this new activity in English-language translation were Brian Lynch's and Peter Jankowski's translations of Paul Celan which appeared in 1986, John F. Deane's translations of Marin Sorescu published in 1987, the same year as Michael O'Loughlin's translations of work by Gerrit Achterberg and 1988 saw the publication of Hugh Maxton's translations of Agnes Nemes Nagy.[15] Raven Arts Press and, in particular, Dedalus Press were the two Irish publishers that were to the fore in producing English-language translations. In addition to bringing out the Marin Sorescu and Agnes Nemes Nagy translations, Dedalus also published translations of work by Miguel Hernandez, Tomas Tranströmer, Francisco de Quevedo, Uffe Harder, Ivan V. Lalic, Margherita Guidacci and Mario Luzi, as well as Arabic translations by Desmond O'Grady and the translations of Denis Devlin and Brian Coffey.[16] However, the inwards translation policy remained problematic for the Arts Council. In a public address to the Irish Translators' Association in 1992, Laurence Cassidy stated, 'this activity of inward translation is one which the Arts Council wishes to encourage strongly. However, I regret to say that there is not enough of such translation enterprise.'[17] Though a considerable number of translations were produced, it was not on the scale envisaged. The publication of translations was not simply a financial problem, it also related to less immediately quantifiable cultural factors. The English language in the late twentieth century has been conspicuously less open than other languages to literary translation, so it was, perhaps, not surprising that Ireland, too, should be affected by this linguistic insularity. There was the further problem of reception, the absence of what Cassidy calls 'gateway persons' in the culture who present foreign writers and literature to a native audience.[18] The success of literary translation can depend not only on the intrinsic excellence of the work in translation but also, on the existence of an appropriate critical infrastructure. If critics, literary editors and educationalists are not particularly interested in foreign literature in translation, the common reader is less likely to hear about the literature and the demand for that literature will remain weak. An important aspect of the reception of literature in general is the process of mediation by which the work is introduced to potential readers. In the case of translation, the need for knowledgeable and interested intermediaries is all the greater where the writer is often totally unknown to the target-language public.

If the phenomena of globalisation and supra-national integration imposed inward translation demands, the set of outward translation relationships in Ireland also generated new cultural needs. The third phase in Arts Council translation policy emerged from the need to address these needs. In 1988, a comprehensive report by Charles Pick on the Irish publishing industry appeared, entitled *Developing Publishing in Ireland*. Pick argued that Irish publishers should widen the market for their titles either through the direct export of books or through the selling on of foreign-language translation rights.[19] A year later, the Arts Council was approached by Liam Mac Cóil and Michael Cronin with an embryonic proposal for the establishment of an agency in Ireland that would have specific responsibility for the promotion abroad of Irish literature in translation. The proposal had evolved from an earlier document drawn up by Liam Mac Cóil which had particularly emphasised the need for Irish-language literature to be made available in languages other than English. Both the Arts Council and Bord na Leabhar Gaeilge were statutorily prevented from assisting foreign publishers who wanted to publish translations of English or Irish-language works by Irish authors. A major obstacle to the publication of translations is the cost of translation itself, and the Irish agencies responsible for Ireland's literatures were powerless to assist. Cronin and Mac Cóil received funding from the Arts Council, Roinn na Gaeltachta (the Department of the Gaeltacht) and Bord na Gaeilge (the Irish-Language Board) to produce a report detailing the need for and the *modus operandi* of an agency specifically dedicated to the promotion of Ireland's literature in translation. They were helped in their task by Jürgen Schneider, a German literary agent. The report by Cronin, Mac Cóil and Schneider appeared in 1990 and was entitled *Literature without Frontiers: Irish Literary Transla-*

tion in the European Context/Litríocht gan Teorainn: An tAistriú Liteartha Éireannach i gComhthéacs na hEorpa.

The report described the existing situation with respect to literary translation in Ireland and outlined the operation of translation schemes and agencies in Belgium, Britain, Denmark, France, Finland, Germany, Italy and the Netherlands. The report included an analysis of four representative bibliographies of works of Irish literature which had been translated into French, German, Italian and Polish. The results were illuminating. The percentage figures for translations of works by Irish authors born after 1945 were 9 per cent French, 5 per cent German, 5 per cent Italian and 3 per cent Polish. In the case of Irish-language works, they represented only 2 per cent of translations in French, 1 per cent in German, 1 per cent in Italy and 0 per cent in Polish.[20] The authors also pointed out that Ireland was the only member-state of the European Community that did not provide financial assistance for the outward translation of its literature. The report made a number of recommendations, arguing that the absence of appropriate structures and schemes meant that 'contemporary Irish literature in both languages, must remain largely unknown to readers outside Ireland'.[21] The report recommended that a national agency be established that would have responsibility for administering grant-assistance for the foreign publication of titles by Irish authors. The agency would represent Ireland at foreign-language book fairs and maintain a database of existing translations of Irish titles in addition to the names of publishers, translators and literary agents. It would publish a newsletter targeting foreign-language publishers, critics and decision makers. The agency would facilitate contacts between publishers and translators for both inward and outward translations.

The report was generally welcomed, but four years were to elapse before the agency known as the Ireland Literature Exchange/ Idirmhalartán Litríocht Éireann was established in 1994. The difficulty lay in persuading potential funders of the cultural and economic importance of literary translation. To many, literary translation appeared to be a somewhat marginal and relatively obscure activity in the bookworld. However, funding was eventually forthcoming from the Cultural Relations Committee of the Department of Foreign Affairs, the Arts Council, Bord na Leabhar Gaeilge and the Arts Council of Northern Ireland. A board was set up under the chairmanship of Micheal Ó Siadhail in 1993 and a director was appointed in 1994. The ILE was located in the Irish Writers'

Centre in Dublin, and its function was to implement the recommendations of the *Literature without Frontiers* report. The rationale for the third
phase of the Arts Council's translation policy was not simply economic –
encouraging Irish publishers to benefit from the secondary windfall of
translation – but also political. Assessing the direction and impact of the
Council's translation policy, Laurence Cassidy claimed:

> It is very important, it is of the most crucial importance that an independent
> country with an independent literature in two languages takes onto itself its
> own representation of that literature and doesn't leave it to London
> [publishing] houses who are really only promoting the authorial end and the
> economic end of the process and are not concerned about the Irish image.[22]

It is noteworthy that it was the move towards European integration and the
incorporation of Ireland into a transnational, multilingual European culture
that prompted the moves towards the defence of Irish cultural specificity in
translation. The internationalisation of the Irish economy and society had
strengthened rather than weakened a sense of difference. In addition, there
is a sense in which the European context provided Irish policy-makers with
the opportunity to move beyond the fixed embrace of Anglo-Irish
relationships, with their long history of unequal distribution of power, to a
more autonomous championing of specific Irish cultural interests. The
policymakers had, in a sense, followed the path of Denis Devlin, Brian
Coffey, Thomas MacGreevy and Samuel Beckett, Irish writers and translators who in the first half of the twentieth century situated themselves in a
European rather than exclusively Anglo-Irish or Irish-Irish context.[23]

TRANSLATION RESISTANCE AND FLUENT STRATEGIES

The contexts of translation are rarely neutral and translation policy
initiatives were not without their critics. The criticisms focused almost
exclusively on the first phase of the Arts Council's translation policy,
the translation of contemporary Irish literature into English. Presenting
The Bright Wave: An Tonn Gheal to the Irish reading public, the publisher and novelist Dermot Bolger stated that:

> Although it was government policy after independence to translate as much
> as possible from English and European literature into Irish . . . no effort
> was made to reverse this process and make living Irish literature available in
> English. In fact, even when I was growing up and perhaps to some extent
> today, the idea of such translation was frowned upon, the general idea being

that those who wished to know what was happening in Irish should be able to read the language in the first place and any concession would dilute the chances of revival of the language.[24]

Translation was the exit visa from the ghetto of linguistic isolationism and would bring the level of achievement of contemporary Irish-language writers to the attention of the English-speaking world. The fact that so many Irish-language poets allowed their work to be translated does indeed point to the desire for a form of recognition in the wider literary community. Interviewed in 1986, Nuala Ní Dhomhnaill decried the lack of response to writing by Irish-language writers:

> Part of creativity is the need to make an impact. You can't say 'I don't care!' though some people do it, but I don't think it's sincere. There is no reaction or feedback, just talking into a void and feeling invisible. I have seventeen years experience of it, and what does it do to you? It makes you bitter. It gives you a ghetto mentality which means that you are constantly looking over your shoulder and on the defensive all the time.[25]

Though the Arts Council supported translations into English, it was individual writers, publishers and translators who decided who and what would be translated. Alan Titley, who wrote the preface to the *Bright Wave* anthology, argued several years later at a round table discussion on translation that the Irish–English translations generated a publicity that was a necessary antidote to prevailing cultural ignorance:

> Without this publicity many people would think, and would like to think, that Irish poetry and Irish literature do not exist at all. Nobody in Ireland must ever be allowed to think that. Nobody must be ever allowed to say that Irish literature is written solely in English. They must be never free to ignore us in our own country.[26]

Translation meant feedback, response, the acknowledgement of another literary tradition and culture. For other writers, however, translation was a form of dispossession that threatened the integrity of writing in Irish. Pól Ó Muirí, the writer and critic, expressed extreme cynicism as to the intellectual and political good faith of the translation enterprise in the Bolger and Kiberd/Fitzmaurice translation anthologies:

> My contention, then, is that this new rapport between Irish poets of both languages, as expressed in these various anthologies is bogus. There is no real desire for an exchange of ideas. We are simply witnessing poets while away the dark winter nights by translating Irish poetry. It occurs to me that translation, in this instance, has a lot more to do with colonialisation – a desire to scavenge rather than a desire to propagate. It is patronage and pity.[27]

Biddy Jenkinson, an Irish-language poet, resists translation of her work into English: 'I prefer not to be translated into English in Ireland. It is a small rude gesture to those who think that everything can be harvested and stored without loss in an English-speaking Ireland.'[28] The desire to speak, maintain and write Irish is primarily motivated by the belief that it contains within it a spirit, an essence, a mind-set that is fundamentally different from English. It is defined, in a sense, by its untranslatability. If this were not the case, there would seem to be little purpose in learning the language as all its literary treasures would already be on display in the shop window of English. The anxiety felt by those hostile to translation practice did not relate only to the pillage implicit in a putative ideal equivalence between the two languages, it also resulted from a fear of the internalisation by Irish speakers of a literary history founded on the reputations of translated writers. Alan Titley, who was active in promoting Irish–English translations, articulates these concerns:

> There are no monoglot English speakers with an understanding of Seán Ó Ríordáin because his work has never been available in translation. Other poets are not much better known and people writing in Irish constantly hear about them because we straddle both cultures and hear what the English-speaking media say about poets whose work has been translated. The fact that Biddy Jenkinson is not more widely read by an Irish-reading public is proof that the work is not the only criterion and that translation has a huge effect – a negative effect in the case of Jenkinson – on the public.[29]

The poet and critic Tomás Mac Síomóin pointed to the relationship between a poetic tradition and public perceptions of a writer. If an Irish-language poet is canonised by a monoglot English-speaking public, influenced by stereotypical representations of the Irish language as pertaining to an archaic, rural way of life, then younger writers are bound to be influenced by aesthetic choices made outside their own language tradition. The publicity, he claims, 'is not in itself a bad thing, but it is done to the exclusion of other poets, whose voices are perhaps better, perhaps more experimental, who are extending the language in ways which render it impossible to translate'.[30] Although the Arts Council specified that any work that was to be translated from Irish into English must already have had a literary life of its own in Irish, the dominant position of English in contemporary Ireland led to an understandable anxiety of influence. Barra Ó Séaghdha argued that a writer in a minority language who is in regular contact with translation runs a risk: 'Subconsciously, with no element of calculation, the degree of future translatability and the values of the English-language audience may become factors that penetrate and weaken the original impulse.'[31]

Much of the translation output from Irish to English in the 1980s and 1990s is eminently readable. The translations of Paul Muldoon, Gabriel Fitzmaurice, Thomas McCarthy and John Montague often read like compositions in their own right. As Douglas Sealy noted in a review of a collection of translations of work by Nuala Ní Dhomhnaill, it was not easy to form a clear or consistent picture of the writer of the original poems. Among the translators were Ciaran Carson, Michael Coady, Peter Fallon, Michael Hartnett, Seamus Heaney, Michael Longley, Medbh McGuckian, Tom McIntyre, Derek Mahon, Paul Muldoon and Eiléan Ní Chuilleanáin. Sealy asks: 'has she [Nuala Ní Dhomhnaill] the smart raciness of Muldoon . . . the clotted verbal richness of McGuckian; the conversational bite of Carson; the ornate elaboration of Longley . . . has she got the bewildering variety of tone supplied by the thirteen translators?'[32] The very fluency of the translations is in itself problematic. Writing on translations in the English-speaking world, Lawrence Venuti notes the preference for what he calls 'fluent strategies'. He defines these strategies as the preference for linear syntax, univocal meaning, current usage and a tendency to shun archaism, unidiomatic constructions, polysemy or any affect that draws attention to the materiality of language. Fluent strategies ultimately obliterate the linguistic and cultural otherness of the source text. Venuti claims that:

> A fluent strategy performs a labour of acculturation which domesticates the foreign text, making it intelligible and even familiar to the target-language reader, providing him or her with the narcissistic experience of recognizing his or her culture in a cultural other, enacting an imperialism that extends the dominion of transparency with other ideological discourses over a different culture.[33]

Venuti's argument must be handled with care. Linguistic incompetence can compromise fluency but the result is likely to be confusion rather than liberation. However, Venuti is right to challenge the intrinsic idealism of fluent strategies where the translation becomes transparent and the translator invisible. Where he is wrong is in supposing that this is always the case. For example, in the case of the Ní Dhomhnaill translations mentioned by Sealy, each translator has his/her unmistakeable form of fluency, so that it is the original poet rather than the translator who becomes invisible.

An effect of fluency is to conceal process, and it is striking in much contemporary translation work in Ireland that so little attention is paid to the act of translation itself. This is true of translation prefaces from the *Bright Wave*, in 1986, to the translations of Cathal Ó Searcaigh's *Homecoming/An Bealach 'na Bhaile*, in 1993. There is no presentation of translation problems or the nature of the translation dynamic in the publications of the European Poetry Translation Network in Ireland, which contain translations by Irish translators of work by Claude Esteban, Bernard Noël, João Miguel Fernandes Jorge and Joaquim Manuel Magalhães.[34] Where they exist, most prefaces to translated work confine themselves to a short bio-critical presentation of the writer's work. In the case of Irish–English translations, references are made to the historical problems of the Irish language and the changing socio-cultural relationships between the two languages on the island. The failure to foreground the act of translation can be seen as resulting from a fear that excessive attention to linguistic detail will bore the general reader. However, the failure to explore the exact nature of formal transformations in translation has two important consequences. Firstly, the question of competence is ignored. The English-language translators who translated poetry from Irish in the *Bright Wave*, for example, had very different degrees of competence in Irish, but the reader is not told whether the translations were direct or were from draft versions in English. Secondly, the translator's work either goes unacknowledged or, perhaps more disconcertingly, with respect to Irish–English translations, the enormous difficulties in translating between two languages that are so strikingly different are elided. The poems read well and, for the monoglot Anglophone reader, nothing in the prefaces indicates the extent of the transformations that must be effected to arrive at a provisional rendering of the radically dissimilar syntactic, lexical and phonological structures of Irish in addition to complex questions of resonance and allusion. In this way, the genuine otherness of the source language and culture is diminished.

The relative lack of self-reflexivity in translation for many years related in part to the absence of an institutional focus for translation studies in Ireland. Despite the fact that the state had been translating since its inception, it was only in 1982 that the first translation studies degree programme was established in the National Institute for Higher Education, Dublin (later to become Dublin City University). No association of translators emerged before the setting up of the Irish Translators' Association in 1986. The neglect of translation as an intellectual discipline in its own

178

right was not, of course, an uniquely Irish phenomenon. For many countries, the emergence of translation studies as an autonomous activity is relatively recent. It is nonetheless striking that in a country where translation had been an integral part of the educational, legal and administrative activities of the state since 1922, sixty years were to elapse before translation studies would begin to feature as a distinct area of academic enquiry. The late development of translation studies was, in part, an effect of the ideology of revivalism. Teaching translation was an open acknowledgement of bilingualism, and danger lay for the apprentice Irish speaker in a disabling dependence on English and the spread of anglicisms or *béarlachas*. Thus, though translation practice was taught in Irish departments, it was, like the teaching of translation in modern language departments, mainly a language exercise. The irony is that ignoring translation leads to the return of the linguistically repressed. The undermining of the lexical and syntactic specificity of Irish is greatly accelerated through a failure to examine the phenomenon of translation in detail. In addition, the extensive translation tradition in Irish remained largely in the realm of close textual scholarship so that its potential contribution to contemporary debates on translation theory and practice went generally unheeded.

UNSETTLING REALITIES

It would be wrong, however, to argue that the dramatic expansion in translation activity in contemporary Ireland has been entirely without reflexive analysis. A number of writers, critics and translators have been alert to the contexts and detail of translation and have differed in their understanding of the nature and aims of the translation process. Commenting on the vogue for translation among Irish writers, the critic and cultural historian, Terence Brown, sees the impulse to translate as a need prompted by the specific pressures of language and culture in modern Ireland. Discussing translation from Irish, he claims:

> What the translation from Irish seems to imply is not a nostalgia for some truly indigenous expression, nor any revivalist enthusiasm, but a sense that the complexity of the Irish poet's contemporary experience requires an interpretive resource which current English language usage somehow fails to supply. It is as if, to adapt the Brian Friel of *Translations*, a linguistic contour does not as yet match the contour of the fact, and the poet must seek for alternative linguistic perspectives from which to survey the landscape.[35]

The unhappiness with 'current English language usage' was, of course, a feature of the theorising of the writers of the Irish Literary Revival, but Brown sees the crisis in language as a crisis of location. Translating Eastern European poets is driven by a desire to deepen 'the local sense of a frighteningly flawed national life'. The unsettling realities of political violence, economic depression and rapid social change in Ireland mean a level of sympathetic response to the predicaments of Eastern European writers and a feeling that the English language of Irish poets is no longer wholly congruent with a world in flux. Brown argues that 'translation as cultural metaphor is therefore a sign of the degree to which in contemporary Ireland inherited definitions of national life, of social origins and expectations fail to account for much individual and collective experience'.[36] Translation is at once a hermeneutic resource and a way of coping.

A source for Brown's argument is the poet Seamus Heaney's reflections on the tasks of the translator. Heaney readily admits the political context of the translation enterprise: 'translation of a text from the Irish language by an Irish writer who speaks English is usually to be perceived in lights other than those of the writer's own career and impulses'.[37] Discussing the genesis of his own translation of the Middle Irish text *Buile Shuibhne*, the tale of a seventh-century Ulster king whom battle and religious censure have driven to insanity, Heaney describes his initial intention as being to make the unionist population more aware of the history of pre-colonial Ulster and, by extension, more sensitive to nationalist grievances. The translation would be read differently by both communities:

> I simply wanted to offer an indigenous text that would not threaten a Unionist (after all, this was just a translation of an old tale, situated for much of the time in what is now Co. Antrim and Co. Down) and that would fortify a Nationalist (after all this old tale tells us we belonged here always and that we still remain unextirpated).[38]

However, the initial political overdeterminedness of the translation was to yield to a more oblique appropriation of the source text through a change in translation strategy. The initial 1972 translation of the text was theoretically-speaking, dynamic, communicative, metaphorically charged. Heaney cites Lowell as an influence and the latter's 'unabashed readiness to subdue the otherness of the original to his own autobiographical neediness'.[39] This led to the conflation of Heaney's personal situation with that of the seventh-century Ulster monarch. When he returned to the translation five years later, Heaney sought a more ascetic, constricted translation, 'more obedient to the metrical containments and the battened-down verbal procedures of the Irish itself'. He argues that 'the closer, line by line, stanza by stanza, end-stopped, obedient, literal approach finally yielded more'. A more literal approach also signalled a political distancing, where the poet values more the 'quarantined otherness of *Buile Shuibhne* as art' more than his complex entanglements with the 'matter of Ulster'.[40]

Heaney is not the only Ulster poet to be drawn by the lodestone of translation. Other Northern poets like Paul Muldoon, Derek Mahon, Ciarán Carson and John Montague have embraced translation in their poetic practice.[41] The engagement with translation has taken place at three levels. Firstly, there is translation as a dialogue with the other language on the island, Irish. Muldoon has published extensive translations of the poetry of Nuala Ní Dhomhnaill while in the case of Ciaran Carson, the dialogue is as much internal as external, Carson having been brought up through Irish in Belfast. Translation here is an act of self-understanding at both a personal and community level.[42] Secondly, there is translation as liberation, escaping from the pressures of Irish politics and history into the playful exuberance of foreign literatures. Translating French (Mahon, Carson, Montague) or classical poetry (Carson, Heaney) allows a release from the tense bipolarities of conflict to explore other worlds of language and expression. Thirdly, there is translation as a way of addressing the conflict but indirectly. As Kathleen Shields has demonstrated in the case of Derek Mahon's translations from the French, translation enables the poet to explore individual and public loyalties in a divided society.[43] Much of contemporary Northern translation practice has favoured fluent, dynamic approaches to source-language material that contrast with Heaney's sobriety in the *Buile Shuibhne* translation. A more restrained, unadorned translation approach to earlier material is not, however, specific to Heaney and one could argue that a concern with the literal is what in Ireland characterises much contemporary English-language translation from pre-twentieth century Irish material. In the 1981 *Duanaire* anthology, Thomas Kinsella and Seán Ó Tuama stress fidelity: the translations are not, 'free "versions" . . . It was taken that the fulfilment of our primary aim required translations of the greatest possible fidelity of content, and the results are as close to the original Irish as we could make them.'[44] They acknowledge the untranslatability of effect linked to earlier Irish prosody, while departures from literal translations of lexical items are recorded in notes to the anthology. In his 1985 translations of the seventeenth-century poems of Dáibhí Ó Bruadair, Michael Hartnett similarly emphasises the difficulty of rendering Gaelic metres and poem-structures in English. Hartnett speaks of his 'insistence that a poet who is such a consummate craftsman should be translated with obsessive care . . . his techniques should be brought across as faithfully as possible'. He does not agree with the adage that the poetry is what gets lost in translation:

> A poet/translator, if he loves the original more than he loves himself, will get the poetry across: he may even get the whole poem across or, at second best, force his own version – within the strictures laid down by the original author – as close as possible to poetry.[45]

However, Hartnett is anxious that his scrupulous attention to poetic detail should not be subsumed to scholarship. His translations are teleological. He tries to keep a West Limerick audience in mind and to convey how Ó Bruadair would have come across to a literate but not scholarly public. To this end, 'I kept to his metres but simplified his diction. This is not meant to be a work of scholarship, but an attempt to restore and popularise.'[46] Though there is a tension between the exegetical proprieties of scholarship and poetically effective translation, it is nonetheless true that Heaney, Kinsella, Ó Tuama and Hartnett are all concerned to preserve the unsettling otherness of the earlier texts. The careful remaking of poems in translation is not so much an act of static reverence as an attempt to convey the complex energies of the Irish texts. Both Heaney and Hartnett refer to earlier scholarly translations by O'Keefe and MacErlean respectively. These contemporary translations are part of a shift from commentary to rhetoric, from translations as respectful commentaries on texts to translations as generators of new discourses.[47] The opposition must not be seen as schismatic. There is no brutal repudiation of scholarly predecessors but a heedful incorporation of their work into more ambitious poetic projects.

The translation discourse surrounding contemporary work is explicit in its disavowal of literalness. The editor of the *Bright Wave* anthology, Dermot Bolger, states his translation policy as follows: 'In giving my instructions to translators, I have stressed that, for this book, I am more concerned that the spirit of the original poem should come across and work as effectively as possible, as against merely reproducing a strictly literal line for line version.'[48] In his introduction to the anthology, Alan Titley is equally wary of the literal. Though expressing a certain scepticism as to the possibility of poetic translation and claiming that it is a task that should be left to poets themselves, he says of the translations in the anthology:

> We are fortunate in these translations in having the best of poets talking to their peers. They recreate one another as kindred spirits across the gulf of language. This is not an operation that proceeds from bags to stitches with the needlework of literalness. One gets the impression of entire poems being relived and refelt, strutting forth anew while putting their best chin forward.[49]

The aim of the translator is to give a different existence rather than a new life to the work. The existences may of course be several, and Liam Mac Cóil attacks what he sees as the essentialism underlying hostility to heterogeneity in translation: 'Maidir liomsa, in ionad bheith ag cur is ag cúiteamh faoin rud atá caillte, b'fhearr liom féachaint ar an rud atá ann, an éagsúlacht.'[50] Difference in translation is less an admission of failure than an affirmation of its potential. Translation as a form of close reading results in diverse interpretations that find expression in the target texts. We mentioned earlier the debates surrounding the fluency strategies of contemporary translation practice in Ireland, but it is important to remember that translation has an experimental, liberatory function that carries with it attendant risks. Translations that are closer to Drydenesque or Lowellian 'imitations' should not be judged and condemned by an immutable standard of philological exactitude but seen as one manifestation of a range of rhetorical responses to the potential for *inventio* in translation. It is, perhaps, the failure to define these responses in the absence of a fully-developed translation studies tradition that has led to the feeling that the reader is not safe from 'the translator's propensities to go it alone when the reader is offguard'.[51]

Introducing his translations of the Spanish poet Francisco de Quevedo (1580–1645), Michael Smith argues that 'the real energy of the poetry, and I believe Borges to be generally correct in his analysis, is that energy directed towards the making of the poem as a literary artifact, a cunning verbal device that invites and entertains inspection and contemplation by the reader'.[52] Smith's translations are described on the front cover as 'versions', and on the back it is stated that Quevedo's poetry 'has been recreated in modern English'. However, in his notes to Quevedo's poems, Smith claims that they 'contain indispensable information for the reader to anchor Quevedo's verse, just as it did for me while *translating*' (my emphasis).[53] No definition of the term 'version' is offered so readers are unsure as to whether what they are reading is a 'recreation' or translation. The status of the 'versions' are unclear. Are they metaphrase, paraphrase or imitation, to borrow Dryden's terminology?[54] Thus, Smith argues that verbal skill is the essence of Quevedo's genius, but there is no explanation offered as to how he went about the task of translation, which would appear all the more difficult because of the linguistic self-consciousness of Quevedo's poetic art. In a review of Smith's earlier Hernandez translations, Lorna Shaughnessy equates version with metaphrase: 'I suspect Michael Smith's "versions" of Hernandez come closer to the stuff of a parallel text than a translation. Perhaps this is why he has opted for the ambiguous category of "version".'[55] John F. Deane's translations of work by the Romanian poet, Marin Sorescu, are also called 'versions', but the translator appears to explain the term in his Introduction to the collection: 'I have worked from English draft versions, from the original model and German and Spanish translations; the poems have been submitted to Sorescu and he has approved them.'[56]

However, the reader without a knowledge of Romanian and without the original text is still uncertain as to what the status is of the 'original model' and the 'English draft versions' in the production of the translations. On the other hand, Hugh Maxton's translations of the Hungarian poet Agnes Nemes Nagy are presented as 'translations' rather than 'versions'. The Irish poet acknowledges that the book was a collaborative translation project and that he worked from draft translations from the Hungarian made by Mária Kórösy and Eszter Molnár. In the commentary, Maxton makes a point of investigating the translation process and discusses the difficulties of translating from Hungarian, pointing to the absence of gender in the language, the prevalence of rhyme in Hungarian poetry and the specific difficulties of cultural allusion in Nemes Nagy's work.[57]

The terminological uncertainty surrounding terms like 'version', 'imitation', 'recreation' and 'translation', if partly a response to theoretical circumstances, can be seen in another light. The poet and translator, Desmond O'Grady, exhorts young poets to look again to the Poundian tradition of 'creative translation', Pound's 'indelibly personal method of transferring poems from their original languages into a modern English that makes poetry'.[58] The creative licence of the translator invigorates the target language and challenges linguistic and cultural parochialism. Wary of the prudent policing of interlingual transfer implied in certain definitions of the term 'translation', some translators have used the more catholic term 'version'. The danger, of course, as Edwin Gentzler points out in his analysis of the Poundian inheritance in the United States, is that licence is given

> to allow translators to intuit good poems from another language without knowledge of the original language or culture, and, as long as they have some poetic sensibility and good taste, now governed by plain speech, and lack of adornment, their translations are accepted.[59]

This danger should not be overstated, however, and it is clear that where contemporary translators in Ireland have had a limited knowledge of the source language they have gone to great lengths to remedy the deficiency and do interpretive and aesthetic justice to the source text. That they should do so demonstrates how much is at stake in translation. In a mischievous analogy the poet and translator, Eiléan Ní Chuilleanáin, sees translation as next to godliness. The translator is as essential to a developed civilisation as a plumber:

> His essential expertise is as necessary for the higher virtues of civilised man – broadmindedness, enterprise, assurance – as for the main luxury of civilized life – uninterrupted human communication, and the endless satisfaction of human curiosity. Translator and plumber, though, both capitalise on basic needs of man, whether civilised or not, and thus inevitably demonstrate the unity of peoples. Languages, histories and traditions, which seem impervious to one another, are revealed as modes of communication.[60]

POLITICAL ECONOMY AND PALIMPSEST

It is translations from Irish into English that have, over the years, attracted much public attention and comment. In any one year, however, the volume of translation into Irish has been significantly greater than English language translations published by Irish publishers. This imbalance is, in part, related to the political economy of translation that has been commented on by a number of translator scholars in the Third World. As Richard Jacquemond points out: 'it is no surprise that the global translational flux is predominantly North–North, while South–South translation is almost non-existent and North–South translation is unequal: cultural hegemony confirms, to a great extent, economic hegemony'.[61] Minority languages are internal colonies that translate more than they are translated. It is the unequal relationship between a major and a minority language which also makes conventional approaches to translation theory and analysis problematic. Jacquemond argues that the North–South translation imbalance has theoretical consequences:

Because translation theory (as well as literary theory in general) has developed on the almost exclusive basis of the European linguistic and cultural experience, it relies on the implicit postulate of an egalitarian relationship between different linguistic and cultural areas and has yet to integrate the recent results of the sociology of interculturality in the colonial and postcolonial contexts.[62]

Where Jacquemond, like so many other post-colonial critics, is mistaken, is to presume that there is a homogenous political economy of translation in Europe itself based on reciprocal equality. It is, indeed, an unease concerning the limits to this reciprocity that has motivated certain translation initiatives in Irish. In 1989, *Conlán* was published. The book contained translations into Irish by Gabriel Rosenstock of selected poems by Seamus Heaney. In 1991 *Byzantium* appeared, co-edited by Gearailt Mac Eoin and Gabriel Rosenstock, and it brought together translations in Irish of a number of W.B. Yeats's better-known poems.[63] Rosenstock, a poet and one of the leading translators into the Irish language, sees these translation projects as an act of cultural reversal, an attempt to counter the trend of translating exclusively from Irish into English: 'One could say that my versions of Heaney (and the volume of Yeats that I co-edited) were an attempt to ensure that the traffic wasn't all one way.'[64] The emphasis on Irish–English translation can also distort the writing of cultural history, and Rosenstock criticises the *Field Day Anthology of Irish Literature* for its indifference to the Irish-language translation tradition: 'I know that the *Field Day Anthology of Irish Literature* featured many translations from the Irish but what of translations into Irish? That is tantamount to saying that translation is not literature, a mere service for the monoglot reader. Translation is manifestly more than that.'[65]

In describing the rationale behind the Heaney translations, Rosenstock rejects the implication that the activity is quixotic or academic in a country where the vast majority of people can read Heaney in the original. He declares:

Heaney is of Irish soil but that soil is much, much older than the English language. The soil is older than the Irish language too and yet it is that language that named the soil and everything that grew out of it. Is it not a logical step to sound out his poetry, to probe those areas of consciousness, memory, inspiration, perception, feeling and sensitivity which would undoubtedly have been expressed in Irish were it not for the vagaries of history?[66]

Translation is a reading of the palimpsest, the Irish-language names and words that inhabit Heaney's world as barely erased presences. Implicit in Rosenstock's *démarche* is the idea that the English of Heaney is, in a sense, ghosted by Irish. The other language is an absence that shadows and informs his English so that translation into Irish bodies forth this absence as real presence. In his introduction to the Yeats's translations, Declan Kiberd emphasises the Gaelic dimension to Yeats's poetic practice. Kiberd quotes Yeats's letter to *The Leader* in 1900 in which he expressed his desire to learn Irish on the grounds that 'the mass of people cease to understand any poetry when they cease to understand the Irish language, which is the language of their imaginations'.[67] Yeats's attempts to learn Irish were notoriously unsuccessful, but Kiberd lists Yeats's borrowings from the Irish-language literary tradition and, in particular, his indebtedness to the translation work of Frank O'Connor. Kiberd claims: 'Má chruthaíonn na haistriúcháin aon ní, léiríonn siad go raibh Yeats "Gaelach", sa mhéid nach féidir linn tuiscint iomlán a fháil ar na dánta gan iad a lárú i dtraidisiún na bardfhilíochta.'[68] As evidence of Yeats's affinities with the older poetic tradition, Kiberd refers to Yeats's praise for generous patrons (Lady Gregory, Hugh Lane, Charles Stewart Parnell), his contempt for the ignorant who despise the artist, his paeans to beautiful women identified with the land of Ireland, and his laments for the declining fortunes of the nobility and the practitioners of poetry. The language of the translations testify to the Gaelic substratum in Yeats's writing, 'léiríonn dul éasca na teanga cé chomh "Gaelach" is a bhí an fear scafánta seo nár fhoghlaim an Ghaeilge féin ariamh'.[69] Translation into Irish, therefore, is less the incorporation of the exotic or remote than a form of collusion with the familiar. Translation is a reading of Yeats's or Heaney's work which stresses Gaelic antecedents and contexts. There are, of course, those who would disagree with the arguments advanced by Rosenstock and Kiberd, but the theorisation of the English–Irish translation practice shows that translation is seen less as an act of patriotic restitution than as an interpretive recontextualisation of a body of work. The politics of the activity, however, have not gone unchallenged. Tomás Mac Síomóin deplores what he describes as the 'ghetto of the colonized mind as exemplified by many Anglo-Irish writers', and claims that 'translating such work with its attendant narrow vision into Irish is a waste of time'. He believes that Irish speakers have nothing to learn from the other culture. Alan Titley defends English–Irish translations as a statement of cultural confidence, echoing Rosenstock's hostility to unidirectional translation: 'If others were translating "from the Irish" we had a right to do the opposite and explore it as a possibility. It was a bold act, an act of imagination and appropriation.'[70] The disagreement centres on the liberatory potential of translation activity and the extent to which such freedom is possible in the charged context of the English–Irish language pair.

PARALLEL MODES OF EXPERIENCE

Contemporary translators in Irish have often sought this freedom elsewhere. The motives for translating from other languages into Irish, apart from genuine interest in the original work, are varied. Firstly, there is the desire to deliver Irish from the fatality of one language pair with its troubled contexts. Secondly, there has been a wish to place Irish in a European rather than an Anglo-Irish context, thus linking up with other minority languages and the older tradition of the Irish language on the European continent. The European Pilot Literary Translation Scheme has partially assisted this movement in that it gives priority to translation from and into minority languages. Thirdly, translation from other languages is seen as a way of opening up and extending the Irish language. Introducing his translations from the French, Breandán Ó Doibhlin laments the cultural uncertainty that can result from obsessive Irish comparisons with English language and literature. He believes that if readers of Irish are introduced to other literatures they may come to appreciate the distinctiveness and value of their own: 'Ní bheadh uaim ach fonn ceoil úr, macalla den saintéad a ghabhann le gach teanga ar leith, a sheinm le cluasa Éireannacha, agus, b'fhéidir, sa tslí sin breis measa a thabhairt dóibh ar ghuth na Gaeilge i measc claisceadal na náisiún.'[71] This cultural self-possession is also related to a history of influence. Translating from French is a way of acknowledging both the influence of French literary models on Irish in earlier periods, and the indirect influence of Irish sources on French literature.[72] Ó Doibhlin, a noted novelist and critic, also points to translation as an act of cultural humility. The fraught history of the Irish language in recent centuries has deprived it of certain linguistic and cultural resources that can be usefully supplied by the translation of French literature:

> Measaim fós, na cáilíochtaí a thugtar suas go coitianta don litríocht sin, a géire agus a grinneas intleachta, a cruinneas cainte, a cuannacht friotail, gur cáilíochtaí iad a rachadh ar sochar do shaothrú na Gaeilge, a fágadh chomh fada sin in éagmais na n-achmhainní agus na n-institiúidí a thugann canúin in aibíocht.[73]

The qualities that Ó Doibhlin refers to are by no means absent from writing in the Irish language, but literature in that language can be supplemented by and reworked through contact with other languages and literatures. In his introduction to the Irish translations of work by the Flemish poet Willem M. Roggeman, Colm Breathnach speaks of the translations' contribution to literature in Irish. They bring 'lón machnaimh agus samhlaíochta', food for thought and imaginative stimulus to the reader.[74] Breathnach further stresses the additive quality of translation in his prefatory remarks to Gabriel Rosenstock's translations of Georg Trakl. The translator has stretched the language and exercised its potential, 'tá aclú agus síneadh nua bainte aige as an teanga'.[75] Translation into Irish has not been confined to poetry, however, and there have translations of drama and prose from Italian, Spanish, Breton and Welsh by translators such as Rita Breatnach, Máire Nic Mhaoláin, Aodh Ó Canainn, Liam Mac Cóil and Uaitéar Mac Gearailt.[76] Much of the prose translation is in the form of school textbooks and books for children which are published by An Gúm.[77] The absence of a wider range of prose translation has attracted criticism. Tomás Mac Síomóin laments the absence of translations in Irish of basic philosophical classics:

> Before we try to translate poetry, that most complex form of human expression which draws on the entire range of man's powers, thought, philosophy, science, economy, politics etc. and the various registers and terminologies used to convey them, we must properly assimilate these terms of reference in prose.[78]

The failure to translate more works of philosophy, science, psychology means that there is greater difficulty in developing an autonomous intellectual life and community in Irish. If English is the conduit for ideas, then Irish speakers will narrow their use of the language to the everyday and pragmatic and find it increasingly difficult to engage confidently in abstract or philosophical debate in their own language. Breandán Ó Doibhlin's translation of Blaise Pascal's *Pensées* into Irish is part of such an attempt to make a part of Europe's intellectual tradition available to the Irish-speaking community. Translation is not simply a question of extending the language, it is also a way of proposing alternative or parallel modes of experience to the speaker of a language. Gabriel Rosenstock claimed that 'the reading experience in Irish which afforded me the greatest pleasure was a translation of a minor novel, *John Splendid*, by Neil Munro, translated as *Iain Aluinn* by Seán Tóibín and published in 1931 by An Gúm.'[79] The pleasure came from a particular evocation of woods and cathedrals that did not feature in the catalogue of experiences and impressions generally available to Irish-language writers. The landscape was different from the landscapes of the West of Ireland or the islands of its coast. Translation was a way of inhabiting other worlds in the language rather than having to choose one specific environment as the inevitable backdrop to lived experience.

The beginning of the 1980s saw the completion of one of the major translation projects in Irish in the twentieth century, the Maynooth Bible. This was the first full translation of the Catholic Bible into Irish and was the fruit of the labours of a group of translators under the general direction of Pádraig Ó Fiannachta, Professor of Irish in Maynooth College. A commission had been set up by the Catholic hierarchy in 1945 to produce an Irish translation of the New Testament, and a number of translations were published: *Lúcás* in 1964; *Matha* in 1966; and *Marcas* in 1972. A steering committee was set up in 1966 to provide a complete version of the Bible in Irish. Pádraig Ó Fiannachta was Secretary to the Committee, and each book was to be published as soon as the translation was completed. The result was that the translations appeared in different forms, sometimes in periodicals, sometimes in book form. The standardisation of Irish also meant that, in producing one single-volume translation, it was necessary to make the spelling and grammar of the older translations conform to the new standards. The teleological intention is apparent in the claim by Ó Fiannachta that the translation of the Bible is aimed at the ordinary reader, 'tá iarracht déanta ar é a bheith inléite . . . ag gnáthléitheoir.'[80]

The Bible was published the same year as the H-Block hunger strikes when ten republican prisoners died on hunger strike for political status. If the political context was fraught, the tone of the prefatory remarks was conciliatory. Cardinal Tomás Ó Fiaich in the Preface or 'Brollach', saluted the 'éacht', the major achievement of the Church of Ireland in translating the Bible three centuries earlier. Ó Fiaich blames the tardiness of the Catholic Church in producing its own translation on the ascendancy of Latin among Irish-speaking Catholics, but expresses the hope that Christians from other Churches will benefit from the new version of the Bible, 'ar an dóigh go mbeidh an t-aistriúchán nua seo ina dhroichead daingean idir Críostaithe uile na hÉireann'.[81] The tense invective of seventeenth-century religious polemic is absent and, instead, translation is seen as an act of ecumenical welcome in a divided society.

The scale of translation into Irish in contemporary Ireland has partly been dictated by the circumstances of a minority language in a predominantly Anglophone culture. However, a significant change with respect to the earlier period of translation activity in the 1930s is that, in literary translation, a greater effort has been made to translate from languages other than English. In addition, the texts chosen have tended to be those which are not widely available in English translations. Hence, a greater linguistic competence on the part of the translators themselves, a recognition of Ireland's diglossia and a desire to culturally re-orient Ireland towards the European continent have stimulated the significant growth in Irish-language translation activity in contemporary Ireland.

REPRESENTING TRANSLATORS

In 1985, Anne Bernard-Kearney proposed that an Irish Translators' Association be founded. On her return to Ireland from a seminar on literary translation in Arles, she felt that Irish translators needed some form of representation at international gatherings and contacted a number of people known for their interest in translation. A steering committee was set up which included Cormac Ó Cuilleanáin, Hugh Maxton, John F. Deane (Secretary), Ronan Sheehan, Pádraig Ó Snodaigh and Anne Bernard-Kearney. The group received a £250 grant from the Arts Council and printed a leaflet inviting translators to join the Irish Translators Association, or Cumann na nAistritheoirí in Éirinn. The association was formally constituted at a meeting held on the premises of Poetry Ireland on the 13 June 1986. The first executive committee was chaired by Cormac Ó Cuilleanáin and included Anne Bernard-Kearney, Michael Cronin, John F. Deane, Olive McKinley, Gabrielle Milch, Joris Mussche, Seosamh Ó Bruadair, Eithne O'Connell, Hans-Christian Oeser, Séamus Ó Tuama, Jennifer Pearson, Ronan Sheehan, Marie Siklo and Kathleen Van Osselaer.[82] The Irish Translators' Association was different from associations in other countries in that there was not a separate association for literary and commercial/technical translators. This was partly for reasons of economies of scale in a small country, but the executive also felt that it was important to stress what translators had in common rather than what separated them. The first two activities of the ITA reflected the dual interests of its members.

In March 1987, Brian Lynch and Peter Jankowski read their translations of Paul Celan at an ITA poetry reading. In May of that year, a Translation Day held at the National Institute for Higher Education, Dublin, included workshops on technical and commercial translation. The ITA compiled a register of translators available for work which has been regularly updated, instituted a code of practice for translators, organised an annual poetry translation competition, drew up a list of recommended translation rates and surveyed the working conditions of translators in Ireland.[83] The ITA also organised seminars on new technology and the translator, the business of translation, translation in Irish, translator training and media translation, as well as seminars in Cork, Galway and Belfast. A professional indemnity insurance policy was negotiated for ITA members, and an annual series of seminars on professional development for translators was launched to provide translators with the requisite skills and expertise to function as effective professionals. The ITA became a candidate member of the *Fédération Internationale des Traducteurs* (FIT) in 1987, and a full member at the FIT World Congress in Belgrade in August 1990. The ITA was given a permanent location in 1992 when it moved into the Irish Writers' Centre in Dublin. A Translation Studies Network was established in 1993 to provide a focus for translating teaching and research in Ireland, and a number of seminars were organised around these issues.

Although the ITA initially made no distinctions between different categories of membership, it was decided at the Extraordinary General Meeting of the Association, on the 24 February 1990, to introduce the category of professional membership. Professional members have to meet a number of strict requirements with regard to qualifications, work experience, language competence and publications portfolios in order to be accepted as professional members of the association. The move to introduce a professional membership category was defended on the grounds that it gave translators greater bargaining power when negotiating at official level, that it was in line with practice in translators' associations in other countries, that it made it easier to sell the services of Irish translators abroad, that it allowed the ITA to charge higher fees and so raise income and that motivating professional members of a body would be easier because they would have a vested professional interest in the success of the body.[84] Fears were expressed that the growing professionalisation of the ITA would lead to the marginalisation of literary translation, but the association in fact organised a number of highly successful events that were showcases for the talents of literary translators: 'Tranverse' (1991); 'Dublin Deutsch' (1991); and 'Seamus Heaney in Translation' (1994). The ITA became a member of the *Conseil Européen des Associations de Traducteurs*

Littéraires (CEATL), a representative organisation for European literary translators in 1992. The different activities and initiatives of the ITA were reported in a quarterly newsletter which first appeared in 1987. The format of the newsletter was changed in March 1992, and a new name, *Translation Ireland*, was adopted in that same year.

PRAGMATIC TRANSLATION, ECONOMIC CHANGE AND NEW TECHNOLOGY

The majority of the members of the Irish Translators' Association are scientific, technical and commercial translators. As we saw in Chapter One, pragmatic translation is a centuries-old activity in Ireland but over the last two decades, there has been unprecedented growth in the area. The first and most obvious reason for this development is Ireland's membership of the European Union. In the 1950s, the Irish economy was heavily dependent on exporting primary agricultural produce to the United Kingdom. Agricultural and food products comprised three quarters of Irish exports, and almost 90 per cent of Irish exports went to the UK market. At the beginning of the 1990s the UK share of Irish exports had dropped to less than 60 per cent and was continuing to fall. Agriculture and food products accounted for less than 20 per cent of total Irish exports and the European share of Irish export markets rose to over 40 per cent.[85] Tourism, a key sector of the Irish economy, saw similar significant changes. In a market that had previously been heavily dependent on North American and British visitors, the number of visitors from mainland Europe to Ireland in the 1980s increased by 165 per cent from 319,000 to 841,000. The number of visitors from Germany rose by 124 per cent, from France by 143 per cent and from Italy by 470 per cent.[86] These developments signalled a shift from a predominantly Anglophone economic environment to a trading situation that was increasingly multilingual. Operating in this new environment meant, therefore, a significant increase in the demand for translation services.

The other factor determining the rapid expansion of translation activity is related to the growth of the software sector in Ireland. The *Strategic Review of the Software Industry in Ireland* published by the National Software Directorate in 1992 identified foreign languages, computing and translation as key elements in the future development of the software sector in Ireland. As the report noted: 'Ireland has become a world centre for software localization and manufacturing, and has developed a complete infrastructure for these functions.'[87] The report also adds that 'the developing infrastructure of software manufacturing support services – translation, disc duplication, printing, etc. – is unique to Ireland and is a significant factor which enables companies to establish and become operational quickly'.[88] The translation of computer manuals and computer software into languages other than their languages of origin is known as software localisation and has become an internationally traded service for Ireland. Software localisation presented the dual advantages of national competitive edge and a potential for clustering, central features of the Industrial Policy Review Group's recommendations for the indigenous and overseas sectors in Ireland.[89] The existence of a software localisation sector servicing international markets was evidence of developments that had radically changed the professional prospects for translators in Ireland.

Like a number of other service industries in Ireland in the pre–informatics age, translation was disadvantaged by geographical location. Freelance translators depended on a postal service where the time-lag factor for continental markets, in particular, could be considerable. Staff translators had to be based in large head offices in metropolitan centres, which militated against the development of the translation profession in Ireland. The shift towards the reticular or network-based economy in developed countries, involving increasing reliance on informatics and telecommunications networks, removed the obstacle of insularity.[90] The development was greatly facilitated by the digitalisation of the Irish trunk transmission network in the 1980s.[91] Fax machines, modems, fax cards, and the internet allow Irish translators to work as peripheral teleworkers in the European market. The shift towards contractual employment in the translation sector in the 1980s also meant a weakening of the geographical imperative which dictated that staff translators had to be physically located in or near the large corporation or organisation for which they worked. The translation work could be done anywhere once the translator had the appropriate computer and telecommunication links.

Software localisation can be subsumed under language technology, a term that is used to describe any technology that is related to or involves the use of language. In 1988, the National Centre for Language Technology was established in Dublin City University. The centre was funded by the European Community's EUROTRA machine translation project. The NCLT researched the integration of terminology into the EURO-

194

TRA machine translation system, the development of criteria for assessing the suitability of sublanguage texts for automatic language processing, the design of specification for tools for the automatic classification of texts and the elaboration of criteria for corpus selections for machine translation.[92] The University of Limerick also became active in the area of language technology and machine translation.[93] The development of language technology in Ireland has been hampered, however, by changes in EU tendering procedures which favour awarding projects to research consortia that involve major industrial partners with large R&D departments. The low level of investment in research and development in Ireland, coupled with a lack of state involvement in the language technology area, has adversely affected potential research development in the area.[94]

TRANSLATING THE MEDIA

Media translation has also emerged as an important area of activity in recent years in Ireland, particularly in the Irish language. This generally takes three forms: translation of material for news broadcasts; dubbing and subtitling. News bulletins are broadcast in Irish by the national radio and television station, Raidió Teilifís Éireann (RTE). There are also news broadcasts by two other radio stations, Raidió na Gaeltachta and Raidió na Life, the former based in the Gaeltacht and the latter in Dublin. As the main source for international news and much national news is English-language the translation activity is continuous. Where uncertainty exists over terminology, for example, the translators consult with either the Translation Section of the Houses of the Oireachtas (Rannóg an Aistriúcháin) or the Terminology Committee for Irish (An Coiste Téarmaíochta).[95] Dubbing has been primarily into Irish of programmes such as the German cartoon series, *Janoschs Traumstunde*. The series, dubbed into Irish as *Scéalta ag Janosch* by the Connemara company 'Telegael', enjoyed considerable success, particularly given the paucity of Irish-language programming for children. Dubbing is, however, expensive and involves more than one person. As Eithne O'Connell points out in 'Media Translation and Lesser-Used Languages – Implications of Subtitles for Irish Language Broadcasting':

> A subtitled version is, by and large, much cheaper and quicker to produce than a dubbed one. Indeed, it is said that subtitles can frequently prove to be up to ten times cheaper than dubbing and while many will be surprised to hear that it can take up to one working week (ie 40 hours) to subtitle a one-

hour television programme, at least only one person is involved in the process so it is still generally much quicker than dubbing.[96]

The establishment of a new television station, Teilifís na Gaeilge, which will broadcast solely in the Irish language could lead to a rise in the number of Irish-language programmes subtitled in English or other languages and sold to domestic or foreign television stations. Subtitling as a translation practice is not, however, without its risks. If programmes were to be systematically subtitled to increase the audience base of the new station or to assist learners of Irish, the danger, O'Connell argues, is that native-speaker competence would be further affected through more exposure to the widely-used majority language. A solution would be the use of 'closed' or 'Teletext' subtitles rather than 'open' or 'burnt-on' sub-titles, though at present only one quarter of Irish television sets are equipped to receive 'closed' subtitles.[97]

Through its BABEL and MEDIA programmes, the European Union has sought to promote the development of the audiovisual industry in Europe. The European industry, unlike its US counterpart, is multilingual, and questions of language and translation are central to its future progress. The appearance of new satellite technology has further implications for media translators in Ireland. European Direct Broadcasting Satellites will be transmitting D2-MAC signals as part of moves to develop High-Definition Television (HDTV) in Europe. D2/MAC Packet is the new French and German television standard that will ultimately replace existing PAL and SECAM standards. The importance of the adoption of this new standard for translators lies in its multiple sound capability. In the old systems, the luminance and chrominance signals (responsible for picture and colour) were interlaced in what was known as frequential multi-plexing. In the transmission of each scanning line, fifty-two microseconds were given over to the transmission of luminance and chrominance signals and twelve microseconds to sound and data signals which were trans-mitted in analog form. The new standard transmits the luminance and chrominance signals in bursts as packets so that there is no interference between different signals and hence no loss of picture quality. This is known as temporal multiplexing. The sound and data signals, which include subtitles and teletext, are transmitted in digital form using duobinary coding. The D2-MAC Standard allows for four separate digital audio channels, which means that a programme can be broadcast simul-taneously in eight different languages.[98] The new standard and satellite technology offers potential outlets for audiovisual material produced in Ireland in both languages. Exploiting these outlets implies, of course, a coherent translation policy with appropriate training objectives for the audiovisual sector in Ireland. In a manner analogous to the potential role of Irish publishers, Irish translators can act as agents for the transmission of European broadcasting material in the English-speaking world. The move would be counter-hegemonic in the sense that globalisation is generally synonymous with unidirectional Anglicisation, the dominance of the English language and Anglo-American culture at the expense of other languages and cultures. English is a language from which, rather than into which, people translate.[99] Using appropriate translation strategies, Irish media translators could carry over audiovisual material from other European languages into English and make the cultural experiences of English-speakers more varied. The experience of a colonial rather than imperial past should make Irish translators more conscious of the need to protect diversity and promote heterogeneity. In this way, the Anglophone translation community in Ireland could make a distinctive contribution to world culture as a non-imperial English-speaking bridge for the European audiovisual industry.

TRANSACTIONS

On 23 September 1980, the Field Day Theatre Company staged its first theatrical production in the Guildhall, Derry. The play was written by Brian Friel and was called *Translations*. It explores the impact of the Ordnance Survey of Ireland in the 1830s on an Irish-speaking community in County Donegal. The most immediate impact of the survey is the anglicisation of placenames in the townland of Baile Beag/Ballybeg. Owen, one of the principal characters, acts as interpreter/translator for the English soldiers involved in carrying out the survey: 'My job is to translate the quaint, archaic tongue that you people persist in speaking into the King's good English.'[100] Owen is not operating in a translation void. Before he enters the stage, translation is already present in the form of Jimmy Jack Cassie's translations from Greek and Latin into Irish, and translation from the classical languages is a constant backdrop to the action of the play. Translation is more than a harmless, scholarly exercise, however, as Manus is quick to point out to his brother Owen, who has just interpreted for the English officers:

MANUS: What sort of translation was that, Owen?
OWEN: Did I make a mess of it?
MANUS: You weren't saying what Lancey was saying!
OWEN: 'Uncertainty in meaning is incipient poetry' – who said that?
MANUS: There was nothing uncertain about what Lancey said: it's a bloody military operation, Owen! and what's Yolland's function? What's 'incorrect' about the place-names we have here?
OWEN: Nothing at all. They're just going to be standardised.
MANUS: You mean changed into English.[101]

Owen is made forcibly aware of the translator's political predicament when he has to translate for Captain Lancey in Act Three. One of the English officers, Lieutenant Yolland, has gone missing, and Lancey threatens reprisals on the local population if he is not found alive. Owen is taken aback at the scale of the reprisals threatened and seeks to interrupt Lancey who swiftly rebukes Owen, saying: 'Do your job. Translate.'[102] Owen, whose first experiences of translation are in the hedge-school of Ballybeg, realises the fraught nature of the translation transaction. Yolland is another of translation's victims. Longing to communicate with Maire, a local woman, his attempts to learn Irish are as unsuccessful as his desire to be accepted by the local community. As one of the play's other translator-figures, Jimmy, puts it, 'you don't cross those borders casually – both sides get very angry'.[103] However, the pressures for translation are not only external, they are also internal. Maire does not want to learn Latin or Greek, she wants to learn English as she intends to emigrate to America. The schoolmaster, Hugh, agrees at the end of the play to teach Maire English but warns, 'don't expect too much. I will provide you with the available words and the available grammar. But will that help you to interpret between privacies? I have no idea.'[104] Hugh dislikes words like 'always' and is wary of atrophied grievance: 'to remember everything is a form of madness'. Another translator in the play, he sees the often uncomfortable relationship between translation and circumstance, 'it can happen that a civilisation can be imprisoned in a linguistic contour which no longer matches the landscape of . . . fact'.[105] Hugh notes the historical fatality of translation process and becomes a part of it, but he acknowledges the contexts, costs and limits of translation in a play that is not comedy but tragedy. The mistranslations of the first two acts invite laughter; those in Act Three are deadly serious.

Friel has not been alone among Ulster writers in drawing attention to the question of language and translation. In a frequently-quoted poem, 'A Grafted Tongue', John Montague speaks of the trauma of language-shift:

> (Dumb,
> bloodied, the severed
> head now chokes to
> speak another tongue:-
>
> As in
> a long suppressed dream,
> some stuttering garb-
> led ordeal of my own)

Translated into the new tongue, you may no longer greet those who speak the old tongue and the poet remarks:

> To grow
> a second tongue, as
> harsh a humiliation
> as twice to be born.[106]

In 'A Lost Tradition' Montague explores the aporias of translation in the renamed landscape:

> The whole landscape a manuscript
> We had lost the skill to read,
> A part of our past disinherited;
> But fumbled like a blind man,
> Along the fingertips of instinct.[107]

The temptation in the case of both Friel and Montague is to read their literary examination of the themes of language and translation as a simple denunciation of the linguistic legacy of colonialism. W.J. Mc Cormack adds the rider that 'rather than see this phenomenon [transliteration of placenames] simply as damning evidence of colonialism, we should additionally see it as a negotiation between languages, even to some extent a compromise imposed by the defeated upon their aggressors'.[108] The historical indictment is certainly present in the work of Friel and Montague, but the ultimate argument for a contemporary audience is that *translation is our condition*. Time and change have meant that it is no longer possible for a painless, unproblematic shift back to the originary Eden of Irish. For the Irish Anglophone, entering into the world of Irish-language, literature and culture is another form of translation with all the difficulty, disorientation and uncertainties that this process implies. Translation is never without consequences. One of the failures of the Revivalist movement in post-Independence Ireland was to assume that translation was transparent, that

199

a natural ability to speak and write in Irish lay below the thin anglicised veneer of the translated Irish.

The world of Jimmy Jack Cassie is the richer for translation. He translates Homer's *Odyssey* into his own emotional longing, and tells Hugh that he will marry Pallas Athene at Christmas. Like the medieval translators of Ireland, he allows the gods of other pantheons to sit happily with native heroes and heroines. In a country of radically and violently conflicting loyalties, translation, as Hugh notes, is 'all we have'. Co-existence implies translating the culture and (political, religious, emotional) language of the other into a language and culture that is strengthened by the presence of the other. The alternative to translation is the muteness of fear. This is not to argue that translation is easy or straightforward. Irish translation history shows that quite the opposite is true. The history also shows, however, the ancient necessity of a practice that at crucial periods in Irish history has provided the openness that has sustained hope. By underlining the central role of translation in the development of the literatures and cultures of Ireland, it may also be possible to make a case for dialogue and renewal. Translating the languages and cultures of Ireland in this century and the next means receptiveness, reciprocity, confidence and courage. The translators should not be found wanting.

Notes

1. Thomas MacDonagh, *Literature in Ireland*, Dublin, Talbot Press, 1920, p. 13.
2. MacDonagh, p. 122.
3. Robert Welch, *Changing States: Transformations in Modern Irish Writing*, London, Routledge, 1993, p. xi.
4. Welch, pp. 4–5.
5. Máirtín Ó Direáin, *Tacar Dánta/Selected Poems*, trans. Tomás Mac Síomóin and Douglas Sealy, Athlone, Goldsmith, 1984.
6. *An Duanaire: Poems of the Dispossessed*, ed., Seán Ó Tuama, trans. Thomas Kinsella, Mountrath, Dolmen Press, 1981.
7. Laurence Cassidy, *Translating the Success of Irish Literature*, Dublin, Arts Council, 1992, p. 3; see also Laurence Cassidy, 'The Arts Council's Translation Policy', *Irish Translator's Association Newsletter*, vol. 2, no. 4, December 1988, p. 8.
8. Interview with Laurence Cassidy, 27 January 1995.
9. Cassidy interview.
10. Further examples of poetry translations are: Mícheál Davitt, *Selected Poems: Rogha Dánta*, Dublin, Raven Arts Press, 1987; Declan Kiberd and Gabriel Fitzmaurice,

eds., *An Crann faoi Bhláth: The Flowering Tree*, Dublin, Wolfhound Press, 1991; Nuala Ní Dhomhnaill, *Pharaoh's Daughter: New and Selected Poems*, trans. several, Dublin, Gallery Press, 1990 and Nuala Ní Dhomnaill, *The Astrakhan Cloak*, trans. Paul Muldoon, Oldcastle, Gallery Press, 1993.

11. Seán Mac Mathúna, *Ding agus Scéalta Eile*, Baile Átha Cliath, An Comhlacht Oideachais, 1983.

12. Laurence Cassidy, 'Translations: breaking into Europe', *Books Ireland*, May 1990, p. 87.

13. Cassidy, *Translating the Success*, p. 1.

14. Cassidy, 'Breaking into Europe', p. 87.

15. Paul Celan, *65 Poems*, trans. Brian Lynch and Peter Jankowski, Dublin, Raven Arts Press, 1986; Gerrit Achterberg, *Hidden Weddings*, trans. Michael O'Loughlin, Dublin, Raven Arts Press, 1987; Marin Sorescu, *The Youth of Don Quixote*, trans. John F. Deane, Dublin, Dedalus, 1987; Agnes Nemes Nagy, *Between*, trans. Hugh Maxton, Dublin, Dedalus/ Budapest, Corvina, 1988.

16. Tomas Tranströmer, *The Wild Market*, trans. John F. Deane, Dublin, Dedalus, 1985; Miguel Hernandez, *Unceasing Lightning*, trans. Michael Smith, Dublin, Dedalus, 1987; Francisco de Quevedo, *On the Anvil*, trans. Michael Smith, Dublin, Dedalus, 1989; *Ten Modern Arab Poets*, trans. Desmond O'Grady, Dedalus, 1992; Denis Devlin, *Translations into English*, ed. Roger Little, Dublin, Dedalus, 1992; Brian Coffey, *Poems and Versions 1929–1990*, Dublin, Dedalus, 1991; Uffe Harder, *The World As If*, trans. John F. Deane, Dublin, Dedalus, 1989; Ivan V. Lalic, *The Passionate Measure*, trans. Francis R. Jones, Dublin, Dedalus, 1990; Mario Luzi, *After Many Years*, trans. Catherine O'Brien, Dublin, Dedalus, 1990; Margherita Guidacci, *In the Eastern Sky*, trans. Catherine O'Brien, Dublin, Dedalus, 1993.

17. Cassidy, *Translating the Success*, p. 3.

18. Cassidy interview.

19. Charles Pick, *Developing Publishing in Ireland: Cothú na Foilsitheoireachta in Éirinn*, The Arts Council, Dublin, 1988, pp. 12–13.

20. Michael Cronin, Liam Mac Cóil and Jürgen Schneider, *Literature without Frontiers: Irish Literary Translation in the European Context/Litríocht gan Teorainn: An tAistriú Liteartha Éireannach i gComhthéacs na hEorpa*, Irish Translators Association, Dublin, 1990, pp. 31–32.

21. Cronin, Mac Cóil and Schneider, p. 60.

22. Cassidy interview.

23. Denis Devlin, *Translations into English*, ed., Roger Little, Dublin, Dedalus, 1992; Brian Coffey, *Poems and Versions 1929–1990*, Dublin, Dedalus, 1991. Much has been written on Beckett and translation but the most useful work is Brian T. Fitch, *Beckett and Babel: An Investigation into the Status of the Bilingual Work*, University of Toronto Press, 1988.

24. Dermot Bolger ed. *The Bright Wave: An Tonn Gheal*, Dublin, Raven Arts Press, 1986, p. 9.

25. Nuala Ní Dhomhnaill, 'Making the Millennium', *Graph*, no. 1, 1986, p. 5.

26. Seán Ó Cearnaigh et al., 'Thoughts on Translation', *Poetry Ireland Review*, no. 39, 1993, p. 70.

27. Pól Ó Muirí, 'A Desire to Scavenge', *Fortnight*, Special Supplement, April 1993, p. 16.
28. Biddy Jenkinson, 'A Letter to an Editor', *Irish University Review*, vol. 4, no. 21, 1991, p. 34.
29. Ó Cearnaigh et al., 'Thoughts on Translation', p. 61.
30. Ó Cearnaigh et al., p. 71.
31. Barra Ó Séaghdha, 'The Tasks of the Translator', *The Irish Review*, no. 14, 1993, p. 144.
32. Douglas Sealy, 'A New Voice for the Seanachie', *The Irish Times*, 8 December 1990.
33. Lawrence Venuti, ed., Introduction, *Rethinking Translation*, London, Routledge, 1992, p. 5.
34. *Poetry Network 1: The Annaghmakerrig Sessions*, Dublin, Dedalus, 1992; *Poetry Network 2: The Annaghmakerrig Sessions*, Dublin, Dedalus, 1992.
35. Terence Brown, 'Translating Ireland', *Krino*, no. 7, 1989, p. 1.
36. Brown, p. 2.
37. Seamus Heaney, 'Earning a Rhyme', *Poetry Ireland Review*, no. 25, 1989, p. 95.
38. Heaney, p. 97.
39. Heaney, p. 98.
40. Heaney, p. 99; p. 100.
41. Ciaran Carson, *First Language*, Oldcastle, Gallery Press, 1993. Kathleen Shields, 'Stocious ships: voluntary exile in Irish translations of Rimbaud's *Bateau ivre*'; paper delivered to Royal Irish Academy Symposium on Modern Languages Studies, November 1994.
42. For comments on language and translation see Ciaran Carson, 'There Was This Man. . . . Ciaran Carson ag caint le Peter Sirr agus Mícheál Ó Cróinín', *Oghma*, 6, 1994, pp. 64–66.
43. Kathleen Shields, 'Derek Mahon's Nerval', *Translation and Literature*, vol. 4, no. 1, 1995, pp. 61–74.
44. Ó Tuama and Kinsella, p. 35.
45. Michael Hartnett, Introduction, Ó *Bruadair*, Dublin, Gallery Press, 1985, p. 13.
46. Hartnett, p. 14.
47. Sherry Simon imports Michel Charles's use of the terms 'commentary' and 'rhetoric' from literary history into translation studies. See Sherry Simon, 'The Language of Cultural Difference: Figures of Alterity in Canadian Translation', Lawrence Venuti, ed., *Rethinking Translation*, London, Routledge, 1992, p. 161.
48. Bolger, *Bright Wave*, p. 9.
49. Alan Titley, 'Introduction', *Bright Wave*, p. 19.
50. 'For my part, instead of arguing about what is lost, I prefer to look at what is there, variety' (my translation), Liam Mac Cóil, 'Ag Aistriú', *Graph*, No. 1, 1986, p. 21.
51. Ciaran Cosgrove, 'Language and Translation', *Poetry Ireland*, Nos. 18/19, 1987, p. 28.
52. Quevedo, *On the Anvil*, p. 15.
53. Quevedo, p. 103.
54. John Dryden, 'On Translation', Rainer Schulte and John Biguenet, eds, *Theories of Translation*, University of Chicago Press, 1992, p. 17.
55. Lorna Shaughnessy, 'Shafts of Fire', *Graph*, no. 3, 1987, p. 16.
56. John F. Deane, Introduction, *Don Quixote*, p. 8.

57. Hugh Maxton, 'The Poetry of Agnes Nemes Nagy: A Commentary', *Between*, pp. 79–91.

58. Desmond O'Grady, 'Ezra Pound and Creative Translation', *Irish Translators' Association Newsletter*, vol. 3, no. 2, 1989, p. 7.

59. Edwin Gentzler, *Contemporary Translation Theories*, London, Routledge, 1993, p. 37.

60. Eiléan Ní Chuilleanáin, 'Poetry in Translation', *Irish Translators' Association Newsletter*, vol. 1, no. 1, 1987, p. 5.

61. Richard Jacquemond, 'Translation and Cultural Hegemony: The Case of French-Arabic Translation', Venuti, ed., *Rethinking Translation*, p. 139.

62. Jacquemond, p. 58.

63. Gabriel Rosenstock and Gearailt Mac Eoin, eds., *Byzantium*, Indreabhán, Cló Iar-Chonnachta, 1991. The translators were Máire Mhac an tSaoi, Douglas Sealy, Seán Mac Mathghamhna, Mícheál Davitt, Paddy Finnegan, Gearailt Mac Eoin, Tomás Tóibín, Mícheál Ó Ruairc, Colm Breathnach, Rosemarie Rowley, Lorcán Ó Treasaigh, Fidelma Ní Ghallchóir, Eithne Strong, Áine Ní Ghlinn and Gabriel Rosenstock.

64. Gabriel Rosenstock, 'Lifting the Veil: Translating Heaney and others – a reverie', *Translation Ireland*, vol. 7, no. 3, 1993, p. 4.

65. Rosenstock, p. 5.

66. Rosenstock, p. 5.

67. Declan Kiberd, 'Réamhrá: W.B. Yeats agus an Ghaeilge', Gabriel Rosenstock and Gearailt Mac Eoin, eds., *Byzantium*, p. 13.

68. 'If these translations demonstrate anything, it is that Yeats was "Gaelic" to the extent that it is not possible to fully understand the poems without situating them in the tradition of bardic poetry' [my translation], Kiberd, p. 16.

69. 'the fluency of the language shows how "Gaelic" was the tall, strapping man who never learned Gaelic [my translation]' Kiberd, p. 17.

70. Ó Cearnaigh et al., p. 62.

71. 'All I would like to do is to play a new tune for Irish ears, an echo of the specific music that attaches to every language, so that in this way they might have more respect for the voice of Irish in the choir of nations' [my translation], Breandán Ó Doibhlin, Réamhrá, *Ón Fhraincís*, Béal Feirste, Lagan Press/Fortnight Educational Trust, 1994, p. 15.

72. For a discussion of one aspect of this influence see Tadhg Ó Dúshláine, *An Eoraip agus Litríocht na Gaeilge: Gnéithe den Bharócachas Eorpach i Litríocht na Gaeilge*, Baile Átha Cliath, An Clóchomhar, 1987.

73. 'I still think that the qualities that are often attributed to that literature [French], sharpness and keenness of intellect, exactness in speech, expressive grace, that these qualities would help the development of Irish which was left for so long without the resources and the institutions that allow for the proper maturation of the vernacular' [my translation], Ó Doibhlin, p. 16.

74. Colm Breathnach, Réamhrá, Willem M. Roggeman, *Cruth an Daonnaí*, trans. Gabriel Rosenstock, Baile Átha Cliath, Coiscéim, 1990, p. 9.

75. Colm Breathnach, Réamhrá, Georg Trakl, *Craorag*, trans. Gabriel Rosenstock, Baile Átha Cliath, Carbad, 1991, p. 12.

76. The list of translations from other languages into Irish is extensive so these titles are merely representative: Paolo Marletta, *Dormitio Viriginis*, trans. Máire Nic Mhaoláin, Baile Átha Cliath, Coiscéim, 1993; Eduardo De Filippo, *De Pretore Vincenzo*, trans. Rita Breatnach, Baile Átha Cliath, Coiscéim, 1993; Juan Ramón Jiménez, *Mise agus Platero*, trans. Aodh Ó Canainn, Baile Átha Cliath, Coiscéim, 1991; Laurent Escudie agus Yann Fanch Jacq, *Taisce an Oileáin*, trans. Uaitéar Mac Gearailt, Indreabhán, Cló Iar-Chonnachta, 1987; J. Selwyn Lloyd, *Saibhreas Chnoic Chaspair*, trans. Liam Mac Cóil, Baile Átha Cliath, An Gúm, 1987.

77. Antain Mag Shamhráin, 'An Gúm', *Irish Translators' Association Newsletter*, vol. 3, no. 2, pp. 9–10.

78. Ó Cearnaigh et al., p. 68.

79. Rosenstock, 'Lifting the Veil', p. 4.

80. Pádraig Ó Fiannachta, 'Focal ón bhFear Eagair', *An Bíobla Naofa*, Maigh Nuad, An Sagart, 1981, n.p.

81. 'in a way that the new translation will be a solid bridge between all Christians in Ireland [my translation]', Tomás Ó Fiaich, 'Brollach', *An Bíobla Naofa*. For discussions relating to the history of the Maynooth and other translations see also Pádraig Ó Fiannachta, ed., *An Bíobla in Éirinn*, Maigh Nuad, An Sagart, 1990.

82. The Chairpersons of the Irish Translators' Association to date have been: Cormac Ó Cuilleanáin (1986–1991); Michael Cronin (1991–1993); Angela Ryan (1993–1994); Gabriele Milch-Skinner (1994–).

83. See Michael Cronin, 'After Fénius Farsaidh: Aspects of Translation in Modern Ireland', *Teanga*, vol. 10, 1990, pp. 109–121.

84. Michael Cronin, 'The Future of the ITA – Discussion Document', *Irish Translators' Association Newsletter*, vol. 2, no. 4, 1988, pp. 6–7.

85. Industrial Policy Review Group, *A Time for Change: Industrial Policy for the 1990s*, Dublin, Stationery Office, 1992, p. 29.

86. Juliette Péchenart and Anne Tangy, 'Gifts of Tongues: Foreign Languages and Tourism Policy in Ireland', Barbara O'Connor and Michael Cronin, eds., *Tourism in Ireland: A Critical Analysis*, Cork University Press, 1993, pp. 162–63.

87. National Software Directorate, *The Software Industry in Ireland: A Strategic Review*, Dublin, Industrial Development Authority, 1992, Section 2–5, n.p.

88. *Software Industry*, Section 4–3, n.p.

89. *A Time for Change*, pp. 70–76.

90. Joel de Rosnay, *Le cerveau planétaire*, Paris, Seuil, 1983, pp. 22–23.

91. See Michael Cronin and John Nolan, 'Language, Technology and the Network-Based Economy', Mladan Jovanovic, ed., *Translation, a Creative Profession/La traduction, une profession créative*, Belgrade, Previdolac, 1991, pp. 320–24.

92. Michael Cronin, 'Translating Technology: Languages in the Reticular Economy', *Teaglaim*, 1, 1993, pp. 17–18.

93. See for an example of research work in the University of Limerick, Norah Power and Gerry O'Neill, 'CASE for Localisation', Reinhard Schäler and Jennifer Pearson, *Proceedings of the First Irish Conference on Language Technology*, 1993, pp. 22–27.

94. Cronin, *Translating Technology*, p. 17.

95. Joachim Fischer, 'Media, Language and Translation in the 1990s: The European Challenge', *Irish Translators' Association Newsletter*, vol. 5, no. 1, p. 3.

96. Eithne O'Connell, 'Media Translation and Lesser-used Languages – Implications of Subtitles for Irish language Broadcasting', F. Eguíluz et al., eds., *Tranvases Culturales: Literatura, Cine, Tranducción*, Victoria, Universided del Pais Vasco, 1994, p. 368.

97. O'Connell, p. 371.

98. Cronin, 'After Fénius Farsaidh', p. 116.

99. See Lawrence Venuti, *The Translator's Invisibility: A History of Translation*, London, Routledge, 1995, pp. 12–17.

100. Brian Friel, *Translations*, London, Faber & Faber, 1981, Act One, p. 29.

101. Friel, Act One, p. 32.

102. Friel, Act Three, p. 61.

103. Friel, p. 68.

104. Friel, p. 67.

105. Friel, Act Two, Scene One, p. 43.

106. John Montague, 'A Grafted Tongue', *New Selected Poems*, Oldcastle, Gallery Press, 1989, pp. 49–50.

107. John Montague, 'A Lost Tradition', p. 47.

108. W.J. Mc Cormack, *From Burke to Beckett: Ascendancy, Tradition and Betrayal in Literary History*, Cork University Press, 1994, p. 251.

BIBLIOGRAPHY

Catalogue of Irish Manuscripts in the Royal Irish Academy.

Catalogue of Irish Manuscripts in British Museum.

Catalogue of the Irish Manuscripts in the Franciscan Library, Killiney.

Clár na Lámhscríbhinní Gaeilge i Leabharlainn Phoiblí Bhéal Feirste.

Clár Lámhscríbhinní Gaeilge Choláiste Ollscoile Chorcaí: Cnuasach Uí Mhurchú.

Clár Lámhscríbhinní Gaeilge Choláiste Ollscoile Chorcaí: Cnuasach Thorna.

Catalogue of Irish Manuscripts in Mount Melleray Abbey, Co. Waterford.

Catalogue of the Irish Manuscripts in the Library of Trinity College Dublin.

Catalogue of Irish Manuscripts in Maynooth College Library.

Lámhscríbhinní Gaeilge Choláiste Phádraig Má Nuad.

Clár Lámhscríbhinní Gaeilge: Leabharlanna na Cléire agus Mionchnuasaigh.

Catalogue of Irish Manuscripts in the National Library of Ireland.

Dictionary of National Biography.

Achterberg, Gerrit, *Hidden Weddings*, trans., Michael O'Loughlin, Dublin, Raven Arts Press, 1987.

An Account of Dr. Keting's History of Ireland and the Translation of it by Dermod O'Connor. Taken out of a Dissertation prefixed to the Memoirs of the Marquis of Clanricard, lately published in London. With some specimens of the said History and Translation. Dublin, Edwin Sandys, 1723.

An Bíobla Naofa, Maigh Nuad, An Sagart, 1981.

An Duanaire: Poems of the Dispossessed, ed., Seán Ó Tuama, trans., Thomas Kinsella, Mountrath, Dolmen Press, 1981.

Aristotle, *On the Art of Poetry*, trans., T.S. Dorsch, Harmondsworth, Penguin, 1978.

Beer, Jeanette ed., *Medieval Translators and their Craft*, Western Michigan University, Medieval Institute Publications, 1989.

Behdad, Ali, *Belated Travellers: Orientalism in the Age of Colonial Dissolution*, Cork University Press, 1994.

Best, R.I. and M.A. O'Brien, *Togail Troí*, Dublin Institute for Advanced Studies, 1966.

Binchy, D.A., 'The Background of Early Irish Literature,' *Studia Hibernica*, 1, 1961, pp. 7–18.

Bolger, Dermot, ed., *The Bright Wave: An Tonn Gheal*, Dublin, Raven Arts Press, 1986.

Bowers, Fredson, ed., *The Dramatic Works of Thomas Decker*, vol. 1, Cambridge University Press, 1953.

Bowers, Fredson, general ed., *The Dramatic Works in the Beaumont and Fletcher Canon*, vol. 1, Cambridge University Press, 1966

Boyle, John, trans., *The Letters of Pliny the Younger with Observations on Each Letter and an Essay on Pliny's Life*, vol. 1, Dublin, 1751.

Bradshaw, Brendan, 'Sword, Word and Strategy in the Reformation in Ireland', *Historical Journal*, vol. 21, 1978, pp. 475–502.

Bradshaw, Brendan, Andrew Hadfield and Willy Maley, eds., *Representing Ireland: Literature and the Origins of Conflict 1534–1660*, Cambridge University Press, 1993.

Brooke, Charlotte, *Reliques of Irish Poetry*, Dublin, Georges Bonham, 1789.

Brown, Terence and Barbara Hayley, eds., *Samuel Ferguson: A Centenary Tribute*, Dublin, Royal Irish Academy, 1987.

Brown, Terence, 'Translating Ireland', *Krino*, no. 7, 1989, pp. 1–4.

Burnet, Gilbert, *The Life of William Bedell, bishop of Kilmore*, London, 1685.

Butt, Isaac, trans., *The Georgics of Virgil*, Dublin, Curry and Company, 1834.

Byrne, Cyril J., Margaret Henry and Pádraig Ó Siadhail, eds., *Celtic Languages and Celtic Peoples*, Halifax, St Mary's University, 1990.

Caerwyn Williams, J.E. and Máirín Ní Mhuiríosa, *Traidisiún Liteartha na nGael*, Baile Átha Cliath, An Clóchomhar, 1978.

Caerwyn Williams, J.E., 'Irish Translations of *Visio Sancti Pauli*', *Éigse*, vol. 6, pp. 127–34.

Calder, George, ed. and trans., *Imtheachta Aeniasa: The Irish Aeneid*, London, Irish Texts Society, 1907.

Calder, George, *Auraicept na n-Éces*, Edinburgh, John Grant, 1917.

Calder, George, ed., *Togail na Tebe*, Cambridge University Press, 1922.

Carney, James, 'Three Old-Irish Accentual Poems', *Ériu*, no. 22, 1971, pp. 23–80.

Carson, Ciaran, *First Language*, Oldcastle, Gallery Press, 1993.

Cassidy, Laurence, 'Translations: breaking into Europe', *Books Ireland*, May 1990, p. 87.

Cassidy, Laurence, 'The Arts Council's Translation Policy', *Irish Translator's Association Newsletter*, vol. 2, no. 4, December 1988, p. 8.

Cassidy, Laurence, *Translating the Success of Irish Literature*, Dublin, Arts Council, 1992.

Celan, Paul, *65 Poems*, trans., Brian Lynch and Peter Jankowski, Dublin, Raven Arts Press, 1986.

Cheyfitz, Eric, *The Poetics of Imperialism: Translation and Colonization from* The Tempest *to* Tarzan, Oxford University Press, 1991.

Coffey, Brian, *Poems and Versions 1929–1990*, Dublin, Dedalus, 1991.

Connolly, Peter, ed., *Literature and the Changing Ireland*, Gerrards Cross, Colin Smythe, 1982.

Copeland, Rita, *Rhetoric, Hermeneutics, and Translation in the Middle Ages*, Cambridge University Press, 1991.

Corcoran, Timothy, 'How English may be taught without Anglicising', *Irish Monthly*, vol. 51, June 1923, pp. 269–73.

Cosgrove, Ciaran, 'Language and Translation', *Poetry Ireland*, nos. 18/19, 1987, pp. 26–30.

Cronin, Michael, 'The Future of the ITA – Discussion Document', *Irish Translators' Association Newsletter*, vol. 2, no. 4, 1988, pp. 6–7.

Cronin, Michael, Liam Mac Cóil and Jürgen Schneider, *Literature without Frontiers: Irish Literary Translation in the European Context/Litríocht gan Teorainn: An tAistriú Liteartha Éireannach i gComhthéacs na hEorpa*, Dublin, 1990.

Cronin, Michael, 'After Fénius Farsaidh: Aspects of Translation in Modern Ireland', *Teanga*, vol. 10, 1990, pp. 109–121.

Cronin, Michael, 'Babel's Suburbs: Irish Verse Translation in the 1980s', *Irish University Review*, vol. 21, no. 1, 1991, pp. 15–26.

Cronin, Michael, 'Movie-Shows from Babel: Translation and the Irish Language', *The Irish Review*, 14, 1993, pp. 56–64.

Cronin, Michael, 'Translating Technology: Languages in the Reticular Economy', *Teaglaim*, 1, 1993, pp. 16–18.

Cunningham, Michael, 'Rotten Story', *The Irish Times*, 2 April 1994.

Cunningham, Michael, 'Babel Bitmap', *Circa*, no. 69, 1994, pp. 35–42.

Curtis, Edmund, 'The Spoken Languages of Medieval Ireland', *Studies*, vol. 8, 1919, pp. 234–54.

Daltún, Séamas, 'Scéal Rannóg an Aistriúchain', *Teangeolas*, 17, 1983, pp. 12–17.

Davitt, Micheál, *Selected Poems: Rogha Dánta*, Dublin, Raven Arts Press, 1987.

de Blácam, Aodh, 'The World of Letters: Poison in the Wells', *Irish Monthly*, vol. 65, pp. 270–81.

de Blácam, Aodh, *Gaelic Literature Surveyed*, Dublin, Talbot Press, 1973.

de Brún, Pádraig, 'A Seventeenth-Century Translation of the First Psalm', *Éigse*, vol. 17, 1977–9, pp. 61–66.

de Courcy Ireland, John, *Ireland's European Tradition*, Drogheda, Vanguard, 1970.

de Courcy Ireland, John and Eoghan Ó hAnluain, eds., *Ireland and the Sea*, Dublin, Cumann Merriman, 1983.

de Filippo, Eduardo, *De Pretore Vincenzo*, trans., Rita Breatnach, Baile Átha Cliath, Coiscéim, 1993.

de Hae and Brighid Ní Dhonnchadha, eds., *Clár Litridheacht na Nua-Ghaeilge*, vol. 1, Baile Átha Cliath, Oifig an tSoláthair, 1938.

de Quevedo, Francisco, *On the Anvil*, trans., Michael Smith, Dublin, Dedalus, 1989.

de Rosnay, Joel, *Le cerveau planétaire*, Paris, Seuil, 1983.

Deane, Seamus, *Celtic Revivals*, London, Faber and Faber, 1985.

Delisle, Jean, 'Projet d'histoire thématique de la traduction', Mladen Jovanović, ed., *Proceedings of XIIth World Congress of FIT*, Belgrade, Prevodilac, 1991, pp. 63–68.

Denman, Peter, *Samuel Ferguson: The Literary Achievement*, Gerrards Cross, Colin Smythe, 1990.

Devlin, Denis, *Translations into English*, ed., Roger Little, Dublin, Dedalus, 1992.

Dillon, Wentworth (Earl of Roscommon), *Q. Horatii Flacci de Arte Poetica Liber ad Pisones*, Dublin, William Heatly, 1733.

Dillon, Wentworth, *An Essay on Translated Verse (1685) and Horace's Art of Poetry Made English (1684)*, Yorkshire, Scolar Press, 1971.

Drummond, William Hamilton, *Ancient Irish Minstrelsy*, Dublin, Hodges and Smith, 1852.

Duffy, Charles Gavan, George Sigerson and Douglas Hyde, *The Revival of Irish Literature*, New York, Lemma, reprinted, 1973.

Ebel, Juila G., 'Translation and Cultural Nationalism in the Reign of Elizabeth', *Journal of the History of Ideas*, vol.30, 1969, pp.593–602.

Eguíluz, F. et al., eds., *Tranvases Culturales: Literatura, Cine, Traducción*, Vitoria, Universidad del Pais Vasco, 1994.

Elliott, Marianne, *Wolfe Tone: Prophet of Irish Independence*, New Haven, Yale University Press, 1989.

Ellis, Roger, ed., *The Medieval Translator*, Cambridge, Brewer, 1989.

Erionnach (George Sigerson), *The Poets and Poetry of Munster*, Dublin, John O'Daly, 1860.

Escudie, Laurent and Yann Fanch Jacq, *Taisce an Oileáin*, trans., Uaitéar Mac Gearailt, Indreabhán, Cló Iar-Chonnachta, 1987.

Fabian, Johannes, *Time and the Other: How Anthropology Makes its Object*, New York, Columbia University Press, 1983.

Falconer, Sheila, ed., *Lorgaireacht an tSoidhigh Naofa*, Dublin Institute of Advanced Studies, 1953.

Falconer, Shiela, 'An Irish Translation of the Gregory Legend', *Celtica*, vol. 4, 1958, pp. 52–95.

Faulkner, Anselm, '*Tóruidheacht na bhFíreun air Lorg Chríosda* (1762): The Translator', *Éigse*, vol. 15, 1973–74, pp. 303–11.

Ferguson, Samuel, 'Hardiman's Irish Minstrelsy No.1', *Dublin University Magazine*, vol. 3, no. 16, April 1834, pp. 456–478.

209

Ferguson, Samuel, 'Hardiman's Irish Minstrelsy No.II', *Dublin University Magazine*, vol. 4, no. 20, August 1834, pp. 152–167.

Ferguson, Samuel, 'Hardiman's Irish Minstrelsy No.III', *Dublin University Magazine*, vol. 4, no. 22, October 1834, pp. 447–467.

Ferguson, Samuel, 'Hardiman's Irish Minstrelsy No. IV', *Dublin University Magazine*, vol. 4, no. 23, November 1834, pp. 514–542.

Ferguson, Samuel, 'The Dublin Penny Journal', *Dublin University Magazine*, vol. 15, no. 85, January 1840, pp. 112–128.

Fischer, Joachim, 'Media, Language and Translation in the 1990s: The European Challenge', *Irish Translators' Association Newsletter*, vol. 5, no. 1, p. 3.

Fitch, Brian T., *Beckett and Babel: An Investigation into the Status of the Bilingual Work*, University of Toronto Press, 1988.

Flower, Robin, *The Irish Tradition*, Oxford, Clarendon Press, 1947.

Francis, Philip, trans., *A Poetical Translation of the works of Horace*, vol. 1, London, 1749.

Francklin, Thomas, trans., *The Tragedies of Sophocles from the Greek*, Dublin, 1778.

Freeman, A. Martin, 'Betha Mhuire Eigiptacdha', *Etudes Celtiques*, vol. 1, 78–113.

Friel, Brian, *Translations*, London, Faber & Faber, 1981.

Gentzler, Edwin, *Contemporary Translation Theories*, London, Routledge, 1993.

Goldring, Maurice, *Faith of Our Fathers: The Formation of Irish Nationalist Ideology 1890–1920*, Dublin, Repsol, 1982.

Graham, Colin, '"Liminal Spaces": Post-Colonial Theories and Irish Culture', *The Irish Review*, no. 16, 1994, pp. 29–43.

Greene, David, 'A Gaelic Version of the Seven Wise Masters', *Béaloideas*, vol. 14, 1945, pp. 219–236.

Greene, David, 'The Irish Versions of the Letter of Prester John', *Celtica*, vol. 2, 1954, pp. 117–45.

Gregory, Lady, *Seventy Years*, Gerrards Cross, Colin Smythe, 1974.

Guidacci, Margherita, *In the Eastern Sky*, trans., Catherine O'Brien, Dublin, Dedalus, 1993.

Gwynn, Edward, 'The Manuscript known as the Liber Flavus Fergusiorum', *Proceedings of the Royal Irish Academy*, vol. 26, 1906–7, pp. 15–41.

Harder, Uffe, *The World As If*, trans., John F. Deane, Dublin, Dedalus, 1989.

Hardiman, James, *Irish Minstrelsy, or Bardic Remains of Ireland with English Poetical Translations*, 2 vols., London, Joseph Robins, 1831.

Harrison, Alan, *Ag Cruinniú Meala*, Dublin, An Clóchomhar, 1988.

Hartnett, Michael, trans., *Ó Bruadair*, Dublin, Gallery Press, 1985.

Heaney, Seamus, 'Earning a Rhyme', *Poetry Ireland Review*, no. 25, 1989, pp. 95–100.

Hermans, Theo, ed., *The Manipulation of Literature: Studies in Literary Translation*, London, Croom Helm, 1985, p. 106.

Hernandez, Miguel, *Unceasing Lightning*, trans., Michael Smith, Dublin, Dedalus, 1987.

Hodges, John, trans., *The Second Satir of Aulus Persius Flaccus*, Dublin, 1705.

Holinshed, Raphael, ed., *Chronicles of England, Scotland and Ireland*, London, Johnson, vi, 1807–8.

Hull, Vernam, 'The Middle Irish Version of Bede's *De Locis Sanctis*', *Zeitschrift für Celtische Philologie*, vol. 17, pp. 225–240.

Hyde, Douglas, *The Conquests of Charlemagne*, London, The Irish Texts Society, 1917.

Hyde, Douglas, *Abhráin Grádh Chúige Connacht: The Love Songs of Connacht*, Shannon, Irish University Press, reprinted, 1969.

Hyde, Douglas, *Beside the Fire*, Dublin, Irish Academic Press, reprinted, 1978.

Industrial Policy Review Group, *A Time for Change: Industrial Policy for the 1990s*, Dublin, Stationery Office, 1992.

Jenkinson, Biddy, 'A Letter to an Editor', *Irish University Review*, vol. 4, no. 21, 1991, pp. 27–34.

Jennings, Brendan, ed., 'Brevis Synopsis Provinciae Hiberniae', *Analecta Hiberniae*, 6, 1934, pp. 12–138.

Jennings, Brendan, 'The Irish Franciscans in Prague', *Studies*, no. 28, 1939, pp. 210–222.

Jiménez, Juan Ramón, *Mise agus Platero*, trans., Aodh Ó Canainn, Baile Átha Cliath, Coiscéim, 1991.

Jovanovic, Mladan, ed., *Translation, a Creative Profession/La traduction, une profession créative*, Belgrade, Previdolac, 1991.

Joyce, James, *A Portrait of the Artist as a Young Man*, Herts., Panther, 1977.

Kallen, Jeffrey L., 'Language maintenance, loss, and ethnicity in the United States: Perspectives on Irish', *Teanga*, vol. 13, 1993, pp. 100–111.

Keating, Geoffrey, *The General History of Ireland*, trans., Dermod O'Connor, 2nd edn, London, Creake, 1726.

Kelly, Louis G., *The True Interpreter: A History of Translation Theory and Practice in the West*, Oxford, Blackwell, 1979.

Kenney, James, *The Sources for the Early History of Ireland*, vol. 1, New York, Columbia University Press, 1929.

Kiberd, Declan and Gabriel Fitzmaurice, eds., *An Crann faoi Bhláth: The Flowering Tree*, Dublin, Wolfhound Press, 1991.

Kiberd, Declan, *Synge and the Irish Language*, 2nd edn., Dublin, Gill & Macmillan, 1993.

Knott, Eleanor, 'An Irish Seventeenth-Century Translation of the Rule of St. Clare', *Ériu*, vol. 15, 1948, pp. 1–187.

Kristeva, Julia, *Étrangers à nous-mêmes*, Paris, Fayard, 1988.

Lalic, Ivan V., *The Passionate Measure*, trans., Francis R. Jones, Dublin, Dedalus, 1990.

Larose, Robert, *Théories contemporaines de la traduction*, Québec, Presses de l'université du Québec, 1989.

Leabhar na nurnaightheadh gcomhchoidchiond agus mheinisdraldachdha na sacrameinteabh, maille le gnathaighthibh agus le hordaighehibh oile, do réir eaglaise na Sagsan. Ata so ar na chur a gclo a Mbaile atha Cliath, a dtigh Sheon Francke alias Franckton, Priontóir an Ríog an Eirin, 1608.

Leerssen, Joseph, *Mere Irish & Fíor-Ghael: Studies in the Idea of Irish Nationality, its Development and Literary Expression prior to the Nineteenth Century*, Amsterdam, John Benjamins, 1986.

Lefevere, André, *Translation, Rewriting and the Manipulation of Literary Fame*, Routledge, London, 1992.

Lennon, Colm, *Richard Stanihurst: The Dubliner 1547–1618*, Dublin, Irish Academic Press, 1981.

Lloyd, J. Selwyn, *Saibhreas Chnoic Chaspair*, trans., Liam Mac Cóil, Baile Átha Cliath, An Gúm, 1987.

Lloyd, David, *Nationalism and Minor Literature: James Clarence Mangan and the Emergence of Irish Cultural Nationalism*, Berkeley, University of California Press, 1987.

Luzi, Mario, *After Many Years*, trans., Catherine O'Brien, Dublin, Dedalus, 1990.

Mac Aogáin, Parthalán, ed., *Graiméir Ghaeilge na mBráthar Mionúr*, Institiúid Ardléinn Bhaile Átha Cliath, 1968.

Mac Cóil, Liam, 'Ag Aistriú', *Graph*, No. 1, 1986, pp. 20–22.

Mac Curtin, Hugh, *A Brief Discourse in Vindication of the Antiquity of Ireland*, Dublin, 1717.

MacDonagh, Thomas, *Literature in Ireland*, Dublin, Talbot Press, 1920.

Mac Eoin, Gearóid, 'Dán ar Chogadh na Traoi', *Studia Hibernica*, vol. 1, 1961, pp. 19–55.

Mac Grianna, Seosamh, *Filí agus Felons*, Cathair na Mart, Foilseacháin Náisiúnta, 1987.

Mac Hale, John, *A Selection of Moore's Melodies*, Dublin, Duffy, 1871.

MacKechnie, John, ed., *Instructio Pie Vivendi et Superna Meditandi*, vol. 2, Dublin, Irish Texts Society, 1946.

Mac Mathúna, Seán, *Ding agus Scéalta Eile*, Baile Átha Cliath, An Comhlacht Oideachais, 1983.

Mac Niocláis, Máirtín, *Seán Ó Ruadháin: Saol agus Saothar*, Baile Átha Cliath, An Clóchomhar, 1991.

Mac Póilín, Aodán, '"Spiritual Beyond the Ways of Men" – Images of the Gael', *The Irish Review*, no. 16, 1994, pp. 1–22.

Mag Shamhráin, Antain, 'An Gúm', *Irish Translators' Association Newsletter*, vol. 3, no. 2, pp. 9–10.

Maginn, William, *Homeric Ballads*, London, Parker, 1850.

Maith agus Dearmad, Sgeul beag d'ar b'ughdar Maria Edgeworth. Rosanna ón ughdar chéadna, trans., Tomás Ó Fíannachtaigh, Baile Átha Cliath, 1833.

Mangan, James Clarence, 'Anthologia Germanica', *Dublin University Magazine*, vol. 7, no. 39, March 1836, pp. 278–302.

Mangan, James Clarence, 'Literae Orientales no. iv', *Dublin University Magazine*, vol. 15, no. 88, April 1840, pp. 377–394.

Marletta, Paolo, *Dormitio Viriginis*, trans., Máire Nic Mhaoláin, Baile Átha Cliath, Coiscéim, 1993.

Martin, F.X. and F.J. Byrne, eds., *The Scholar Revolutionary: Eoin MacNeill (1867–1945) and the Making of the New Ireland*, Shannon, Irish University Press, 1973.

Matthiesen, J., *Translation, an Elizabethan Art*, Cambridge, Harvard University Press, 1931.

Maurrais, Jacques, 'Petite histoire des législations linguistiques au Royaume-Uni', *L'Action Nationale*, no. 80, 1990, pp. 35–41.

McAdoo, H.R., 'The Irish Translations of the Book of Common Prayer', *Éigse*, vol. 2, 1940, pp. 251–57.

Mc Cormack, W.J., *From Burke to Beckett: Ascendancy, Tradition and Betrayal in Literary History*, Cork University Press, 1994.

McGrath, Fergal, *Education in Ancient and Medieval Ireland*, Dublin, 'Studies' Special Publications, 1979.

Meyer, Kuno, ed., *Sanas Chormaic*, Lampeter, Llanerch Publishers, reprint ed., 1994.

Meyer, Robert, 'The Sources of the Middle Irish Alexander', *Modern Philology*, vol. 47, no. 1, 1949, pp. 1–7.

Milton, John, *The Works of John Milton*, vol. 6, New York, Columbia University Press, 1932.

Montague, John, 'A Grafted Tongue', *New Selected Poems*, Oldcastle, Gallery Press, 1989.

Montgomery, Henry R., *Specimens of the Early Native Poetry of Ireland in English*, Dublin, James McGlashan, 1846.

Moore, Thomas, *The Poetical Works of Thomas Moore*, vol. 1, London, Longman, 1840.

Murphy, Arthur, trans., *The Works of Cornelius Tacitus*, 4 vols., London, 1793.

Murphy, Gerard, *The Ossianic Lore and Romantic Tales of Medieval Ireland*, Cork, Mercier Press, 1971.

National Software Directorate, *The Software Industry in Ireland: A Strategic Review*, Dublin, Industrial Development Authority, 1992.

Nemes Nagy, Agnes *Between*, trans., Hugh Maxton, Dublin, Dedalus/Budapest, Corvina, 1988.

Nettlau, Max, 'On Some Irish Translations from Medieval European Literature', *Revue Celtique*, vol. 10, 1889, pp. 178–191.

Ní Chuilleanáin, Eiléan, 'Poetry in Translation', *Irish Translators' Association Newsletter*, vol. 1, no. 1, 1987, p. 5.

Ní Dhomhnaill, Nuala, 'Making the Millennium', *Graph*, no. 1, 1986, pp. 5–9.

Ní Dhomhnaill, Nuala, *Pharaoh's Daughter: New and Selected Poems*, trans., several, Dublin, Gallery Press, 1990.

Ní Dhomhnaill, Nuala, *The Astrakhan Cloak*, trans., Paul Muldoon, Oldcastle, Gallery Press, 1993.

Nietzsche, Friedrich, *The Gay Science*, trans., Walter Kaufmann, New York, Random House, 1974.

Niranjana, Tejaswini, *Siting Translation: History, Post-Structuralism and the Colonial Context*, Berkeley, University of California Press, 1992.

Ní Shéaghdha, Nessa, 'Translations and Adaptations into Irish', *Celtica*, vol. 16, 1984, pp. 107–124.

Ní Shéaghdha, Nessa, 'Collectors of Irish Manuscripts: Motives and Methods', *Celtica*, vol. 17, 1985, pp. 1–28.

Ó Buachalla, Breandán, *I mBéal Feirste Cois Cuain*, Baile Átha Cliath, An Clóchomhar, 1968.

Ó Buachalla, Breandán, 'Arthur Brownlow: A Gentleman more Curious than Ordinary', *Ulster Local History*, vol. 7, no. 2, 1982, pp. 24–28.

Ó Buachalla, Breandán, 'In a Hovel by the Sea', *The Irish Review*, vol. 14, 1993, pp. 48–55.

Ó Catháin, Diarmaid, 'Dermot O'Connor, Translator of Keating', *Eighteenth-Century Ireland: Iris an dá chultúr*, vol. 2, 1987, pp. 67–87.

Ó Cearnaigh, Seán, et al., 'Thoughts on Translation', *Poetry Ireland Review*, no. 39, 1993, pp. 61–71.

Ó Ciosáin, Éamon, *An t-Éireannach 1934–1937: Páipéar Sóisialach Gaeltachta*, Baile Átha Cliath, An Clóchomhar, 1993.

Ó Cléirigh, Tomás, *Aodh Mac Aingil agus an Scoil Nua-Ghaeilge i Lobháin*, Baile Átha Cliath, An Gúm, 1985.

O'Connell, F.W. and R.M. Henry, eds., *An Irish Corpus Astronomiae*, London, David Nutt, 1915.

O'Connor, Barbara and Michael Cronin, eds., *Tourism in Ireland: A Critical Analysis*, Cork University Press, 1993.

Ó Conchúir, Breandán, *Scríobhaithe Chorcaí 1700–1850*, Baile Átha Cliath, An Clóchomhar, 1982.

Ó Cuív, Brian, 'Flaithrí Ó Maolchonaire's Catechism of Christian Doctrine', *Celtica*, vol. 1, 1950, pp. 161–206.

Ó Cuív, Brian, 'Irish Translations of Thomas à Kempis's *De Imitatione Christi*', *Celtica*, vol. 2, 1954, pp. 252–274.

Ó Cuív, Brian, 'An Eighteenth-Century Account of Keating and his Foras Feasa ar Éirinn', *Éigse*, vol. 9, 1958–61, pp. 263–269.

Ó Cuív, Brian, ed., *Seven Centuries of Irish Learning 1000–1700*, Dublin, Stationery Office, 1961

Ó Cuív, Brian, *The Linguistic Training of the Mediaeval Irish Poet*, Dublin Institute for Advanced Studies, 1973.

O'Curry, Eugene, *On the Manners and Customs of the Ancient Irish*, W.K. Sullivan, ed., 3 vols., London, Williams and Norgate, 1873.

Ó Díreáin, Máirtín, *Tacar Dánta/Selected Poems*, trans., Tomás Mac Síomóin and Douglas Sealy, Athlone, Goldsmith, 1984.

Ó Doibhlin, Breandán, *Ón Fhraincis*, Béal Feirste, Lagan Press/Fortnight Educational Trust, 1994.

O'Donovan, John, ed., *Annals of the Kingdom of Ireland*, 3rd ed., 7 vols., Dublin, de Búrca, 1990.

Ó Dúill, Gréagóir, *Samuel Ferguson: Beatha agus Saothar*, Baile Átha Cliath, An Clóchomhar, 1993.

Ó Dúshláine, Tadhg, *An Eoraip agus Litríocht na Gaeilge: Gnéithe den Bharócachas Eorpach i Litríocht na Gaeilge*, Baile Átha Cliath, An Clóchomhar, 1987.

Ó Fiannachta, Pádraig, ed., *An Bíobla in Éirinn*, Maigh Nuad, An Sagart, 1990.

O'Grady, Desmond, 'Ezra Pound and Creative Translation', *Irish Translators' Association Newsletter*, vol. 3, no. 2, 1989, p. 7.

O'Grady, Standish Hayes, *Caithréim Thoirdhealbhaigh*, London, Irish Texts Society, 1929.

O'Grady, Standish Hayes, *Silva Gadelica*, vol. 2, New York, Lemma, reprinted, 1970.

Ó Fachtna, Anselm, '"An Bheatha Chrábhaidh" agus "An Bheatha Dhiaga"', *Éigse*, vol. 10, 1961–63, pp. 89–95.

Ó Fachtna, Anselm, ed., *An Bheatha Dhiaga nó an tSlighe Ríoghdha*, Institiúid Ardléinn Bhaile Átha Cliath, 1967.

Ó Faireacháin, Roibeárd, 'Regarding an Gúm', *Bonaventura*, Summer 1937, pp. 175–6.

Ó Fiach, Tomás, *Gaelscrínte san Eoraip*, Baile Átha Cliath, Foilseacháin Ábhair Spioradálta, 1986.

Ó Fiannachta, Pádraig, 'A Fragment of an Irish Romantic Tale', *Irish Ecclesiastical Record*, vol. 109, 1968, pp. 166–81.

O'Leary, Peter, *Papers on Irish Idiom*, T.F. O'Rahilly, ed., Dublin, Browne and Nolan, 1929

Ó Maolchonaire, Flaithrí, *Desiderius*, ed., Thomas F. O'Rahilly, Dublin, Stationery Office, 1941.

Ó Maonaigh, Cainneach, *Smaointe Beatha Chríost*, Baile Átha Cliath, Institiúid Ard-Léighinn, 1944.

Ó Maonaigh, Cainneach, *Scáthán Shacramuinte na hAithridhe*, Institiúid Ardléinn Bhaile Átha Cliath, 1952.

Ó Maonaigh, Cainneach, 'Scríbhneoirí Gaeilge an Seachtú hAois Déag', *Studia Hibernica*, vol. 2, 1962, pp. 182–208.

Ó Maonaigh, Cainneach, ed., *Seanmónta Chúige Uladh*, Institiúid Ard-Léinn Bhaile Átha Cliath, 1965.

Ó Mórdha, Séamus P., 'Údar *Toruidheacht na bhFireun air Lorg Chriosda'*, *Studia Hibernica*, vol. 3, 1963, pp. 155–72.

Ó Muirí, Pól, 'A Desire to Scavenge', *Fortnight*, Special Supplement, April 1993, pp. 15–17.

O'Rahilly, Cecile, ed., *Trompa na bhFlaitheas*, Dublin Institute for Advanced Studies, 1955.

O'Rahilly, Cecile, ed., *Eachtra Uilliam*, Dublin Institute for Advanced Studies, 1949.

O'Rahilly, Thomas F., review of *The Conquests of Charlemagne*, ed., Douglas Hyde, *Studies*, vol. 8, 1919, pp. 668–670.

Ó Riain, Seán, *Pleanáil Teanga in Éirinn 1919–1985*, Baile Átha Cliath, Carbad, 1994.

Ó Séaghdha, Barra, 'The Tasks of the Translator', *The Irish Review*, no. 14, 1993, pp. 143–47.

Ó Súilleabháin, Pádraig, ed., *Rialachas San Froinsias*, Insitiúid Ard Léinn Bhaile Átha Cliath, 1953.

Ó Súilleabháin, Pádraig, ed., *Beatha San Froinsias*, Baile Átha Cliath Institiúid Ard Léinn Bhaile Átha Cliath, 1957.

Ó Súilleabháin, Pádraig, 'Varia', *Éigse*, vol. 9, 1958–61, pp. 233–242.

Ó Súilleabháin, Pádraig, ed., *Buaidh na Neamhchroiche*, Institiúid Ard Léinn Bhaile Átha Cliath, 1972.

Paul St-Pierre, 'Translation as a Discourse of History', *TTR*, vol. 6, no. 1, 1993, pp. 61–82.

Perkins, Jill, *Joyce and Hauptmann. Before Sunrise*. James Joyce's Translation, with an Introduction and Notes by Jill Perkins, San Marino, Huntington Library, 1978.

Pick, Charles, *Developing Publishing in Ireland: Cothú na Foilsitheoireachta in Éirinn*, Dublin, 1988.

Poetry Network 1: The Annaghmakerrig Sessions, Dublin, Dedalus, 1992.

Poetry Network 2: The Annaghmakerrig Sessions, Dublin, Dedalus, 1992.

Power, Maura, ed., *An Irish Astronomical Text*, London, Irish Texts Society, 1914.

Pratt, Mary Louise, *Imperial Eyes: Travel Writing and Transculturation*, London, Routledge, 1992.

Puttenham, George, *The Arte of English Poesie (1589)*, eds., Gladys Doidge Wilcock and Alice Walker, Cambridge University Press, 1936.

Quin, Gordon, ed., *Stair Ercuil agus a bás*, Dublin, Irish Texts Society, 1939.

Quinn, Bob, *Atlantean: Ireland's North African and Maritime Heritage*, London, Quartet, 1986.

Quintillian, *The Institutio Oratoria of Quintillian*, trans., H.E. Butler, vol. 4, London, Heinemann, 1922.

Rafael, Vicente, *Contracting Colonialism: Translation and Christian Conversion in Tagalog Society under Early Spanish Rule*, Ithaca, Cornell University Press, 1988.

Rafroidi, Patrick, *L'Irlande et le romantisme*, Paris, Éditions Universitaires, 1972.

Richardson, John, trans., *Seanmora ar na Priom Phoncibh, na Chreideamh: Sermons upon the Principal Points of Religion*, London, 1711.

Richardson, John, trans., *The Church Catechism Explained by Way of Question and Answer; And Confirm'd by Scripture Proofs*, London, 1712.

Richter, Michael, *Medieval Ireland – The Enduring Tradition*, Dublin, Gill and Macmillan, 1988.

Robinson, F.N., 'The Irish Lives of Guy of Warwick and Bevis of Hampton', *Zeitschrift für Celtische Philologie*, vol. 6, 1908, pp. 9–180 and pp. 273–338.

Roggeman, Willem M., *Cruth an Daonnaí*, trans., Gabriel Rosenstock, Baile Átha Cliath, Coiscéim, 1990.

Rosenstock, Gabriel and Gearailt Mac Eoin, eds., *Byzantium*, Indreabhán, Cló Iar-Chonnachta, 1991.

Rosenstock, Gabriel, 'Lifting the Veil: Translating Heaney and others – a reverie', *Translation Ireland*, vol. 7, no. 3, 1993, pp. 4–6.

Ryan, John, ed., *Essays and Studies presented to Professor Eoin MacNeill*, Dublin, Three Candles, 1940.

Saddlemyer, Ann, ed., *The Translations and Adaptations of Lady Gregory and her Collaborations with Douglas Hyde and W.B. Yeats*, Gerrards Cross, Colin Smythe, 1970.

Schäler, Reinhard and Jennifer Pearson, *Proceedings of the First Irish Conference on Language Technology*, 1993, pp. 22–27.

Schulte, Rainer and John Biguenet, eds., *Theories of Translation*, Chicago, Chicago University Press, 1992.

Sealy, Douglas, 'A New Voice for the Seanachie', *The Irish Times*, 8 December 1990.

Serres, Michel, *Le parasite*, Paris, Grasset, 1980.

Seymour, M.C., 'The Irish Version of "Mandeville's Travels"', *Notes and Queries*, vol. 208, 1963, pp. 364–366.

Seymour, St John D., *Anglo-Irish Literature 1200–1582*, Cambridge University Press, 1929.

Shaughnessy, Lorna, 'Shafts of Fire', *Graph*, no. 3, 1987, pp. 15–16.

Sheehan, Ronan, 'Spectacles', *Graph*, no. 7, Winter 1989–1990, pp. 3–5.

Sheridan, Thomas, trans., *The Philoctetes of Sophocles*, Dublin, 1725.

Sheridan, Thomas, trans., *The Satyrs of Persius*, Dublin, 1728.

Sheridan, Thomas, trans., *Homer's Battle of the Frogs and Mice with the Remarks of Zoilus*, Dublin, 1727.

Shields, Kathleen, 'Derek Mahon's Nerral', *Translation and Literature*, vol. 4, no. 1, 1995, pp. 61–74.

Shuckburgh, E.S., *Two Biographies of William Bedell*, Cambridge, Cambridge University Press, 1902.

Sigerson, George, *Bards of the Gael and Gall*, 2nd edn., London, Fisher Unwin, 1907.

Simms, J.G., 'John Toland (1670–1722), a Donegal Heretic', *Irish Historical Studies*, vol. XVI, no. 63, 1969, 304–20.

Simon, Sherry, *Le Trafic des langues: traduction et littérature dans la littérature québécoise*, Montreal, Boréal, 1995.

Skerrett, R.A.Q., 'Two Irish Translations of the *Liber de Passione Christi*', *Celtica*, vol. 6, 1963, pp. 82–117.

Skirne, Peter, Rosemary E. Wallbank-Turner and Jonathan West, eds., *Connections: Essays in Honour of Eda Sagarra on the Occasion of her 60th Birthday*, Stuttgart, Verlag Hans-Dieter Heinz, 1993.

Smith Clark, William, *The Early Irish Stage: The Beginnings to 1720*, Oxford, Clarendon, 1955.

Sonzogni, Marco, 'Courtly Love in Ireland: Synge's Translations of Petrarch', *Translation Ireland*, vol. 9, no. 1, pp. 7–11.

Sorescu, Marin, *The Youth of Don Quixote*, trans., John F. Deane, Dublin, Dedalus, 1987.

Spenser, Edmund, *A View of the Present State of Ireland*, ed., W.L. Renwick, Oxford, Clarendon, 1970.

Stanford, William Bedell, 'Towards a History of Classical Influences in Ireland', *Proceedings of the Royal Irish Academy*, vol. 70 section C, 1970, pp. 13–91.

Stanford, William Bedell, *Ireland and the Classical Tradition*, Dublin, Allen Figgis, 1976.

Stanihurst, Richard, *Aeneid*, ed., E. Arber, Constable, London, 1880.

Stewart, James, 'Párliament na mBan', *Celtica*, vol. 7, 1966, pp. 135–141.

Stokes, Whitley, *Three Irish Glossaries*, London and Edinburgh, 1862.

Stokes, Whitley, 'On the materia medica of the Medieval Irish', *Revue Celtique*, no. 9, 1888, pp. 222–44.

Stokes, Whitley, 'The Gaelic Abridgement of Ser Marco Polo', *Zeitschrift für Celtische Philologie*, vol. 1, 1897, pp. 245–273, pp. 362–438.

Stokes, Whitley, ed., *In Cath Catharda*, Leipzig, Verlag von S. Hirzel, 1909, Irische Texte iv/2.

Stokes, Whitley and John Strachan, *Thesaurus Palaeohibernicus*, 2 vols., rpt., Dublin Institute for Advanced Studies, 1975.

Synge, John Millington, *Collected Works*, vol. 2, Oxford University Press, 1966.

Tate, N. and N. Brady, trans., *A New Version of the Psalms of David*, London, 1696.

Ten Modern Arab Poets, trans., Desmond O'Grady, Dublin, Dedalus, 1992.

Tiomna Nuadh ar dTighearna agus ar slanaightheora Iosa Criosd, ar na tarruing go firinneach as Gréigis gu Gáoidheilg. Re Uilliam Ó Domhnuill. Ata so ar na chur a gclo a mbaile Atha Cliath, a dtigh Mhaighistir Uilliam Uiséir Chois an Droichid, ré Seón Francke. 1602.

Titley, Alan, *An t-Urscéal Gaeilge*, Baile Átha Cliath, An Clóchomhar, 1991.

Todd, J.H., ed., *Irish Nennius*, Dublin, Irish Archaeological Society, 1848.

Trakl, Georg, *Craorag*, trans., Gabriel Rosenstock, Baile Átha Cliath, Carbad, 1991.

Tranströmer, Tomas, *The Wild Market*, trans., John F. Deane, Dublin, Dedalus, 1985.

Tyrrell, Robert, 'Translation as a Fine Art', *Hermathena*, vol. 6, no. 13, 1887, pp. 147–158.

Ua Súilleabháin, Seán, 'Sgathán an Chrábhaidh: Foinsí an Aistriúcháin', *Éigse*, vol. 24, 1990, pp. 26–36.

Vallancey, Charles, *Essay on the Antiquity of the Irish Language*, Dublin, Powell, 1772.

Venuti, Lawrence, ed., *Rethinking Translation*, London, Routledge, 1992.

Venuti, Lawrence, *The Translator's Invisibility: A History of Translation*, London, Routledge, 1995.

Walker, Ellis, trans., *Epicteti Enchiridion*, London, Sam Keble, 1692.

Welch, Robert, *A History of Verse Translation from the Irish 1789–1897*, Gerrards Cross, Colin Smythe, 1988.

Welch, Robert, *Changing States: Transformations in Modern Irish Writing*, London, Routledge, 1993.

Wetenhall, Edward, trans., *The Wish being the Tenth Satire of Juvenal*, Dublin, 1675.

Williams, N.J.A., 'The Source of Imtheacta Generodeis', *Éigse*, vol. 17, 1977–79, pp. 297–300.

Williams, Nicholas, *I bPrionta i Leabhar*, Baile Átha Cliath, An Clóchomhar, 1986

Wulff, Winifred, *Rosa Anglica*, London, Irish Texts Society, 1929.

Yeats, William Butler, *Essays and Introductions*, London, Macmillan, 1951.

Yeats, William Butler, *Autobiographies*, London, Macmillan, 1955.

Zuber, Roger, *Les 'Belles Infidèles' et la formation du goût classique*, Paris, Armand Colin, 1968.

INDEX

Abbey Theatre, 139
Achterberg, Gerrit, 171
Act for the English Order, Habit and Language (1537), 8, 48, 52
Act of Uniformity (1560), 52
Act of Union (1801), 100
    repeal of, 103, 116, 132
Alexander the Great, 16
    Epistola ad Aristotelem, 35
alienation, 4–5
Anacreon
    Odes, 120–1
Anastasius, 13
An Coiste Téarmaíochta, 196
Anglo-Irish literature, 102, 113, 114, 120
    see also Hiberno-English
An Gúm, 189, 190
    state translation enterprise, 156–61
    see also Coiste na Leabhar
Annals of the Four Masters, 64, 65, 133
Anster, John, 122–3
antiquarian tradition, 94–5, 104–7, 114, 120, 124, 125, 132–3, 139, 148
Aquinas, Thomas, 14
    De Mixtione Elementorum, 27, 28
    De Motu Cordis, 27
    Gualterus de dosibus, 27
    Operationibus Occultis Naturae, 27
Aristeion-European Literary and Translation Prizes, 171
Arnold, Matthew, 74, 121
    Celticism of, 20, 109
Arts Council, 171, 174, 191
    Author's Royalty Scheme, 170
    bilingual policy, 169, 170
    translation policy, 169–72, 174, 177
Ascendancy class, 67, 94, 98, 132
astronomical texts, translations of, 65
    see also Middle Ages
Atkinson, Professor Robert, 152

Bacon, Francis, 14
'barbarity' of native Irish, 51–2
bardic tradition, 19, 33, 34, 39, 63, 70, 82, 187
Bartholomeus of Pisa
    Liber Confirmitatum, 65
Beckett, Samuel, 4, 38, 140, 174
Bedell, William, 56–7, 67, 73, 81, 107
Behan, Brendan, 4, 140
Behdad, Ali, 113
Benjamin, Walter, 31
Benoît de Sainte Maure
    Roman de Troie, 15
Bernard of Gordon
    Lilium Medicinae, 26, 27, 39
Betha Mhuire Eigiptachdha, 33, 34
Bhailís, Nioclás, 54
Bible
    Douai Bible, 61
    Psalms, 72
    translated into Irish, 99
        Maynooth Bible, 190–1
        New Testament, 52, 53–5, 190
        Old Testament, 56–7, 68, 73, 81
Black Death, 23
Boethius, 13, 14
Bolger, Dermot
    The Bright Wave, 170, 174–5, 178
Book of Ballymote, 21
Bord na Gaeilge, 172
Bord na Leabhar Gaeilge, 170, 172, 174
Bourke, Angela, 4
Boyle, John
    Letters of Pliny the Younger, 80
Boyle, Robert, 57, 68
Boyle, Roger, 68
Brady, Nicholas, 72, 73
Breathnach, Colm, 189
brehons, 8, 9
Bristed, Ezekiel, 70–1

220